P9-CDW-307

ABOUT THIS BOOK

For over sixty-five years, the United States war machine has been on automatic pilot. Since World War II we have been conditioned to believe that America's motives in 'exporting' democracy are honorable, even noble. In this startling and provocative book, William Blum, a leading dissident chronicler of US foreign policy and the author of controversial bestseller *Rogue State*, argues that nothing could be further from the truth. Moreover, unless this fallacy is unlearned, and until people understand fully the worldwide suffering American policy has caused, we will never be able to stop the monster.

ABOUT THE AUTHOR

WILLIAM BLUM is one of the United States' leading non-mainstream experts on American foreign policy. He left the State Department in 1967, abandoning his aspiration of becoming a Foreign Service Officer because of his opposition to what the US was doing in Vietnam. He then became a founder and editor of the *Washington Free Press*, the first 'alternative' newspaper in the capital.

Blum has been a freelance journalist in the US, Europe, and South America. His stay in Chile in 1972–73, writing about the Allende government's 'socialist experiment,' and then its tragic overthrow in a CIA-designed coup, instilled in him a personal involvement and an even more heightened interest in what his government was doing in various corners of the world.

His book *Killing Hope: US Military and CIA Interventions Since World War II* has received international acclaim. Noam Chomsky called it 'Far and away the best book on the topic.' In 1999 he was one of the recipients of Project Censored's awards for 'exemplary journalism.' Blum is also the author of *Rogue State: A Guide to the World's Only Superpower*, *West-Bloc Dissident: A Cold War Memoir*, and *Freeing the World to Death: Essays on the American Empire*. His books have been translated into 27 foreign-language editions. In January 2006, a tape from Osama bin Laden stated that 'it would be useful' for Americans to read *Rogue State*, to gain a better understanding of their enemy.

Blum currently sends out a monthly Internet newsletter, the *Anti-Empire Report*.

AMERICA'S DEADLIEST EXPORT

DEMOCRACY

THE TRUTH ABOUT US FOREIGN POLICY AND EVERYTHING ELSE

WILLIAM BLUM

Fernwood Publishing
HALIFAX & WINNIPEG

Zed Books
LONDON | NEW YORK

America's Deadliest Export: Democracy – the Truth about US Foreign Policy and Everything Else was first published in 2013.

Published in Canada by Fernwood Publishing Ltd,
32 Oceanvista Lane, Black Point, Nova Scotia BOJ 1BO
and 748 Broadway Avenue, Winnipeg, Manitoba R3G 0X3
www.fernwoodpublishing.ca

Published in the rest of the world by Zed Books Ltd,
7 Cynthia Street, London N1 9JF, UK and
Room 400, 175 Fifth Avenue, New York, NY 10010, USA
www.zedbooks.co.uk

Copyright © William Blum 2013

The right of William Blum to be identified as the author of this work has been asserted by him in accordance with the Copyright, Designs and Patents Act, 1988

Fernwood Publishing Company Limited gratefully acknowledges the financial support of the Government of Canada through the Canada Book Fund and the Canada Council for the Arts, the Nova Scotia Department of Communities, Culture and Heritage, the Manitoba Department of Culture, Heritage and Tourism under the Manitoba Book Publishers Marketing Assistance Program and the Province of Manitoba, through the Book Publishing Tax Credit, for our publishing program.

Typeset in Monotype Bulmer
by illuminati, Grosmont
Cover designed by Rogue Four Design
Printed and bound in the United States of America

Distributed in the USA exclusively by Palgrave Macmillan, a division of St Martin's Press, LLC, 175 Fifth Avenue, New York, NY 10010, USA

All rights reserved. No part of this publication may be reproduced, stored in a retrieval system or transmitted in any form or by any means, electronic, mechanical, photocopying or otherwise, without the prior permission of Zed Books Ltd.

A catalogue record for this book is available from the British Library
Library of Congress Cataloging in Publication Data available

Library and Archives Canada Cataloguing in Publication
    Blum, William
        America's deadliest export : democracy- the truth about
    US foreign policy and everything else / William Blum.
    Includes bibliographical references.
    ISBN 978-1-55266-559-6
        1. United States—Foreign relations—1945-.   2. Democracy—United States.
    I. Title.
    E183.7.B59 2013   327.73   C2012-907758-5

ISBN 978 1 78032 446 3 hb   (Zed Books)
ISBN 978 1 78032 445 6 pb   (Zed Books)
ISBN 978 1 55266 559 6   (Fernwood Publishing)

CONTENTS

Introduction   1

1   US foreign policy vs the world   15

2   Terrorism   39

3   Iraq   53

4   Afghanistan   79

5   Iran   88

6   George W. Bush   106

7   Condoleezza Rice   111

8   Human rights, civil liberties, and torture   114

9   WikiLeaks   131

10 Conspiracies   146

11 Yugoslavia   154

12 Libya   161

13 Latin America   170

14 Cuba   186

15 The Cold War and anti-communism   199

16 The 1960s   226

17 Ideology and society   230

18 Our precious environment   243

19 The problem with capitalism   247

20 The media   269

21 Barack Obama   285

22 Patriotism   304

23 Dissent and resistance in America   314

24 Religion   323

25 Laughing despite the empire   329

26 But what can we do?   334

    Notes   339

    Index   353

INTRODUCTION

The secret to understanding US foreign policy is that there is no secret. Principally, one must come to the realization that the United States strives to dominate the world, for which end it is prepared to use any means necessary. Once one understands that, much of the apparent confusion, contradiction, and ambiguity surrounding Washington's policies fades away. To express this striving for dominance numerically, one can consider that since the end of World War II the United States has

- endeavored to overthrow more than 50 foreign governments, most of which were democratically elected;[1]
- grossly interfered in democratic elections in at least 30 countries;[2]
- attempted to assassinate more than 50 foreign leaders;[3]
- dropped bombs on the people of more than 30 countries;[4]
- attempted to suppress a populist or nationalist movement in 20 countries.[5]

The impact on world consciousness in recent decades of tragedies such as in Rwanda and Darfur has been more conspicuous than the American-caused tragedies because the first two each took place in one area and within a relatively short period of time. Despite the extensive documentation of the crimes of US foreign policy, because of the very breadth of American interventions and the time period of sixty-eight years it's much more difficult for the world to fully grasp what the United States has done.

In total: since 1945, the United States has carried out one or more of the above-listed actions, on one or more occasions, in seventy-one countries (more than one-third of the countries of the world),[6] in the process of which the US has ended the lives of several million people, condemned many millions more to a life of agony and despair, and has been responsible for the torture of countless thousands. US foreign policy has likely earned the hatred of most of the people in the world who are able to more or less follow current news events and are familiar with a bit of modern history.

Oderint dum metuant – 'Let them hate so long as they fear' – was attributed to one or another prominent leader of Ancient Rome.

Shortly before the US invasion of Iraq in March 2003, career diplomat John Brady Kiesling, the political counselor at the US embassy in Athens, resigned over the Iraq policy. 'Has "oderint dum metuant" really become our motto?' he asked in his letter of resignation, referring to the fact that more than one member of the Bush administration had used the expression.[7]

Following the US invasion of Afghanistan in October 2001, former CIA director James Woolsey commented about worries that storming Baghdad would incite Islamic radicals and broaden support for them: 'The silence of the Arab public in the wake of America's victories in Afghanistan,' he said, proves that 'only fear will re-establish respect for the U.S.... We need to read a little bit of Machiavelli.' (In the same talk, Woolsey further established himself as a foreign policy pundit by stating: 'There is so much evidence with respect to [Saddam Hussein's] development of weapons of mass destruction and ballistic missiles ... that I consider this point beyond dispute.'[8])

Speaking at the graduation ceremony of the US Military Academy in West Point, New York, in June 2002, President George W. Bush told America's future warriors that they were 'in a conflict between good and evil' and that 'We must uncover terror cells in 60 or more countries.'[9] The United States institutional war machine was, and remains, on automatic pilot.

When the plans for a new office building for the military, which came to be known as The Pentagon, were brought before the Senate on August 14, 1941, Senator Arthur Vandenberg of Michigan was puzzled. 'Unless the war is to be permanent, why must we have permanent accommodations for war facilities of such size?' he asked. 'Or is the war to be *permanent*?'[10]

'Wars may be aberrant experiences in the lives of most human individuals, but some nations are serial aggressors,' observed *The Black Commentator* in the fourth year of the war in Iraq. 'American society is unique in having been formed almost wholly by processes of aggression against external and internal Others.'[11]

It can be said that American history is the history of an empire in the making, since the first British settler killed the first native American.

All countries, it is often argued, certainly all powerful countries, have always acted belligerent and militaristic, so why condemn the United States so much? But that is like arguing that since one can find anti-Semitism in every country, why condemn Nazi Germany? Obviously, it's a question of magnitude. And the magnitude of US aggression puts it historically into a league all by itself, just as the magnitude of the Nazis' anti-Semitism did. Is the world supposed to uncritically accept terribly aggressive behavior because it's traditional and expected? Somehow normal? Is that any way to build a better world?

Full spectrum dominance

A number of expressions and slogans associated with the Nazi regime in Germany have become commonly known in English.

Sieg Heil! – Hail Victory!

Arbeit macht frei – Work makes you free.

Denn heute gehört uns Deutschland und morgen die ganze Welt – Today Germany, tomorrow the world.

Ich habe nur den Befehlen gehorcht! – I was only following orders!

But none perhaps is better known than *Deutschland über alles* – Germany above all.

Thus I was taken aback, in June 2008, when I happened to come across the website of the United States Air Force (www. airforce.com) and saw on its first page a heading 'Above all'. Lest you think that this referred simply and innocently to planes high up in the air, this page linked to another site (www.airforce. com/achangingworld) where 'Above all' was repeated even more prominently, with links to sites for 'Air Dominance,' 'Space Dominance,' and 'Cyber Dominance,' each of which in turn repeated 'Above all'. These guys don't kid around. They're not your father's imperialist warmongers. If they're planning for a new 'thousand-year Reich', let's hope that their fate is no better than the original, which lasted twelve years.

Here's how the gentlemen of the Pentagon have sounded in the recent past on the subject of space.

> We will engage terrestrial targets someday – ships, airplanes, land targets – from space. … We're going to fight *in* space. We're going to fight *from* space and we're going to fight *into* space. (General Joseph Ashy, Commander-in-Chief of the U.S. Space Command[12])

> With regard to space dominance, we have it, we like it, and we're going to keep it. (Keith R. Hall, Assistant Secretary of the Air

Force for Space and Director of the National Reconnaissance Office[13])

> During the early portion of the 21st century, space power will also evolve into a separate and equal medium of warfare. ... The emerging synergy of space superiority with land, sea, and air superiority will lead to Full Spectrum Dominance. ... Development of ballistic missile defenses using space systems and planning for precision strikes from space offers a counter to the worldwide proliferation of WMD [weapons of mass destruction]. ... Space is a region with increasing commercial, civil, international, and military interests and investments. The threat to these vital systems is also increasing. ... Control of Space is the ability to assure access to space, freedom of operations within the space medium, and an ability to deny others the use of space, if required. ('United States Space Command: Vision for 2020'[14])

> Space represents a fundamentally new and better way to apply military force. (US Strategic Command[15])

Washington's ambition for world domination is driven not by the cause of a deeper democracy or freedom, a more just world, ending poverty or violence, or a more liveable planet, but rather by economics and ideology.

Michael Parenti has observed:

> The objective is not just power for its own sake but power to insure plutocratic control of the planet, power to privatize and deregulate the economies of every nation in the world, to hoist upon the backs of peoples everywhere – including the people of North America – the blessings of an untrammeled 'free market' corporate capitalism. The struggle is between those who believe that the land, labor, capital, technology, and markets of the world should be dedicated to maximizing capital accumulation for the few, and those who believe that these things should be used for the communal benefit and socio-economic development of the many.[16]

It can thus be appreciated that to the American power elite one of the longest lasting and most essential foreign policy goals has been preventing the rise of any society that might serve as a good example of an alternative to the capitalist model. This was the essence of the Cold War. Cuba and Chile were two examples of several such societies in the socialist camp which the United States did its best to crush.

Like most powerful leaders – past, present, and future – American officials would have the rest of us believe that the policies they pursue in their quest for domination are beneficial to their own people and to most of the world, even if the blessings are not always immediately recognizable. They would like nothing better than to remake the world in America's image, with free enterprise, 'individualism', something called 'Judeo-Christian values,' and some other thing they call 'democracy' as core elements. Imagine, then, what a shock September 11, 2001 was to such men; not simply the kind of shock that you and I experienced on that fateful day, but the realization that someone had dared to 'diss' the empire, a traumatic shock to the political nervous system. American leaders assume that US moral authority is as absolute and unchallengeable as US military power. 'The messianism of American foreign policy is a remarkable thing,' a Russian parliamentary leader noted in 2006. 'When Secretary of State Condoleezza Rice speaks it seems like Khrushchev reporting to the party congress: "The whole world is marching triumphantly toward democracy but some rogue states prefer to stay aside from that road, etc. etc."'[17]

And here is Michael Ledeen, former official of the Reagan administration, later a fellow at one of the leading conservative think tanks, American Enterprise Institute, speaking shortly before the US invasion of Iraq in 2003:

> If we just let our own vision of the world go forth, and we embrace it entirely, and we don't try to be clever and piece together clever diplomatic solutions to this thing, but just wage a total war against these tyrants, I think we will do very well, and our children will sing great songs about us years from now.[18]

It was difficult to resist. A year after the dreadful invasion and catastrophic occupation of Iraq I sent Mr Ledeen an email reminding him of his words and saying simply: 'I'd like to ask you what songs your children are singing these days.' I did not expect a reply, and I was not disappointed.

Future president Theodore Roosevelt, who fought in Cuba at the turn of the last century with the greatest of gung-ho-ism, wrote: 'It is for the good of the world that the English-speaking race in all its branches should hold as much of the world's surface as possible.'[19] One can find similar sentiments without end expressed by American leaders since the 1890s.

After the attacks of September 11, 2001 many Americans acquired copies of the Quran in an attempt to understand why Muslims could do what they did. One can wonder, following the invasion of Iraq, whether Iraqis bought Christian bibles in search of an explanation of why the most powerful nation on the planet had laid such terrible waste to their ancient land, which had done no harm to the United States.

Wars of aggression

Has there ever been an empire that didn't tell itself and the rest of the world that it was unlike all other empires, that its mission was not to plunder and control but to enlighten and liberate?

The *National Security Strategy*, a paper issued by the White House in September 2002, states:

> In keeping with our heritage and principles, we do not use our strength to press for unilateral advantage. We seek instead to create a balance of power that favors human freedom: conditions in which all nations and all societies can choose for themselves the rewards and challenges of political and economic liberty.

However, later in the same report we read:

It is time to reaffirm the essential role of American military
strength. We must build and maintain our defenses beyond challenge ... Our forces will be strong enough to dissuade potential
adversaries from pursuing a military build-up in hopes of surpass-
ing, or equaling, the power of the United States. ... To forestall or
prevent ... hostile acts by our adversaries, the United States will, if
necessary, act preemptively.

'Preemptive war' is what the post-World War II International
Military Tribunal at Nuremberg, Germany, called a war of aggression. 'To initiate a war of aggression,' the Tribunal declared,
'therefore, is not only an international crime, it is the supreme
international crime differing only from other war crimes in that
it contains within itself the accumulated evil of the whole.'

Six months after issuing the National Security Strategy, the
United States carried out an attack on Iraq which was less – that
is, worse – than 'preemptive': there was no provocation or threat
of any kind from Iraq. The 1941 attack on Pearl Harbor in Hawaii
by imperial Japan was certainly more preemptive. As Noam
Chomsky has pointed out:

Japanese leaders knew that B-17 Flying Fortresses were coming
off the Boeing production lines and were surely familiar with the
public discussions in the US explaining how they could be used to
incinerate Japan's wooden cities in a war of extermination, flying
from Hawaiian and Philippine bases – 'to burn out the industrial
heart of the Empire with fire-bombing attacks on the teeming
bamboo ant heaps,' as retired Air Force General Chennault
recommended in 1940, a proposal that 'simply delighted' President
Roosevelt. Evidently, that is a far more powerful justification for
bombing military bases in US colonies than anything conjured
up by Bush–Blair and their associates in their execution of 'preemptive war.'[20]

The Germans insisted that their invasion of Poland in 1939
was justified on the grounds of preemption. Poland, declared
the Nazis, was planning to invade Germany. (Nineteenth-century

German Chancellor Otto Bismarck once asserted that 'Preventive war is like committing suicide out of fear of death.') In 2003, and for some years subsequent, it was the United States saying that Iraq was an 'imminent threat' to invade the US or Israel or whoever, even when no weapons of mass destruction had been located in Iraq and no plausible motive for Iraq invading the US or Israel could be given. The claim of an imminent Iraqi threat eventually fell of its own weight, as did many other prominent Bush administration assertions about the US invasion.

Intelligence of the political kind

American leaders have convinced a majority of the American people of the benevolence of their government's foreign policy. To have persuaded Americans of this, as well as a multitude of other people throughout the world – in the face of overwhelming evidence to the contrary, such as the lists of US international atrocities shown above – must surely rank as one of the most outstanding feats of propaganda and indoctrination in all of history.

I think there are all kinds of intelligence in this world: musical, scientific, mathematical, artistic, academic, literary, mechanical, and so on. Then there's political intelligence, which I would define as the ability to see through the nonsense which the politicians – echoed by the media – of every society feed their citizens from birth on to win elections and assure continuance of the prevailing ideology. A lack in the American citizenry of any of the other types of intelligence, though perhaps personally detrimental, does not kill. A widespread deficiency of political intelligence, however, can and does allow the taking of the lives of large numbers of innocent people in places like Iraq, Afghanistan, Pakistan, Yugoslavia, and Vietnam. The American people alone have the power to influence the extremists who, in one election after another, in the form of Democrats or Republicans, come to power in the United States and proceed to create havoc and disaster in one new killing field after another. But the citizenry fall for US government propaganda justifying its military actions as regularly and as naively as Charlie Brown falling for Lucy's football.

The American people are very much like the children of a Mafia boss who do not know what their father does for a living, and don't want to know, but then wonder why someone just threw a firebomb through the living room window.

Now why is that? Why are these people so easily indoctrinated? Are they just stupid? I think a better answer is that they have certain preconceptions; consciously or unconsciously, they have certain basic beliefs about the United States and its foreign policy, and if you don't deal with these basic beliefs you'll be talking to a stone wall. This book deals with many of these basic beliefs, or what can also be called 'myths.'

It is not at all uncommon to grow to adulthood in the United States, even graduate from university, and not be seriously exposed to opinions significantly contrary to these prevailing myths, and know remarkably little about the exceptionally harmful foreign policy of the government. It's one thing for historical myths to rise in the absence of a written history of a particular period, such as our beliefs concerning the Neanderthals; but much odder is the rise of such myths in the face of a plethora of historical documents, testimony, films, and books.

To describe this on a personal level: I remember the good warm feeling I used to have in my teens and twenties, and even into my thirties, whenever I heard good ol' Bob Hope dishing out his good ol' American humor to the good ol' American GIs scattered all over the world. I never gave any thought to what the good ol' American GIs were actually *doing* all over the world in the first place. But would good ol' Bob Hope be entertaining good ol' American GIs embarked on anything less than honorable missions? Could the nice, young, clean-cut American boys who laughed so heartily at the same jokes I laughed at be up to no good? Had our soldiers *ever* been up to no good? Nothing I had been exposed to in any school or mainstream media had left me with that impression in any firm or lasting way. The question had never even crossed my mind.

On the infrequent occasion that I encountered someone of dissident views they invariably did not have the facts at their fingertips, did not argue their case very well, did not understand – as I myself did not – my basic beliefs/myths. Their effect upon my thinking was thus negligible. It took the horror of Vietnam inescapably thrown into my face by protesters and their media coverage to initiate a whole new personal intellectual process. The process would likely have begun much sooner had I been able to read something like the present book.

Democracy is a beautiful thing,
except that part about letting just any old jerk vote

> The people can have anything they want.
> The trouble is, they do not want anything.
> At least they vote that way on election day.
>
> (Eugene Debs, American socialist leader,
> early twentieth century)

Why was the 2008 presidential primary vote for Ohio congressman Dennis Kucinich so small when anti-Iraq War sentiment in the United States was apparently so high – millions had marched against it on repeated occasions, with perhaps not a single demonstration of any size in support – and Kucinich was easily the leading anti-war candidate in the Democratic race, indeed the only genuine one after former senator Mike Gravel withdrew? Even allowing for his being cut out of several televised national debates, Kucinich's showing was remarkably poor. In Michigan, on January 15, it was only Kucinich and Hillary Clinton running. Clinton got 56 percent of the vote, the 'uncommitted' vote (for candidates who had withdrawn but whose names were still on the ballot) was 39 percent, and Kucinich received but 4 percent. And Clinton had been the leading pro-war hawk of all the Democratic candidates.

I think much of the answer may lie in the fact that the majority of the American people – like the majority of people elsewhere in the world – aren't very sophisticated politically or intellectually, and many of them weren't against the war for very cerebral reasons. Their opposition often stemmed from things like the large number of American soldiers who'd been killed or wounded; the fact that the United States was not 'winning'; that America's reputation in the world was being soiled; that numerous other Americans had expressed their opposition to the war; that President Bush suffered from multiple verbal and character shortcomings with television comedians regularly making fun of him – or because of a number of other reasons we couldn't even guess at. There is not much that is particularly perceptive or learned in this collection of reasons, no special insight into history, foreign relations, international law, warfare, economics, propaganda, or ideology – the basis of the 'political intelligence' referred to above; which makes it so much easier for a politician who actually supports a war to sell herself as an anti-war candidate when the occasion calls for it.

Activists like myself are often scoffed at for saying the same old things to the same old people; just spinning our wheels, we're told, 'preaching to the choir' or 'preaching to the converted.' But long experience as speaker, writer and activist in the area of foreign policy tells me it just ain't so. From the questions and comments I regularly get from my audiences, via email and in person, I can plainly see that there are numerous significant information gaps and misconceptions in the choir's thinking, often leaving them unable to see through the newest government lie or propaganda trick; they're unknowing or forgetful of what happened in the past that illuminates the present; or knowing the facts but unable to apply them at the appropriate moment; vulnerable to being led astray by the next person who offers a specious argument that opposes what they currently believe, or think they believe. The choir needs to be frequently reminded and enlightened.

As cynical as many Americans may think the members of the choir are, the choir is frequently not cynical enough about the power elite's motivations. No matter how many times they're lied to, they still often underestimate the government's capacity for deceit, clinging to the belief that their leaders somehow mean well. As long as people believe that their elected leaders are well intentioned, the leaders can, and do, get away with murder. Literally. This belief is the most significant of the myths the present book deals with.

One reason for confusion among the electorate is that the two main parties, the Democrats and Republicans, while forever throwing charges and counter-charges at each other, actually hold indistinguishable views concerning foreign policy, a similarity that is one of the subjects of this book. What is the poor voter to make of all this?

Apropos of this we have the view of the American electoral system from a foreigner, Cuban leader Raúl Castro. He has noted that the United States pits two identical parties against one another, and joked that a choice between a Republican and Democrat is like choosing between himself and his brother Fidel. 'We could say in Cuba we have two parties: one led by Fidel and one led by Raúl, what would be the difference?' he asked. 'That's the same thing that happens in the United States ... both are the same. Fidel is a little taller than me, he has a beard and I don't.'[21]

In sum, even when the hearts of the choir may be in the right place, their heads still need working on, on a recurring basis. And, in any event, very few people are actually born into the choir; they achieve membership only after being preached to, multiple times.

The essays that make up the book are a combination of new and old; combined, updated, expanded, refined; many first appeared in one form or another in my monthly online *Anti-Empire Report*, or on my website, at various times during the past eight years or so; where a date is specified at the beginning of the piece it's the date it was first written and should be read from that vantage point (although in some cases it may differ markedly from the original). This book is for current and, hopefully, future members of the choir.

1

US FOREIGN POLICY vs THE WORLD

Mit der dummheit kämpfen Götter selbst vergebens.
('With stupidity, even the gods struggle in vain.')

Friedrich Schiller (1759–1805)

I'm often told by readers of their encounters with Americans who support the outrages of US foreign policy no matter what facts are presented to them, no matter what arguments are made, no matter how much the government's statements are shown to be false. My advice is to forget such people. They would support the outrages even if the government came to their home, seized their firstborn, and hauled them away screaming, so long as the government assured them it was essential to fighting terrorism (or communism), and threw in a little paean to democracy, freedom, and God. My rough guess is that these people constitute no more than 15 percent of the American population. I suggest that we concentrate on the rest, who are reachable.

Inasmuch as I cannot see violent revolution succeeding in the United States (something deep inside tells me that we couldn't quite match the government's firepower, not to mention its viciousness), I can offer no solution to stopping the imperial beast other than: educate yourself and as many others as you can, increasing the number of those in the opposition until it

reaches a critical mass, at which point... I can't predict the form
the explosion will take or what might be the trigger.

As to the education, I like to emphasize certain points that
try to deal with the underlying intellectual misconceptions and
emotional 'hang-ups' I think Americans have which stand in
the way of their seeing through the propaganda. Briefly, here
are some of the main points (explained in more detail in later
chapters):

1. Far and away the most important lesson to impart to the American mind and soul: regardless of our lifetime of education to
   the contrary, US foreign policy does not 'mean well.' The facts
   presented in this book should leave no doubt of that thesis, but
   the progressive political activist must be conscious of it at all
   times. I like to ask the American True Believers: what would
   the United States have to do in its foreign policy to cause you
   to stop supporting it?

2. The United States is not concerned with this thing called
   'democracy', no matter how many times every American
   president uses the word each time he opens his mouth. As
   noted in the Introduction, since 1945 the US has attempted to
   overthrow more than fifty governments, most of which were
   democratically elected, and grossly interfered in democratic
   elections in at least thirty countries. The question is: what do
   American leaders mean by 'democracy'? The last thing they
   have in mind is any kind of economic democracy – the closing
   of the gap between the desperate poor and those for whom
   too much is not enough. The first thing they have in mind is
   making sure the target country has the political, financial, and
   legal mechanisms in place to make it hospitable to corporate
   globalization.

3. Anti-American terrorists are not motivated by hatred or envy
   of freedom or democracy, or by American wealth, secular

government, or culture, as we've been told many times. They are motivated by decades of awful things done to their homelands by US foreign policy. It works the same way all over the world. In the period of the 1950s to the 1980s in Latin America, in response to a long string of harmful American policies, there were countless acts of terrorism against US diplomatic and military targets as well as the offices of US corporations. The US bombing, invasion, occupation, and torture in Iraq, Afghanistan, and elsewhere in recent years have created thousands of new anti-American terrorists. We'll be hearing from them for a very long time.

4. The United States is not actually against terrorism per se, only those terrorists who are not allies of the empire. There is a lengthy and infamous history of Washington's support for numerous anti-Castro terrorists, even when their terrorist acts were committed in the United States. At this moment, Luis Posada Carriles remains protected by the US government, though he masterminded the blowing up of a Cuban airplane that killed 73 people. He's but one of hundreds of anti-Castro terrorists who've been given haven in the United States over the years. The United States has also provided close support to terrorists, or fought on the same side as Islamic jihadists, in Kosovo, Bosnia, Iran, Libya, and Syria, including those with known connections to al-Qaeda, to further foreign policy goals more important than fighting terrorism.

5. Iraq was not any kind of a threat to the United States. Of the never-ending lies concerning Iraq, this is the most insidious, the necessary foundation for all the other lies.

6. There was never any such animal as the International Communist Conspiracy. There were, as there still are, people living in misery, rising up in protest against their condition, against an oppressive government, a government usually supported by the United States.

That oh-so-precious world where words have no meaning

In December 1989, two days after bombing and invading the defenseless population of Panama, killing as many as a few thousand totally innocent people, guilty of no harm to any American, President George H.W. Bush declared that his 'heart goes out to the families of those who have died in Panama.'[1] When a reporter asked him, 'Was it really worth it to send people to their death for this? To get [Panamanian leader Manuel] Noriega?' Bush replied: 'Every human life is precious, and yet I have to answer, yes, it has been worth it.'[2]

A year later, preparing for his next worthwhile mass murder, the first US invasion of Iraq, Bush Sr. said: 'People say to me: "How many lives? How many lives can you expend?" Each one is precious.'[3]

At the end of 2006, with Bush's son now president, White House spokesman Scott Stanzel, commenting about American deaths reaching 3,000 in the second Iraq War, said that Bush 'believes that every life is precious and grieves for each one that is lost.'[4] In February 2008, with American deaths about to reach 4,000, and Iraqi deaths as many as a million or more, George W. Bush asserted:

> When we lift our hearts to God, we're all equal in his sight.
> We're all equally precious.... In prayer we grow in mercy and
> compassion.... When we answer God's call to love a neighbor as
> ourselves, we enter into a deeper friendship with our fellow man.[5]

Inspired by such noble – dare I say *precious?* – talk from its leaders, the American military machine likes to hire like-minded warriors. Here is Erik Prince, founder of the military contractor Blackwater, whose employees in Iraq killed people like others flick away a mosquito, in testimony before Congress: 'Every life, whether American or Iraqi, is precious.'[6]

While his killing of thousands of Iraqis was proceeding merrily along in 2003, the second President George Bush was moved to say: 'We believe in the value and dignity of every human life.'[7]

Both father and son are on record expressing their deep concern for God and prayer both before and during their mass slaughters. 'I trust God speaks through me,' said Bush the younger in 2004. 'Without that, I couldn't do my job.'[8]

After his devastation of Iraq and its people, Bush the elder said: 'I think that, like a lot of others who had positions of responsibility in sending someone else's kids to war, we realize that in prayer what mattered is how it might have seemed to God.'[9]

God, one can surmise, might have asked George Bush, father and son, about the kids of Iraq. And the adults. And, in a testy, rather ungodlike manner, might have snapped: 'So stop wasting all the precious lives already!'

In the now-famous exchange on television in 1996 between Madeleine Albright and reporter Lesley Stahl, the latter was speaking of US sanctions against Iraq, and asked the then-US ambassador to the UN, and Secretary of State-to-be: 'We have heard that a half million children have died. I mean, that's more children than died in Hiroshima. And... and you know, is the price worth it?'

Albright replied: 'I think this is a very hard choice, but the price... we think the price is worth it.'[10]

Ten years later, Condoleezza Rice, continuing the fine tradition of female Secretaries of State and the equally noble heritage of the Bush family, declared that the current horror in Iraq was 'worth the investment' in American lives and dollars.[11]

The worldwide eternal belief that American foreign policy has a good side that can be appealed to

On April 6, 2011, in the midst of NATO/US bombing of his country, Libyan leader Muammar Gaddafi wrote a letter to President Barack Obama in which he said:

> We have been hurt more morally than physically because of what
> had happened against us in both deeds and words by you. Despite
> all this you will always remain our son whatever happened ... Our
> dear son, Excellency, Baraka Hussein Abu Oubama, your inter-
> vention in the name of the U.S.A. is a must, so that Nato would
> withdraw finally from the Libyan affair.[12]

Gaddafi's hope that writing to Obama could move the American
president to put an end to the bombing of Libya turned out, as
we know, to be unrealistic.

Before the American invasion in March 2003, Iraq tried to
negotiate a peace deal with the United States. Iraqi officials,
including the chief of the Iraqi Intelligence Service, wanted
Washington to know that Iraq no longer had weapons of mass
destruction and offered to allow American troops and experts
to conduct a search; they also offered full support for any US
plan in the Arab–Israeli peace process, and to hand over a man
accused of being involved in the World Trade Center bombing
in 1993. If this is about oil, they added, they would also talk
about US oil concessions.[13] Washington's reply was its 'Shock
and Awe' bombing.

In 2002, before the coup in Venezuela that briefly ousted President Hugo Chávez, some of the plotters went to Washington to
get a green light from the Bush administration. Chávez learned of
this visit and was so distressed by it that he sent officials from his
government to plead his own case in Washington. The success of
this endeavor can be judged by the fact that the coup took place
very shortly thereafter.[14]

In 1994, it was reported that the spokesperson of the Zapatista
rebels in Mexico, Subcomandante Marcos, said that 'he expects
the United States to support the Zapatistas once US intelligence
agencies are convinced the movement is not influenced by Cubans
or Russians.' 'Finally,' Marcos said, 'they are going to conclude
that this is a Mexican problem, with just and true causes.'[15] Yet

for many years, before and after these remarks, the United States provided the Mexican military with all the tools and training needed to crush the Zapatistas.

Maurice Bishop of Grenada in 1983, Cheddi Jagan of British Guiana in 1961, the Guatemalan foreign minister in 1954, all made their appeals to Washington to be left in peace.[16] The governments of all three countries were overthrown by the United States.

In 1945 and 1946, Vietnamese leader Ho Chi Minh, a genuine admirer of America and the Declaration of Independence, wrote at least eight letters to President Harry Truman and the State Department asking for America's help in winning Vietnamese independence from the French. He wrote that world peace was being endangered by French efforts to reconquer Indochina and he requested that 'the four powers' (US, USSR, China, and Great Britain) intervene in order to mediate a fair settlement and bring the Indochinese issue before the United Nations.[17] Ho Chi Minh received no reply. He was, after all, some kind of communist.

The myth of the good war

The reason so many Americans support US war crimes is that they're convinced that no matter how bad things may look, the government means well. And one of the foundation stones for this edifice of patriotic faith is the Second World War, a historical saga that all Americans are taught about from childhood on. We all know what its real name is: 'The Good War.'

Which leads me to recommend a book, *The Myth of the Good War*, by Jacques Pauwels, published in 2002. It's very well done, well argued and documented, an easy read. I particularly like the sections dealing with the closing months of the European campaign, during which the United States and Great Britain contemplated stabbing their Soviet ally in the back with maneuvers like a separate peace with Germany, using German troops to fight the Russians, and sabotaging legal attempts by various Communist parties and other elements of the European left to share in (highly earned) political power after the war; the most dramatic example of this being the US taking the side of the Greek neo-fascists against the Greek left, who had fought the Nazis courageously. Stalin learned enough about these schemes to at least partially explain his postwar suspicious manner toward his 'allies.' In the West we called it 'paranoia.'[18]

The enduring mystique of the Marshall Plan

Amidst all the political upheavals in North Africa and the Middle East in 2011 the name 'Marshall Plan' kept being repeated by political figures and media around the world as the key to rebuilding the economies of those societies to complement the supposed political advances. But *caveat emptor*; let the buyer beware.

During my years of writing and speaking about the harm and injustice inflicted upon the world by unending United States interventions, I've often been met with resentment from those who accuse me of chronicling only the negative side of US foreign policy and ignoring the many positive sides. When I ask the person to give me some examples of what s/he thinks show the virtuous face of America's dealings with the world in modern times, one of the things mentioned – almost without exception – is the Marshall Plan. This is usually described along the lines of: 'After World War II, the United States unselfishly built up Europe economically, including its wartime enemies, and allowed them to compete with the US.' Even those today who are very cynical about US foreign policy, who are quick to question the White House's motives in Afghanistan, Iraq, and elsewhere, have little problem in accepting this picture of an altruistic America of the period 1948–1952. But let us have a closer look at the Marshall Plan.

After World War II, the United States, triumphant abroad and undamaged at home, saw a door wide open for world supremacy. Only the thing called 'communism' stood in the way, politically, militarily, economically, and ideologically. Thus it was that the entire US foreign policy establishment was mobilized to confront this 'enemy', and the Marshall Plan was an integral part of this campaign. How could it be otherwise? Anti-communism had been the principal pillar of US foreign policy from the Russian Revolution up to World War II, pausing for the war until the closing months of the Pacific campaign when Washington put challenging communism ahead of fighting the Japanese. Even the dropping of the atom bomb on Japan – when the Japanese had already been defeated – can be seen as more a warning to the Soviets than a military action against the Japanese.[19]

After the war, anti-communism continued as the leitmotif of American foreign policy as naturally as if World War II and the alliance with the Soviet Union had not happened. Along with the CIA, the Rockefeller and Ford Foundations, the Council on Foreign Relations, certain corporations, and a few other private institutions, the Marshall Plan was one more arrow in the quiver of those striving to remake Europe to suit Washington's desires:

1. Spreading the capitalist gospel – to counter strong postwar tendencies toward socialism.
2. Opening markets to provide new customers for US corporations – a major reason for helping to rebuild the European economies; e.g. a billion dollars (at twenty-first-century prices) of tobacco, spurred by US tobacco interests.
3. Pushing for the creation of the Common Market (the future European Union) and NATO as integral parts of the West European bulwark against the alleged Soviet threat.
4. Suppressing the left all over Western Europe, most notably sabotaging the Communist parties in France and Italy in their

bids for legal, non-violent, electoral victory. Marshall Plan funds were secretly siphoned off to finance this endeavor, and the promise of aid to a country, or the threat of its cutoff, was used as a bullying club; indeed, France and Italy would certainly have been exempted from receiving aid if they had not gone along with the plots to exclude the Communists from any kind of influential role.

The CIA also skimmed large amounts of Marshall Plan funds to covertly maintain cultural institutions, journalists, and publishers, at home and abroad, for the omnipresent and heated propaganda of the Cold War; the selling of the Marshall Plan to the American public and elsewhere was entwined with fighting 'the red menace'. Moreover, in their covert operations, CIA personnel at times used the Marshall Plan as cover, and one of the Plan's chief architects, Richard Bissell, then moved to the CIA, stopping off briefly at the Ford Foundation, a long-time conduit for CIA covert funds. 'Twas one big happy, scheming family.

The Marshall Plan imposed all kinds of restrictions on the recipient countries, all manner of economic and fiscal criteria which had to be met, designed for a wide-open return to free enterprise. The US had the right not only to control how Marshall Plan dollars were spent, but also to approve the expenditure of an equivalent amount of the local currency, giving Washington substantial power over the internal plans and programs of the European states; welfare programs for the needy survivors of the war were looked upon with disfavor by the United States; even rationing smelled too much like socialism and had to go or be scaled down; nationalization of industry was even more vehemently opposed by Washington.

The great bulk of Marshall Plan funds returned to the United States, or never left, being paid directly to American corporations to purchase American goods. The US Agency for International

Development (AID) stated in 1999: 'The principal beneficiary of America's foreign assistance programs has always been the United States.'[20]

The program could be seen as more a joint business operation between governments than an American 'handout'; often it was a business arrangement between American and European ruling classes, many of the latter fresh from their service to the Third Reich, some of the former as well; or it was an arrangement between congressmen and their favorite corporations to export certain commodities, including a lot of military goods. Thus did the Marshall Plan help lay the foundation for the military–industrial complex as a permanent feature of American life.

It is very difficult to find, or put together, a clear, credible description of how the Marshall Plan played a pivotal or indispensable role in the recovery in each of the sixteen recipient nations. The opposing view, at least as clear, is that the Europeans – highly educated, skilled and experienced – could have recovered from the war on their own without an extensive master plan and aid program from abroad, and indeed had already made significant strides in this direction before the Plan's funds began flowing. Marshall Plan funds were not directed primarily toward the urgently needed feeding of individuals or rebuilding their homes, schools, or factories, but at strengthening the economic superstructure, particularly the iron, steel and power industries. The period was in fact marked by deflationary policies, unemployment, and recession. The one unambiguous outcome was the full restoration of the propertied classes.[21]

Why do they hate us? Part 1

Here is President Dwight Eisenhower in a March 1953 National Security Council Meeting: Why can't we 'get some of the people in these downtrodden countries to like us instead of hating us?'[22]

The United States is still wondering, and is no closer to an understanding than Good Ol' Ike was sixty years ago. The American people and their leaders appear to still believe what Frances Fitzgerald observed in her study of American history textbooks:

> According to these books, the United States had been a kind of Salvation Army to the rest of the world: throughout history, it had done little but dispense benefits to poor, ignorant, and diseased countries. ... the United States always acted in a disinterested fashion, always from the highest of motives; it gave, never took.[23]

I almost feel sorry for the American troops scattered round the world on military bases situated on other people's land. They're 'can-do' Americans, accustomed to getting their way, accustomed to thinking of themselves as the best, and they're frustrated as hell, unable to figure out 'why they hate us', why we can't win them over, why we can't at least wipe them out. Don't they want freedom and democracy? At one time or another the can-do boys tried writing a comprehensive set of laws and regulations, even a constitution, for Iraq; setting up mini-bases in neighborhoods; building walls to block off areas; training and arming 'former' Sunni insurgents to fight Shias and al-Qaeda; enlisting Shias to help fight, against whomever; leaving weapons or bomb-making material in public view to see who picks it up, then pouncing on them; futuristic vehicles and machines and electronic devices to destroy roadside bombs; setting up their own Arabic-language media, censoring other media; classes for detainees on anger control, an oath of peace, and the sacredness of life and property; regularly revising the official reason the United States was in the country in the first place... one new tactic after another, and when all else fails call it a 'success' and give it a nice inspiring action name, like 'surge'... and nothing helps. They're can-do Americans, using good ol' American know-how and Madison Avenue savvy, sales campaigns, public relations, advertising, selling the US brand, just like they do it back home; employing psychologists and anthropologists... and nothing helps. And how can it if the product you're selling is toxic, inherently, from birth, if you're totally ruining your customers' lives, with no regard for any kind of law or morality. They're can-do Americans, accustomed to playing by the rules – theirs; and they're frustrated as hell.

Here now the Google Cavalry rides up on its silver horse. Through its think tank (or 'think/do tank'), Google Ideas, the company paid for eighty former Muslim extremists, neo-Nazis, US gang members and other former radicals to gather in Dublin in June, 2011 ('Summit Against Violent Extremism', or SAVE) to explore how technology can play a role in 'de-radicalization' efforts around the globe. Now is that not Can-do ambitious?

The 'formers,' as they have been dubbed by Google, were surrounded by 120 thinkers, activists, philanthropists, and business leaders. The goal was to dissect the question of what draws some people, particularly young people, to extremist movements and why some of them leave. The person in charge of this project was Jared Cohen, who spent four years on the State Department's Policy Planning staff, and was soon to be an adjunct fellow at the Council on Foreign Relations (CFR), focusing on counter-radicalization, innovation, technology, and statecraft.[24]

So... it's 'violent extremism' that's the big mystery, the target for all these intellectuals to figure out. Why does violent extremism attract so many young people all over the world? Or, of more importance probably to the State Department and CFR types, why do violent extremists single out the United States as their target of choice?

Readers of my rants do not need to be enlightened as to the latter question. There is simply an abundance of terrible things US foreign policy has done in every corner of the world. As to what attracts young people to violent extremism, consider this:

what makes a million young Americans willing to travel to places like Afghanistan and Iraq to risk life and limb to kill other young people, who have never done them any harm, and to commit unspeakable atrocities and tortures?

Is this not extreme behavior? Can these young Americans not be called 'extremists' or 'radicals'? Are they not violent? Do the Google experts understand their behavior? If not, how will they ever understand the foreign Muslim extremists? Are the experts prepared to examine the underlying phenomenon – the deep-seated belief in 'American exceptionalism' drilled into every cell and nerve ganglion of American consciousness from pre-kindergarten on? Do the esteemed experts, then, have to wonder about those who believe in 'Muslim exceptionalism'?

In 2009, Ayman al-Zawahiri, al Qaeda's second-in-command, declared: 'He [Obama] is trying to say: "Do not hate us ... but we will continue to kill you".'[25]

Why do they hate us? Part 2

For some time in 2005 the Pentagon was engaged in fighting against the American Civil Liberties Union, members of Congress, and others who were pushing for the release of new photos and videos of prisoner 'abuse' (otherwise known as 'torture') in the American gulag. The Pentagon was blocking release of these materials because, they claimed, it would inflame anti-American feelings and inspire terrorist acts abroad. This clearly implied that so-called anti-Americans come to their views as a result of American actions or behavior. Yet, the official position of the Bush administration, repeated numerous times and never rescinded by the Obama administration, is that the motivation behind anti-American terrorism has nothing to do with anything the United States does abroad, or has ever done, but has to do with personal defects of the terrorists.[26]

In a similar vein, Undersecretary of State for Public Diplomacy Karen Hughes toured the Middle East in 2005 for the stated purpose of correcting the 'mistaken' impressions people have of the United States, which, she would have the world believe, are the root cause of anti-American hatred and terrorism; it was all a matter of misunderstanding, image, and public relations. At her confirmation hearing in July, Hughes said: 'The mission of public diplomacy is to engage, inform, and help others understand our policies, actions and values.'[27] But what if the problem is that the Muslim world, like the rest of the world, understands America only too well?

Predictably, this confidante of President Bush (this being her only qualification for the position) uttered one inanity after another on her tour. Here she is in Turkey: 'to preserve the peace, sometimes my country believes war is necessary,' and declaring that women are faring much better in Iraq than they did under Saddam Hussein.[28] When her remarks were angrily challenged by Turkish women in the audience, Hughes replied: 'Obviously we have a public relations challenge here ... as we do in different places throughout the world.'[29] Right, Karen, it's all just PR, nothing of any substance to worry your banality-filled little head about.

The *Arab News,* a leading English-language Middle East daily, summed up Hughes's performance thus: 'Painfully clueless.'[30]

The *Washington Post* reported that Hughes's 'audiences, especially in Egypt, often consisted of elites with long ties to the United States, but many people she spoke with said the core reason for the poor U.S. image remained U.S. policies, not how those policies were marketed or presented.'[31] Might she and her boss learn anything from this? Nah.

Why do they hate us? Part 3

The Pentagon awarded three contracts in June 2005, worth up to $300 million, to companies it hoped would inject more creativity into US psychological operations to improve foreign public opinion about the United States, particularly their opinion of the American military. 'We would like to be able to use cutting-edge types of media,' said Col. James A. Treadwell, director of the Joint Psychological Operations Support Element.

Dan Kuehl, a specialist in information warfare at the National Defense University, added: 'There are a billion-plus Muslims that are undecided. How do we move them over to being more support-ive of us? If we can do that, we can make progress and improve security.'[32] And so it goes. And so it has gone since September 11, 2001. The world's only superpower has felt misunderstood, unloved. 'How do I respond when I see that in some Islamic countries there is vitriolic hatred for America?' asked George W. a month after 9/11. 'I'll tell you how I respond: I'm amazed. I'm amazed that there's such misunderstanding of what our country is about that people would hate us. I am – like most Americans, I just can't believe it because I know how good we are.'[33]

Psychological operations, information warfare, cutting-edge media ... surely there's a high-tech solution. But again – what if it's not a misunderstanding? What if the people of the world simply don't believe that we're so good? What if they – in their foreign ignorance and Al Jazeera brainwashing – have come to the bizarre conclusion that saturation bombing, invasion, occupa-tion, destruction of homes, torture, depleted uranium, killing a hundred thousand, and daily humiliation of men, women and children do not indicate good intentions?

Why can't the US government talk about why they hate us?

Following an act of terrorism, we rarely receive from our officials and media even a slightly serious discussion of the terrorists' motivation. Was there any kind of deep-seated grievance or re-sentment with anything or anyone American being expressed?

Any perceived wrong they wished to make right? Anything they sought to obtain revenge for? And why is the United States the most common target of terrorists?

But such questions are virtually forbidden in the mainstream world. At a White House press briefing in January 2010, Assistant to the President for Counterterrorism and Homeland Security, John Brennan, was asked a question by veteran reporter Helen Thomas concerning an attempt by 'the underwear bomber,' Umar Farouk Abdulmutallab, to blow up a US airliner on Christmas Day 2009:

> THOMAS: What is really lacking always for us is you don't give the motivation of why they want to do us harm. ... What is the motivation? We never hear what you find out or why.
>
> BRENNAN: Al Qaeda is an organization that is dedicated to murder and wanton slaughter of innocents ... [They] attract individuals like Mr. Abdulmutallab and use them for these types of attacks. He was motivated by a sense of religious sort of drive. Unfortunately, al Qaeda has perverted Islam, and has corrupted the concept of Islam, so that [they're] able to attract these individuals. But al Qaeda has the agenda of destruction and death.
>
> THOMAS: And you're saying it's because of religion?
>
> BRENNAN: I'm saying it's because of an al Qaeda organization that uses the banner of religion in a very perverse and corrupt way.
>
> THOMAS: Why?
>
> BRENNAN: I think ... this is a long issue, but al Qaeda is just determined to carry out attacks here against the homeland.
>
> THOMAS: But you haven't explained why.[34]

You've got to be carefully taught

It needs to be repeated: the leading myth of US foreign policy, the one which entraps more Americans than any other, is the belief that the United States, in its foreign policy, means well. American leaders may make mistakes, they may blunder, they may lie, they may even on the odd occasion cause more harm than good, but *they do mean well*. Their intentions are honorable, if not divinely inspired. Of that most Americans are certain. And as long as a person clings to that belief, it's rather unlikely that s/he will become seriously doubtful and critical of the official stories.

It takes a lot of repetition while an American is growing up to inculcate this message into their young consciousness, and lots more repetition later on. The education of an American true-believer is ongoing, continuous ... schoolbooks, comicbooks, church sermons, Hollywood films, all forms of media, all the time; hardened into historical concrete. Here is Michael Mullen, chairman of the Joint Chiefs of Staff, the highest military officer in the United States, writing in the *Washington Post* in 2009:

> We in the U.S. military are likewise held to a high standard. Like the early Romans, we are expected to do the right thing, and when we don't, to make it right again ... And it's why each civilian casualty for which we are even remotely responsible sets back our efforts to gain the confidence of the Afghan people months, if not years. It doesn't matter how hard we try to avoid hurting the innocent, and we do try very hard. It doesn't matter how proportional the force we deploy, how precisely we strike. It doesn't even matter if the enemy hides behind civilians. What matters are the death and destruction that result and the expectation that we could have avoided it ... Lose the people's trust, and we lose the war ... I see this sort of trust being fostered by our troops all over the world. They are building schools, roads, wells, hospitals and power stations. They work every day to build the sort of infrastructure that enables local governments to stand on their own. But mostly, even when they are going after the enemy, they are building friendships. They are building trust. And they are doing it in superb fashion.[35]

How many young service members have heard such a talk from Mullen or other officers? How many of them have not been impressed, even choked up? How many Americans reading or hearing such stirring words have not had a lifetime of reinforcement reinforced once again? How many could even imagine that Admiral Mullen is spouting a bunch of crap? The great majority of Americans will swallow it. When Mullen declares 'What matters are the death and destruction that result and the expectation that we could have avoided it,' he's implying that there was no way to avoid it. But of course it could have been easily avoided by simply not dropping any bombs on the Afghan people.

You tell the true believers that the truth is virtually the exact opposite of what Mullen has said and they look at you as if you just got off the Number 36 bus from Mars. Bill Clinton bombed Yugoslavia for seventy-eight days and nights in a row. His military and political policies destroyed one of the most progressive countries in Europe. And he called it 'humanitarian intervention.' It's still regarded by almost all Americans, including many, if not most, 'progressives,' as just that. Propaganda is to a democracy what violence is to a dictatorship.

God bless America. And its bombs

When they bombed Korea, Vietnam, Laos, Cambodia, El Salvador and Nicaragua I said nothing because I wasn't a communist.

When they bombed China, Guatemala, Indonesia, Cuba, and the Congo I said nothing because I didn't know about it.

When they bombed Lebanon and Grenada I said nothing because I didn't understand it.

When they bombed Panama I said nothing because I wasn't a drug dealer.

When they bombed Iraq, Afghanistan, Pakistan, Somalia, and Yemen I said nothing because I wasn't a terrorist.

When they bombed Yugoslavia and Libya for 'humanitarian' reasons I said nothing because it sounded so honorable.

Then they bombed my house and there was no one left to speak out for me. But it didn't really matter. I was dead.[36]

It has become a commonplace to accuse the United States of choosing as its bombing targets only people of color, those of the Third World, or Muslims. But it must be remembered that one of the most sustained and ferocious American bombing campaigns of modern times – seventy-eight consecutive days – was carried out against the people of the former Yugoslavia: white, European, Christians. The United States is an equal-opportunity bomber. The only qualifications for a country to become a target are: (a) it poses an obstacle – could be anything – to a particular desire of the American Empire; (b) it is virtually defenseless against aerial attack; (c) it does not possess nuclear weapons.

A Mecca of hypocrisy, a Vatican of double standards

On February 21, 2008, following a demonstration against the United States' role in Kosovo's declaration of independence, rioters in the Serbian capital of Belgrade broke into the US embassy and set fire to an office. The attack was called 'intolerable' by Secretary of State Condoleezza Rice,[37] and the American ambassador to the United Nations, Zalmay Khalilzad, said he would ask the UN Security Council to issue a unanimous statement 'expressing the council's outrage, condemning the attack, and also reminding the Serbian government of its responsibility to protect diplomatic facilities.'[38]

This is of course standard language for such situations. But what the media and American officials didn't remind us is that in May 1999, during the US/NATO bombing of Serbia, then part of Yugoslavia, the Chinese embassy in Belgrade was hit by a US missile, causing considerable damage and killing three embassy employees. The official Washington story on this – then, and still now – is that it was a mistake. But this is almost certainly a lie. According to a joint investigation by the *Observer* of London and *Politiken* newspaper in Denmark, the embassy was bombed because it was being used to transmit electronic communications for the Yugoslav army after the army's regular system was made inoperable by the bombing. The *Observer* was told by 'senior military and intelligence sources in Europe and the US' that the embassy bombing was deliberate, which was 'confirmed in detail by three other Nato officers – a flight controller operating in Naples, an intelligence officer monitoring Yugoslav radio traffic from Macedonia and a senior [NATO] headquarters officer in Brussels.'[39]

Moreover, the *New York Times* reported at the time that the bombing had destroyed the embassy's intelligence-gathering nerve center, and two of the three Chinese killed were intelligence officers. 'The highly sensitive nature of the parts of the embassy that were bombed suggests why the Chinese ... insist the bombing was no accident. ... "That's exactly why they don't buy our explanation",' said a Pentagon official.[40] There were several other good reasons not to buy the story as well.[41]

In April 1986, after the French government refused the use of its airspace to US warplanes headed for a bombing raid on Libya, the planes were forced to take another, longer route. When they reached Libya they bombed so close to the French embassy that the building was damaged and all communication links knocked out.[42]

And in April 2003, the US ambassador to Russia was summoned to the Russian Foreign Ministry due to the fact that the residential quarter of Baghdad where the Russian embassy was located was bombed several times by the United States during its invasion of Iraq.[43] There had been reports that Saddam Hussein was hiding in the embassy.[44]

So, we can perhaps chalk up the State Department's affirmations about the inviolability of embassies as yet another example of US foreign policy hypocrisy. But I think that there is some satisfaction in that American foreign policy officials, as morally damaged as they must be, are not all so unconscious that they don't know they're swimming in a sea of hypocrisy. The *Los Angeles Times* reported in 2004 that

> The State Department plans to delay the release of a human rights report that was due out today, partly because of sensitivities over the prison abuse scandal in Iraq, U.S. officials said. One official ... said the release of the report, which describes actions taken by the U.S. government to encourage respect for human rights by other nations, could 'make us look hypocritical.'[45]

And in 2007 the *Washington Post* informed us that Chester Crocker, former Assistant Secretary of State and current member of the State Department's Advisory Committee on Democracy Promotion, noted that 'we have to be able to cope with the argument that the U.S. is inconsistent and hypocritical in its promotion of democracy around the world. That may be true.'[46]

The empire's deep dark secret

'In my opinion, any future defense secretary who advises the president to again send a big American land army into Asia or into the Middle East or Africa should have his head examined,' declared Obama's Secretary of Defense, Robert Gates, on February 25, 2011.

Remarkable. Every one of the many wars the United States has engaged in since the end of World War II has been presented to the American people, explicitly or implicitly, as a war of necessity, not a war of choice; a war urgently needed to protect American citizens, American allies, vital American 'interests,' freedom and/or democracy, or kill dangerous anti-American terrorists and various other bad guys. Here is President Obama speaking of Afghanistan: 'But we must never forget this is not a war of choice. This is a war of necessity.'[47]

This being the case, how can a future administration say it will not go to war if any of these noble causes is seriously threatened? The answer, of course, is that these noble causes are irrelevant. The United States goes to war where and when it wants, and if a noble cause is not self-evident, the government, with indispensable help from the American media, will manufacture one. Secretary Gates is now admitting that there is a choice involved. Well, Bob, thanks for telling us. You were Bush's Secretary of Defense as well, and before that spent twenty-six years in the CIA and the National Security Council. You sure know how to keep a secret.

Reforming the Indonesian military, for forty years
(June 13, 2005)

On May 25, 2005 President Bush stated that it makes sense for the United States to maintain close military ties with Indonesia, despite the objections of human rights activists who say such coordination should be withheld until Indonesia does more to address human rights abuses by its military. 'We want young officers from Indonesia coming to the United States,' said Bush. 'We want there to be exchanges between our military corps – that will help lead to better understandings.' Bush made his remarks after meeting with the Indonesian president, who, Bush added, 'told me he's in the process of reforming the military, and I believe him.'[48] (In May 2002, Indonesian Defense Minister Matori met with US Defense Secretary Rumsfeld at the Pentagon. Matori said his government had begun to 'reform the military.' Rumsfeld believed him enough to call for 'military-to-military relations' to be 're-established.')[49]

Indonesian officials saying they're going to reform the military is like officials in Nevada saying they're going to crack down on gambling. For forty years the Indonesian military has engaged in mass murder and other atrocities, in Jakarta, East Timor, Aceh, Papua, and elsewhere, taking the lives of well over a million people,

including several Americans in recent years. For forty years relations between the US and Indonesian militaries have been one of
the very closest of such contacts in the Third World for the United
States, despite the occasional objections and prohibitions from
Congress. For forty years, American officials have been saying
that they have to continue training and arming Indonesia's military
because the contact with the American military will have some
kind of ennobling effect. For forty years it has had no such effect
at all. As Senator Tom Harkin (D.-Iowa) observed in 1999: 'I have
seen no evidence in my 24 years in Congress of one instance where
because of American military involvement with another military
that the Americans have stopped that foreign army from carrying
out atrocities against their own people. No evidence, none.'[50]

Yet the pretense continues, for what else can an American official say? Something like the following? 'We don't care how brutal
the Indonesian military is because they got rid of Sukarno and his
irritating nationalism and neutralism for us, and for forty years
they've been killing people we call communists, killing people
we call terrorists, and protecting our oil, natural gas, mining, and
other corporate interests against Indonesian protestors. Now if
that's not freedom and democracy, I don't know what is.'

[As we'll see from State Department cables in the WikiLeaks
chapter, the Obama administration renewed military ties with
Indonesia in spite of serious concerns expressed by American
diplomats that the Indonesian military's human rights abuses in
the province of West Papua were stoking unrest in the region.

The United States also overturned a ban on training the Indonesian Kopassus army special forces – despite the Kopassus's
long history of arbitrary detention, torture, and murder – after
the Indonesian president threatened to derail President Obama's
trip to the country in November 2010.]

2

TERRORISM

A safer world for Americans...
if they don't leave home

Supporters of US foreign policy have been repeating the point ever since the attacks of September 11, 2001: US counterterrorism policy has worked. How do they know? Because there haven't been any successful terrorist attacks in the United States in all the years since that infamous day.

True, but there weren't any terrorist attacks in the United States in the six years *before* September 11, 2001 either, the last one being the Oklahoma City bombing of April 19, 1995. The absence of terrorist attacks in the US appears to be the norm, with or without a War on Terror.

More significantly, in the years since 9/11 the United States has been the target of terrorist attacks on scores of occasions, not even counting those in Iraq or Afghanistan – attacks on military, diplomatic, civilian, Christian, and other targets associated with the United States; in the Middle East, South Asia, and the Pacific; more than a dozen times in Pakistan alone. The attacks include the October 2002 bombings of two nightclubs in Bali, Indonesia, which killed more than 200 people, almost all of them Americans and citizens of their Australian and British war allies; the following year brought the heavy bombing of the US-managed Marriott Hotel in Jakarta, Indonesia, the site of diplomatic receptions and 4th of July celebrations held by the American embassy; and other horrendous attacks in later years on US allies in Madrid and London because of the war.

Land of the free, home of the War on Terror

David Hicks is a 31–year-old Australian who in a plea-bargain with a US military court served nine months in prison, largely in Australia. That was after five years at Guantánamo Bay, Cuba, without being charged with a crime, without a trial, without a conviction. Under the deal, Hicks agreed not to talk to reporters for one year (a terrible slap in the face of free speech), to forever waive any profit from telling his story (a slap – mon Dieu! – in the face of free enterprise), to submit to US interrogation and testify at future US trials or international tribunals (an open invitation to the US government to hound the young man for the rest of his life), to renounce any claims of mistreatment or unlawful detention (a requirement which would be unconstitutional in a civilian US court). 'If the United States were not ashamed of its conduct, it wouldn't hide behind a gag order,' said Hicks's attorney Ben Wizner of the American Civil Liberties Union.[1]

Like so many other 'terrorists' held by the United States in recent years, Hicks had been 'sold' to the American military for a bounty offered by the US, a phenomenon repeated frequently in Afghanistan and Pakistan. US officials had to know that, once they offered payments to a very poor area to turn in bodies, almost anyone was fair game.

Other 'terrorists' have been turned in as reprisals for all sorts of personal hatreds and feuds. Many others – abroad and in the United States – have been incarcerated by the United States simply for working for, or merely contributing money to, charitable organizations with alleged or real ties to a 'terrorist organization,' as determined by a list kept by the State Department, a list conspicuously political.

It was recently disclosed that an Iraqi resident of Britain is being released from Guantánamo after four years. His crime? He refused to work as an informer for the CIA and MI5, the British security service. His business partner is still being held in Guantánamo, for the same crime.[2]

Finally, there are those many other poor souls who have been picked up simply for being in the wrong place at the wrong time. 'Most of these guys weren't fighting. They were running,' General Martin Lucenti, former deputy commander of Guantánamo, has pointed out.[3]

Thousands of people have been thrown into hell on earth for no earthly reason. The world media have been overflowing with their individual tales of horror and sadness for years. Guantánamo's former commander, General Jay Hood, said: 'Sometimes we just didn't get the right folks.'[4] Not that the torture they were put through would be justified if they were in fact 'the right folks.'

Hicks was taken into custody in Afghanistan in 2001. He was a convert to Islam and like others from many countries had gone to Afghanistan for religious reasons, had wound up on the side of the Taliban in the civil war that had been going on since the early 1990s, and had received military training at a Taliban camp. The United States has insisted on calling such camps 'terrorist training camps,' or 'anti-American terrorist training camps,' or 'al-Qaeda terrorist training camps.' Almost every individual or group not in love with US foreign policy that Washington wants to stigmatize is charged with being associated with, or being a member of, al-Qaeda, as if there's a precise and meaningful distinction between people retaliating against the atrocities of American imperialism while being a member of al-Qaeda and retaliating against the atrocities of American imperialism while *not* being a member of al-Qaeda; as if al-Qaeda gives out membership cards to fit into your wallet, and there are chapters of al-Qaeda that put out a weekly newsletter and hold a potluck on the first Monday of each month.

It should be noted that for nearly half a century much of southern Florida has been one big training camp for anti-Castro terrorists. None of their groups – which have carried out many hundreds of serious terrorist acts in the US as well as abroad, including bombing a passenger airplane in flight – is on the State Department list. Nor were the Contras of Nicaragua in the 1980s, heavily supported by the United States, about whom former CIA director Stansfield Turner testified: 'I believe it is irrefutable that a number of the Contras' actions have to be characterized as terrorism, as State-supported terrorism.'[5] The same applies to groups in Kosovo and Bosnia, with close ties to al-Qaeda, including Osama bin Laden, in the recent past, but which have allied themselves with Washington's agenda in the former Yugoslavia since the 1990s. Now we learn of US support for a Pakistani group called Jundullah and led by a Taliban, which has taken responsibility for the kidnappings and deaths and of more than a dozen Iranian soldiers and officials in cross-border attacks.[6] Do not hold your breath waiting for the name Jundullah to appear on the State Department list of terrorist organizations; nor any of the several other ethnic militias being supported by the CIA to carry out terrorist bombing and assassination attacks in Iran.[7]

The same political selectivity applies to many of the groups which *are* on the list, particularly those opposed to American or Israeli policies.

Amid growing pressure from their home countries and international human rights advocates, scores of Guantánamo detainees have been quietly repatriated in the past three years. Now a new analysis by lawyers who have represented detainees at this twenty-first-century Devil's Island says this policy undermines

Washington's own claims about the threat posed by many of the prison camp's residents. The report, based on US government case files for Saudi detainees sent home over the past three years, shows inmates being systematically freed from custody within weeks of their return. In half the cases studied, the detainees had been turned over to US forces by Pakistani police or troops in return for financial rewards. Many others were accused of terrorism connections in part because their Arab nicknames matched those found in a computer database of al-Qaeda members, documents show. In December, a survey by the Associated Press found that 84 percent of released detainees – 205 out of 245 individuals whose cases could be tracked – were set free after being released to the custody of their native countries. 'There are certainly bad people in Guantánamo Bay, but there are also other cases where it's hard to understand why the people are still there,' said Anant Raut, co-author of the report, who has visited the detention camp three times. 'We were struggling to find some rationality, something to comfort us that it wasn't just random. But we didn't find it.'

The report states that many of the US attempts to link the detainees to terrorism groups were based on evidence the authors describe as circumstantial and 'highly questionable,' such as the travel routes the detainees had followed in flying commercially from one Middle Eastern country to another. American officials have associated certain travel routes with al-Qaeda, when in fact, says the report, the routes 'involve ordinary connecting flights in major international airports.' With regard to accusations based on similar names, the report states: 'This accusation appears to be based upon little more than similarities in the transliterations of a detainee's name and a name found on one of the hard drives.'

Raut said he was most struck by the high percentage of Saudi detainees who had been captured and turned over by Pakistani forces. In effect, he said, for at least half the individuals in his report the United States 'had no first-hand knowledge of their activities' in Afghanistan before their capture and imprisonment.[8]

When Michael Scheuer, the former CIA officer who headed the Agency's Osama bin Laden unit, was told that the largest group in Guantánamo came from custody in Pakistan, he declared: 'We absolutely got the wrong people.'[9] Never mind. They were all treated equally: all thrown into solitary confinement; shackled blindfolded, forced to undergo excruciating physical contortions for long periods, denied medicine; sensory deprivation and sleep deprivation were used, alomg with two dozen other methods of torture which American officials do not call torture. (If you tortured these officials, they might admit that it's 'torture lite.')

'The idea is to build an antiterrorist global environment,' a senior American defense official said in 2003, 'so that in 20 to 30 years, terrorism will be like slave-trading, completely discredited.'[10]

When will the dropping of bombs on innocent civilians by the United States, and invading and occupying their country, without their country attacking or threatening the US, become completely discredited? When will the use of depleted uranium and cluster bombs and CIA torture renditions become things that even men like George W. Bush, Dick Cheney, and Donald Rumsfeld will be too embarrassed to defend?

Australian/British journalist John Pilger has noted that in George Orwell's *1984* 'three slogans dominate society: war is peace, freedom is slavery and ignorance is strength. Today's slogan, war on terrorism, also reverses meaning. The war is terrorism.'

Saved again, thank the Lord, saved again
(August 18, 2006)

> Our government has kept us in a perpetual state of fear – kept us in a continuous stampede of patriotic fervor – with the cry of grave

national emergency. Always there has been some terrible evil at home or some monstrous foreign power that was going to gobble us up if we did not blindly rally behind it by furnishing the exorbitant funds demanded. Yet, in retrospect, these disasters seem never to have happened, seem never to have been quite real. (General Douglas MacArthur, 1957[11])

So now we've (choke) just been (gasp) saved from the simultaneous blowing up of as many as ten airplanes headed toward the United States from the UK. Wow, thank you Brits, thank you Homeland Security. And thanks for preventing the destruction of the Sears Tower in Chicago, saving lower Manhattan from a terrorist-unleashed flood, smashing the frightful Canadian 'terror plot' with seventeen arrested, ditto the three Toledo terrorists, and squashing the Los Angeles al-Qaeda plot to fly a hijacked airliner into a skyscraper.

The Los Angeles plot of 2002 was proudly announced by George W. in 2006. It has since been totally discredited. Declared one senior counterterrorism official: 'There was no definitive plot. It never materialized or got past the thought stage.'[12]

And the scare about ricin in the UK, which our own Mr Cheney used as part of the build-up for the invasion of Iraq, telling an audience on January 10, 2003: 'The gravity of the threat we face was underscored in recent days when British police arrested … suspected terrorists in London and discovered a small quantity of ricin, one of the world's deadliest poisons.' It turned out there was not only no plot, there was no ricin. The Brits discovered almost immediately that the substance wasn't ricin but kept that secret for more than two years.[13]

From what is typical in terrorist scares, it is likely that the individuals arrested in the UK on August 10, 2006 were guilty of what George Orwell, in *1984*, called 'thoughtcrimes.' That is to say, they haven't actually *done* anything. At most, they've *thought* about doing something the government would label 'terrorism.'

Perhaps not even very serious thoughts, perhaps just venting their anger at the exceptionally violent role played by the UK and the US in the Middle East and thinking out loud how nice it would be to throw some of that violence back in the face of Blair and Bush. And then, the fatal moment for them that ruins their lives forever: their angry words are heard by the wrong person, who reports them to the authorities. (In the Manhattan flood case the formidable, dangerous 'terrorists' made mention on an Internet chat room about blowing something up.[14])

Soon a government agent provocateur appears, infiltrates the group, and then actually *encourages* the individuals to think and talk further about terrorist acts, to develop real plans instead of youthful fantasizing, and even provides the individuals with some of the means for carrying out these terrorist acts, like explosive material and technical know-how, money and transportation, whatever is needed to advance the plot. It's known as 'entrapment,' and it's supposed to be illegal, it's supposed to be a powerful defense for the accused, but the authorities get away with it all the time; and the accused get put away for a very long time. And because of the role played by the agent provocateur, we may never know whether any of the accused, on their own, would have gone much further, if at all, like actually making a bomb, or, in the present case, even making transatlantic flight reservations, since many of the accused reportedly did not even have passports. Government infiltrating and monitoring is one thing; encouragement, pushing the plot forward, and scaring the public to make political capital from it are quite something else.

Prosecutors have said that the seven men in Miami charged with conspiring to blow up the Sears Tower in Chicago and FBI buildings in other cities had sworn allegiance to al-Qaeda. This came after meeting with a confidential government informant who was posing as a representative of the terrorist group. Did they swear or hold such allegiance, one must wonder, *before* meeting with the informant? 'In essence,' reported the *Independent*, 'the entire case rests upon conversations between Narseal Batiste, the apparent ringleader of the group, with the informant, who was posing as a member of al-Qaeda but in fact belonged to the [FBI] South Florida Terrorist Task Force.' Batiste told the informant that 'he was organizing a mission to build an "Islamic army" in order to wage jihad.' He provided a list of things he needed: boots, uniforms, machine guns, radios, vehicles, binoculars, bullet-proof vests, firearms, and $50,000 in cash. Oddly enough, one thing that was not asked for was any kind of explosive material. After sweeps of various locations in Miami, government agents found no explosives or weapons. 'This group was more aspirational than operational,' said the FBI's deputy director, while one FBI agent described them as 'social misfits.' And, added the *New York Times*, investigators openly acknowledged that the suspects 'had only the most preliminary discussions about an attack.' Yet Cheney later hailed the arrests at a political fundraiser, calling the group a 'very real threat.'[15]

It was perhaps as great a threat as the suspects in the plot to unleash a catastrophic flood in lower Manhattan by destroying a huge underground wall that holds back the Hudson River. That was the story first released by the authorities; after a while it was replaced by the claim that the suspects were actually plotting something aimed at the subway tunnels that run under the river.[16] Which is more reliable, one must wonder, information on Internet chat rooms or WMD tips provided by CIA Iraqi informers? Or information obtained, as in the current case in the UK, from Pakistani interrogators of the suspects, none of the interrogators being known to be ardent supporters of Amnesty International.

And the three men arrested in Toledo, Ohio, in February 2006 were accused of – are you ready? – plotting to recruit and train terrorists to attack US and allied troops overseas. For saving us from this horror we have a paid FBI witness to thank. He had been an informer with the FBI for four years, and most likely was paid for each new lead he brought in. In the Sears case, the FBI paid almost $56,000 to two confidential informants, and government officials also granted one of them immigration parole so he could remain in the country.[17]

There must be millions of people in the United States and elsewhere who have thoughts about 'terrorist acts.' I might well be one of them when I read about a gathering of Bush, Cheney, and assorted neocons that's going to take place. Given the daily horror of Iraq, Afghanistan, Lebanon, and Palestine in recent times, little of which would occur if not for the government of the United States of America and its allies, the numbers of people having such thoughts must be multiplying rapidly. If I had been at an American or British airport as the latest scare story unfolded, waiting in an interminable line, having my flight canceled, or being told I can't have any carry-on luggage, I may have found it irresistible at some point to declare loudly to my fellow suffering passengers: 'Y'know, folks, this security crap is only gonna get worse and worse as long as the United States and Britain continue to invade, bomb, overthrow, occupy, and torture the world!' How long would it be before I was pulled out of line and thrown into some kind of custody?

If General MacArthur were alive today, would he dare to publicly express the thoughts cited above?

Policymakers and security experts, reports the Associated Press, say that 'Law enforcers are now willing to act swiftly against al-Qaeda sympathizers, even if it means grabbing wannabe terrorists whose plots may be only pipe dreams.'[18]

The capture of dangerous would-be terrorists has been a growth industry in the United States ever since the events of September 11, 2001. Do you remember the 'shoe bomber'? Richard Reid was his name and he was aboard an American Airlines flight from Paris to Miami on December 22, 2001; he tried to detonate explosives hidden in his shoes, didn't succeed, and was overpowered by attendants and passengers. It's because of him that we have to take our shoes off at the airport.

There was also 'the underwear bomber,' Umar Farouk Abdulmutallab, referred to above, who tried to set off plastic explosives sewn into his underwear while aboard a Northwest Airlines flight as the plane approached Detroit airport in 2009. But he failed to detonate them properly, producing only some popping noises and a flame; another passenger jumped him and restrained him as others put out the fire. It's because of Mr Abdulmutallab that we now virtually have to take our underwear off at airports.

And the reason we have strict rules about carrying liquids and gels aboard an airplane? We can thank some other young clowns in Europe in 2006 with pipe dreams about blowing up ten airliners with liquid explosives; they scarcely made it to step one. Since the 'bomb made from liquids and gels' story was foisted upon the public, several chemists and other experts have pointed out the technical near-impossibility of manufacturing such a bomb in a moving airplane, if for no other reason than the necessity of spending at least an hour or two in the airplane bathroom.

Then there was Faisal Shahzad, the 'Times Square bomber,' who on May 1, 2010 parked his car in the heart of New York City, tried to detonate various explosive devices in the car, but succeeded in producing only smoke. He then walked away from the car, after which he was arrested. It's because of him that cars are no longer permitted in Times Square. (No, that's a joke, but maybe not for long.)

The incompetence of these would-be bombers in being unable to detonate their explosives is remarkable. You'd think they could have easily gotten that critical and relatively simple part of the operation down pat beforehand. What I find even more remarkable is that neither of the two men aboard the airplanes thought of going into the bathroom, closing the door, and then trying to detonate the explosives. An 8-year-old child would have thought of that. Are we supposed to take the 'threat' posed by such men seriously?

'The Department of Homeland Security would like to remind passengers that you may not take any liquids onto the plane. This includes ice cream, as the ice cream will melt and turn into a liquid.' This was actually heard by one of my readers at Atlanta airport in 2012. He laughed out loud. He informs me that he didn't know what was more bizarre, that such an announcement was made or that he was the only person that he could see who reacted to its absurdity.

Another example of the frightful terrorist threat was in October 2010 when we were told that two packages addressed to Chicago had been found aboard American cargo planes, one in Dubai, the other in England, containing what might, or might not, be an explosive device; which might, or might not, have exploded. Authorities said it was not known if the intent was to detonate the packages in flight or in Chicago.

Now get this. Terrorists, we are told, are shipping bombs in packages to the United States. They of course would want to make the packages as innocuous looking as can be, right? Nothing that would provoke any suspicion in the mind of an already very suspicious American security establishment, right? So what do we have? The packages were mailed from *Yemen*... and addressed to *Jewish synagogues* in Chicago... Well folks, nothing to see here, just keep moving.[19]

A tale of two terrorists

Zacarias Moussaoui, the only person ever charged in the United States in connection with the September 11, 2001 attacks, testifying at his 2006 trial in Alexandria, Virginia: the sobbing

September 11 survivors and family members who testified against him were 'disgusting'... He and other Muslims want to 'exterminate' American Jews... executed Oklahoma City bomber Timothy McVeigh was 'the greatest American.'[20] Moussaoui expressed his willingness to kill Americans 'any time, anywhere'... 'I wish it had happened not only on the 11th, but the 12th, 13th, 14th, 15th and 16th.'[21]

Orlando Bosch, one of the masterminds behind the October 6, 1976 bombing of a Cuban passenger plane, blown out of the sky with seventy-three people on board, including the entire young Cuban fencing team, interviewed on April 8, 2006 by Juan Manuel Cao of Channel 41 in Miami:

CAO: Did you down that plane in 1976?

BOSCH: If I tell you that I was involved, I will be inculpating myself ... and if I tell you that I did not participate in that action, you would say that I am lying. I am therefore not going to answer one thing or the other.

CAO: In that action 73 persons were killed...

BOSCH: No chico, in a war such as us Cubans who love liberty wage against the tyrant [Fidel Castro], you have to down planes, you have to sink ships, you have to be prepared to attack anything that is within your reach.

CAO: But don't you feel a little bit for those who were killed there, for their families?

BOSCH: Who was on board that plane? Four members of the Communist Party, five north Koreans, five Guyanese ... Who was there? Our enemies.

CAO: And the fencers? The young people on board?

BOSCH: I saw the young girls on television. There were six of them. After the end of the competition, the leader of the six dedicated their triumph to the tyrant. She gave a speech filled with praise for the tyrant. We had already agreed in Santo Domingo, that everyone who comes from Cuba to glorify the tyrant had to run the same risks as those men and women that fight alongside the tyranny.

CAO: If you ran into the family members who were killed in that plane, wouldn't you think it difficult ... ?

BOSCH: No, because in the end those who were there had to know that they were cooperating with the tyranny in Cuba.

The difference between Zacarias Moussaoui and Orlando Bosch is that one of them was put on trial and sentenced to life in prison while the other walks around Miami a free man, free enough to be interviewed on television. In 1983 the City Comission of Miami declared a 'Dr Orlando Bosch Day.'[22]

Bosch had a partner in plotting the bombing of the Cuban airliner: Luis Posada, a Cuban-born citizen of Venezuela. He lives as a free man in the United States. His extradition has been requested by Venezuela for several crimes, including the downing of the airliner, part of the plotting having taken place in Venezuela. But the Bush and Obama administrations have refused to send him to Venezuela, for, despite his horrible crime, he's an ally of the empire; Venezuela and Cuba are not. Nor will Washington try him in the US for the crime. However, the Convention for the Suppression of Unlawful Acts Against the Safety of Civil Aviation (1973), of which the United States is a signatory, gives Washington no discretion. Article 7 says that the state in which 'the alleged offender is found shall, if it does not extradite him, be obliged, without exception whatsoever and whether or not the offence was committed in its territory, to submit the case to its competent authorities for the purpose of prosecution.'[23] Extradite or prosecute. The United States does neither.

3

IRAQ

Iraq. Began with big lies. Ending with big lies. Never forget.

'Most people don't understand what they have been part of here,' said Command Sgt. Major Ron Kelley as he and other American troops prepared to leave Iraq in mid-December 2011. 'We have done a great thing as a nation. We freed a people and gave their country back to them.'

'It is pretty exciting,' said another young American soldier in Iraq. 'We are going down in the history books, you might say.'[1]

Ah yes, the history books, the multi-volume, leather-bound, richly-embossed set of 'The Greatest Destructions of One Country by Another.' The newest volume can relate, with numerous graphic photos, how the modern, educated, advanced nation of Iraq was reduced to a quasi-failed state; how the Americans, beginning in 1991, bombed for twelve years, with one dubious excuse or another; then invaded, then occupied, overthrew the government, tortured without inhibition, killed wantonly; how the people of that unhappy land lost everything...

The loss of a functioning educational system. A 2005 UN study revealed that 84 percent of the higher education establishments had been 'destroyed, damaged and robbed.' The intellectual stock was further depleted as many thousands of academics and other professionals fled abroad or were kidnapped or assassinated; hundreds of thousands, perhaps a million, other Iraqis, most of them from the vital, educated middle class, left for Jordan, Syria or Egypt, many after receiving death threats. 'Now I am isolated,' said a middle-class Sunni Arab, who decided to leave. 'I have no government. I have no protection from the government. Anyone can come to my house, take me, kill me and throw me in the trash.'[2]

Loss of a functioning health-care system. And loss of the public's health. Deadly infections including typhoid and tuberculosis rampaged through the country. Iraq's network of hospitals and health centers, once admired throughout the Middle East, was severely damaged by the war and looting.

The UN's World Food Program reported that 400,000 Iraqi children were suffering from 'dangerous deficiencies of protein.' Deaths from malnutrition and preventable diseases, particularly among children, already a problem because of the twelve years of US-imposed sanctions, increased as poverty and disorder made access to a proper diet and medicines ever more difficult.

Thousands of Iraqis lost an arm or a leg, frequently from unexploded US cluster bombs, which became land mines; cluster bombs are a class of weapons denounced by human rights groups as a cruelly random scourge on civilians, especially children who pick them up.

Depleted uranium particles, from exploded US ordnance, float in the Iraqi air, to be breathed into human bodies and to radiate forever, and infect the water, the soil, the blood, and the genes, producing malformed babies. And the use of napalm as well. And white phosphorous. The most awful birth defects result. The BBC told of doctors in the Iraqi city of Fallujah reporting a high level of birth defects, with some blaming weapons used by the United States during its fierce onslaughts of 2004 and subsequently, which left much of the city in ruins. The level of heart defects among newborn babies was said to be thirteen times higher than in Europe. The BBC correspondent also saw children in the city who were suffering from paralysis or brain damage, and a photograph of one baby who was born with three heads. He added that he heard many times that officials in Fallujah had warned women that they should not have children. One doctor in the city had compared data about birth defects from before 2003 – when she saw about one case every two months – with the situation in 2010, when she saw cases every day. 'I've seen footage of babies born with an eye in the middle of the forehead, the nose on the forehead,' she said.[3]

('Years from now when America looks out on a democratic Middle East, growing in freedom and prosperity, Americans will speak of the battles like Fallujah with the same awe and reverence that we now give to Guadalcanal and Iwo Jima' [in World War II] – George W. Bush[4])

The supply of safe drinking water, effective sewage disposal, and reliable electricity all generally fell well below pre-invasion levels, producing constant hardship for the public, in temperatures reaching 115 degrees. To add to the misery, people waited all day in the heat to purchase gasoline, due in part to oil production, the country's chief source of revenue, being less than half its previous level.

The water and sewerage system and other elements of the infrastructure had been purposely destroyed by US bombing in the first Gulf War of 1991. By 2003, the Iraqis had made great strides in repairing the most essential parts of it. Then came Washington's renewed bombing.

The American military assaulted at least one hospital to prevent it from giving out casualty figures from US attacks that contradicted official US figures, which the hospital had been in the habit of doing.

Numerous homes were broken into by US forces, the men taken away, the women humiliated, the children traumatized; on many occasions, the family said that the American soldiers helped themselves to some of the family's money.

no

There was destruction and looting of the country's ancient heritage, perhaps the world's greatest archive of the human past. Sites were left unprotected by the US military, which was busy protecting oil facilities.

Iraq's legal system, outside of the political sphere, was once one of the most impressive and secular in the Middle East; now, religious law increasingly prevails.

Women's rights, previously enjoyed, fell under great danger of being subject to harsh Islamic law. There is today a Shiite religious ruling class in Iraq, which tolerates physical attacks on women for showing a bare arm or for picnicking with a male friend. Men can be harassed for wearing shorts in public, as can children playing outside in shorts.

> I see that Frontline on PBS this week has a documentary called 'Bush's War'. That's what I've been calling it for a long time. It's not the 'Iraq War.' Iraq did nothing. Iraq didn't plan 9/11. It didn't have weapons of mass destruction. It DID have movie theaters and bars and women wearing what they wanted and a significant Christian population and one of the few Arab capitals with an open synagogue. But that's all gone now. Show a movie and you'll be shot in the head. Over a hundred women have been randomly executed for not wearing a scarf. (Filmmaker Michael Moore, March 24, 2008)

Sex trafficking, virtually nonexistent previously, has become a serious issue.

Jews, Christians, and other non-Muslims have lost much of the security they had enjoyed in Saddam's secular society; many have emigrated. The Kurds of Northern Iraq evicted Arabs from their homes. Arabs evicted Kurds in other parts of the country.

A gulag of prisons run by the US and the new Iraqi government featured a wide variety of torture and abuse; a human-rights disaster area. Only a very small portion of the many tens of thousands imprisoned by US forces were convicted of any crime.

Paul Bremer, head of the Coalition Provisional Authority, the first US occupation administration of Iraq in 2003, made free enterprise a guiding rule, shutting down 192 state-owned businesses where the World Bank estimated 500,000 people were working.[5]

Many people were evicted from their homes because they were Baathist, Saddam Hussein's party. US troops took part in some of the evictions. They also demolished homes in fits of rage over the killing of one of their buddies.

When US troops didn't find who they were looking for, they took who was there; wives were held until the husband turned himself in, a practice which Hollywood films stamped in the American mind as being a particular evil of the Nazis; it's also an example of collective punishment of civilians, forbidden under the Geneva Convention.

Continual American bombing assaults on neighborhoods left an uncountable number of destroyed homes, workplaces, mosques, bridges, roads, and everything else that goes into the making of modern civilized life.

Haditha, Fallujah, Samarra, Ramadi... names that will live in infamy for the wanton destruction, murder, and assaults upon human beings and human rights carried out in those places by US forces.

American soldiers and private security companies regularly killed people and left the bodies lying in the street; civil war, death squads, kidnapping, car bombs, rape, each and every day... Iraq became the most dangerous place on earth. US-trained Iraqi military and police forces killed even more, as did the insurgency. An entire new generation growing up on violence and sectarian ethics; this will poison the Iraqi psyche for many years to come.

US intelligence and military police officers often freed dangerous criminals in return for a promise to spy on insurgents.

Iraqis protesting about particular issues were shot by US forces on several occasions.

At various times, Iraqi newspapers were closed down by the American occupation for what they printed; reporters were shot by American troops; the US killed, wounded, or jailed reporters from Al Jazeera television, closed the station's office, and banned it from certain areas because occupation officials didn't like the news the station was reporting; the Pentagon planted paid-for news articles in the Iraqi press to serve propaganda purposes.

> This war [in Iraq] is the most important liberal, revolutionary U.S. democracy-building project since the Marshall Plan ... it is one of the noblest things this country has ever attempted abroad. (Thomas Friedman, much-acclaimed *New York Times* foreign affairs analyst, November 2003[6])

> President Bush has placed human rights at the center of his foreign policy agenda in unprecedented ways. (Michael Gerson, columnist for the *Washington Post*, and former speech-writer for George W. Bush, 2007[7])

> [The war in Iraq] is one of the noblest endeavors the United States, or any great power, has ever undertaken. (David Brooks, NPR commentator and *New York Times* columnist, 2007[8])

If this is what leading American public intellectuals believed and imparted to their audiences, is it any wonder that the media can short-circuit people's critical faculties altogether? It should also be noted that these three journalists were all with 'liberal' media.

> It is a common refrain among war-weary Iraqis that things were better before the U.S.-led invasion in 2003. (*Washington Post*, May 5, 2007)

It was indeed common. National Public Radio foreign correspondent Loren Jenkins, serving in NPR's Baghdad bureau in 2006, met with a senior Shiite cleric, a man who was described in the NPR report as 'a moderate' and as a person trying to lead his followers into practicing peace and reconciliation. He had been jailed by Saddam Hussein and forced into exile. Jenkins asked him: 'What would you think if you had to go back to Saddam Hussein?' The cleric replied that he'd 'rather see Iraq under Saddam Hussein than the way it is now.'[9]

That same year, in a BBC interview, UN Secretary General Kofi Annan agreed when it was suggested that some Iraqis believe life is worse now than it was under Saddam Hussein's regime.

> I think they are right in the sense of the average Iraqi's life. If I were an average Iraqi obviously I would make the same compari-son, that they had a dictator who was brutal but they had their streets, they could go out, their kids could go to school and come back home without a mother or father worrying, 'Am I going to see my child again?'[10]

No matter... drum roll, please... Stand tall American GI hero! And don't even *think* of ever apologizing or paying any repara-tions. Iraq is forced by Washington to continue paying reparations to Kuwait for Iraq's invasion in 1990 (an invasion instigated in no small measure by the United States). And – deep breath here! – Vietnam has been compensating the United States. Since 1997 Hanoi has been paying off about $145 million in debts left by the defeated South Vietnamese government for American food and infrastructure aid. Thus, Hanoi is reimbursing the United States for part of the cost of the war waged against it.[11] How much will Iraq be paying the United States?

On December 14, 2011, at the Fort Bragg, North Carolina mili-tary base, Barack Obama stood before an audience of soldiers to speak about the Iraq War. It was a moment in which the president of the United States found it within his heart and soul – as well as within his oft-praised (supposed) intellect – to proclaim:

> This is an extraordinary achievement, nearly nine years in the making. And today, we remember everything that you did to make it possible. ... Years from now, your legacy will endure. In the names of your fallen comrades etched on headstones at Arlington,

and the quiet memorials across our country. In the whispered words of admiration as you march in parades, and in the freedom of our children and grandchildren. ... So God bless you all, God bless your families, and God bless the United States of America. ... You have earned your place in history because you sacrificed so much for people you have never met.

Does Mr Obama, the Peace Laureate, believe the words that come out of his mouth? Barack H. Obama believes only in being the president of the United States. It is the only strong belief the man holds.

But freedom has indeed reigned – for the great multinationals to extract everything they can from Iraq's resources and labor without the hindrance of public interest laws, environmental regulations, or worker protections.

Yet, despite all of the above, when the subject is Iraq and the person I'm having a discussion with has no other argument left to defend US policy, at least at the moment, I may be asked:

'Just tell me one thing, are you glad that Saddam Hussein is out of power?'

And I say: 'No.'

And the person says: 'No?'

And I say: 'No. Tell me, if you went into surgery to correct a knee problem and the surgeon mistakenly amputated your entire leg, what would you think if someone then asked you: Are you glad that you no longer have a knee problem? The people of Iraq no longer have a Saddam problem.'

And many Iraqis actually supported him.

US foreign policy, the mainstream media, and Alzheimer's

There's no letup, is there? The preparation of the American mind, the world mind, for the next gala performance of D&D – Death and Destruction. The bunker-buster bombs are now

30,000 pounds each one, six times as heavy as the previous delightful model. But the Masters of War still want to be loved; they need for you to believe them when they say they have no choice, that Iran is the latest threat to life as we know it, no time to waste.

The preparation of minds was just as fervent before the invasion of Iraq in March 2003. And when it turned out that Iraq did not have any kind of arsenal of weapons of mass destruction (WMD)... well, our power elite found other justifications for the invasion, and didn't look back. Some berated Iraq: 'Why didn't they tell us that? Did they *want* us to bomb them?'

In actuality, before the US invasion high Iraqi officials had stated clearly on repeated occasions that they had no such weapons. In August 2002, Iraqi Deputy Prime Minister Tariq Aziz told American newscaster Dan Rather on CBS: 'We do not possess any nuclear or biological or chemical weapons.'[12] In December, Aziz stated to Ted Koppel on ABC: 'The fact is that we don't have weapons of mass destruction. We don't have chemical, biological, or nuclear weaponry.'[13] Hussein himself told Rather in February 2003: 'These missiles have been destroyed. There are no missiles that are contrary to the prescription of the United Nations [as to range] in Iraq. They are no longer there.'[14]

Moreover, General Hussein Kamel, former head of Iraq's secret weapons program, and a son-in-law of Saddam Hussein, told the UN in 1995 that Iraq had destroyed its banned missiles and chemical and biological weapons soon after the Persian Gulf War of 1991.[15]

There are yet other examples of Iraqi officials telling the world that the WMD were non-existent.

And if there were still any uncertainty remaining, in July 2010 Hans Blix, former chief United Nations weapons inspector, who led a doomed hunt for WMD in Iraq, told a British inquiry into the 2003 invasion that those who were '100 percent certain there were weapons of mass destruction' in Iraq turned out to have 'less than zero percent knowledge' of where the purported hidden caches might be. He testified that he had warned British Prime Minister Tony Blair in a February 2003 meeting – as well as US Secretary of State Condoleezza Rice in separate talks – that Hussein might have no weapons of mass destruction.[16]

Those of you who don't already have serious doubts about the American mainstream media's knowledge and understanding of US foreign policy should consider this: despite the two revelations on Dan Rather's CBS programs, and the other revelations noted above, in January 2008 we find CBS reporter Scott Pelley interviewing FBI agent George Piro, who had interviewed Saddam Hussein before he was executed:

> PELLEY: And what did he tell you about how his weapons of mass destruction had been destroyed?
>
> PIRO: He told me that most of the WMD had been destroyed by the U.N. inspectors in the '90s, and those that hadn't been destroyed by the inspectors were unilaterally destroyed by Iraq.
>
> PELLEY: He had ordered them destroyed?
>
> PIRO: Yes.
>
> PELLEY: So why keep the secret? Why put your nation at risk? Why put your own life at risk to maintain this charade?[17]

The United States and Israel are preparing to attack Iran because of their alleged development of nuclear weapons, which Iran has denied on many occasions. Of the Iraqis who warned the United States that it was mistaken about the WMD, Saddam Hussein was executed, Tariq Aziz is awaiting execution. Which Iranian officials is USrael going to hang after their country is laid to waste?

Would it have mattered if the Bush administration had fully believed Iraq when it said it had no WMD? Probably not. There is ample evidence that Bush knew this to be the case, or at a minimum should have seriously suspected it; the same applies to Tony Blair. Saddam Hussein did not sufficiently appreciate just how psychopathic his two adversaries were. Bush was determined to vanquish Iraq, for the sake of Israel, for control of oil, and for expanding the empire with new bases, though in the end most of this didn't work out as the empire expected; for some odd reason, it seems that the Iraqi people resented being bombed, invaded, occupied, demolished, and tortured.

But if Iran is in fact building nuclear weapons, we have to ask: is there some international law that says that the US, the UK, Russia, China, Israel, France, Pakistan, and India are entitled to nuclear weapons, but Iran is not? If the United States had known that the Japanese had deliverable atomic bombs, would Hiroshima and Nagasaki have been destroyed? Israeli military historian Martin van Creveld has written: 'The world has witnessed how the United States attacked Iraq for, as it turned out, no reason at all. Had the Iranians not tried to build nuclear weapons, they would be crazy.'[18]

Examine a map: Iran sits directly between two of the United States' great obsessions – Iraq and Afghanistan... directly between two of the world's greatest oil regions – the Persian Gulf and Caspian Sea... it's part of the encirclement of the two leading potential threats to American world domination – Russia and China... Tehran will never be a client state or obedient poodle to Washington. How could any good, self-respecting Washington imperialist resist such a target? Bombs Away!

The sign has been put out front: 'Iraq is open for business'

In 2005, the British NGO Platform, issued a report, *Crude Designs: The Rip-Off of Iraq's Oil Wealth*, disclosing the American occupation's massive giveaway of the sovereign nation's most valuable commodity, oil. Among its findings:

The report revealed how an oil policy with origins in the US
State Department is on course to be adopted in Iraq, soon after
the December elections, with no public debate and at enormous
potential cost. The policy allocates the majority of Iraq's oilfields
– accounting for at least 64% of the country's oil reserves – for
development by multinational oil companies.

The estimated cost to Iraq over the life of the new oil contracts
is $74 to $194 billion, compared with leaving oil development in
public hands. The contracts would guarantee massive profits to
foreign companies, with rates of return of 42 to 162 percent. The
kinds of contracts that will provide these returns are known as
production sharing agreements. PSAs have been heavily promoted
by the US government and oil majors and have the backing of
senior figures in the Iraqi Oil Ministry. However, PSAs last for
25–40 years, are usually secret, and prevent governments from
later altering the terms of the contract.[19] *Crude Designs* author
and lead researcher Greg Muttitt says: 'The form of contracts
being promoted is the most expensive and undemocratic option
available. Iraq's oil should be for the benefit of the Iraqi people,
not foreign oil companies.'[20]

Noam Chomsky remarked: 'We're supposed to believe that the
US would've invaded Iraq if it was an island in the Indian Ocean
and its main exports were pickles and lettuce. This is what we're
supposed to believe.'[21]

Another charming tale about the noble mission

On April 6, 2004 Lieutenant General Ricardo Sanchez was in
Iraq in video teleconference with President Bush, Secretary of
State Colin Powell, and Secretary of Defense Donald Rumsfeld.
One major American offensive was in operation, another about to
be launched. According to Sanchez's memoir, Powell was talking
tough that day:

'We've got to smash somebody's ass quickly,' Powell said. 'There has to be a total victory somewhere. We must have a brute demonstration of power.' Then Bush spoke: 'At the end of this campaign al-Sadr must be gone. At a minimum, he will be arrested. It is essential he be wiped out. Kick ass! If somebody tries to stop the march to democracy, we will seek them out and kill them! We must be tougher than hell! This Vietnam stuff, this is not even close. It is a mind-set. We can't send that message. It's an excuse to prepare us for withdrawal. ... There is a series of moments and this is one of them. Our will is being tested, but we are resolute. We have a better way. Stay strong! Stay the course! Kill them! Be confident! Prevail! We are going to wipe them out! We are not blinking!'
(*Wiser in Battle: A Soldier's Story*, pp. 349–50)

Who would have thought? Bush has been vindicated
(December 11, 2007)

We're making progress in Iraq! The 'surge' is working, we're told. Never mind that the war is totally and perfectly illegal. Not to mention totally and perfectly, even exquisitely, immoral. It's making progress. That's a good thing, isn't it? Meanwhile, the al-Qaeda types have greatly increased their number all over the Middle East and South Asia, so their surge is making progress too. Good for them. And speaking of progress in the War on Terror, is anyone progressing faster and better than the Taliban?

The American progress is measured by a decrease in violence, the White House has decided – a daily holocaust has been cut back to a daily multiple catastrophe. And who's keeping the count? Why, the same good people who have been regularly feeding us a lie for the past five years about the number of Iraqi deaths, completely ignoring the epidemiological studies. (Real Americans don't do Arab body counts.) An analysis by the *Washington Post* left the administration's claim pretty much in tatters. The article opened with: 'The U.S. military's claim that violence has decreased sharply in Iraq in recent months has come under scrutiny from many experts within and outside the government, who contend that some of the underlying statistics are questionable and selectively ignore negative trends.' The article then continued in the same critical vein.[22]

To the extent that there may have been a reduction in violence, we must also keep in mind that, thanks to this lovely little war, there are several million Iraqis either dead or in exile abroad, or in bursting American and Iraqi prisons; there must also be a few million more wounded who are homebound or otherwise physically limited; so the number of potential victims and killers has been greatly reduced. Moreover, extensive ethnic cleansing has taken place in Iraq (another good indication of progress, n'est-ce pas?) – Sunnis and Shiites are now living more in their own special enclaves than before, none of those stinking mixed communities with their unholy mixed marriages, so violence of the sectarian type has also gone down.[23] On top of all this, US soldiers have been venturing out a lot less (for fear of things like... well, dying), so the violence against our noble lads is also down. Remember that insurgent attacks on American forces is how the Iraqi violence (post-2003 invasion) all began in the first place.

Oh, did I mention that 2007 was the deadliest year for US troops since the war began?[24] It's been the same worst year for American forces in Afghanistan.

One of the signs of the reduction in violence in Iraq, the administration would like us to believe, is that many Iraqi families are returning from Syria, where they had fled because of the violence. The *New York Times*, however, reported that 'Under intense pressure to show results after months of political stalemate, the [Iraqi] government has continued to publicize figures that exaggerate the movement back to Iraq.' The count, it turns out, included all Iraqis crossing the border, for whatever reason. A United Nations survey found that 46 percent were leaving Syria because they could not afford to stay; 25 percent said they fell victim to a stricter Syrian visa policy; and only 14 percent said they were returning because they had heard about improved security.[25]

How long can it be before vacation trips to 'Exotic Iraq' are flashed across our television screens? 'Baghdad's Beautiful Beaches Beckon.' Just step over the bodies. Indeed, the State Department has recently advertised for a 'business development/ tourism' expert to work in Baghdad, 'with a particular focus on tourism and related services.'[26]

We've been told often by American leaders and media that the US forces can't leave because of the violence, because there would be a bloodbath. Now there's an alleged significant decrease in the violence. Is that being used as an argument to get out – a golden opportunity for the United States to leave, with head held high? Of course not.

The past is unpredictable: leaving Iraq vs leaving Vietnam
(August 10, 2007)

As the call for withdrawal of American forces from Iraq grows louder, those who support the war are rewriting history to paint a scary picture of what happened in Vietnam after the United States military left in March 1973.

They speak of invasions by the North Vietnamese communists, but fail to point out that a two-decades-long civil war had simply continued after the Americans left, minus a good deal of the horror that US bombs and chemical weapons had been causing.

They speak of the 'bloodbath' that followed the American withdrawal, a term that implies killing of large numbers of civilians who didn't support the communists. But this never happened. If it had taken place the anti-communists in the United States who supported the war in Vietnam would have been more than happy to publicize a 'commie bloodbath.' It would have made big headlines all over the world. The fact that you can't find anything of the sort is indicative of the fact that nothing like a bloodbath took place. It would be difficult to otherwise disprove this negative.

'Some 600,000 Vietnamese drowned in the South China Sea attempting to escape,' proclaimed the conservative WorldNetDaily website recently.[27] Has anyone not confined to a right-wing happy farm ever heard of this before?

They mix Vietnam and Cambodia together in the same thought, leaving the impression that the horrors of Pol Pot included Vietnam. This is the conservative National Review Online:

> Six weeks later, the last Americans lifted off in helicopters from the
> roof of the U.S. embassy in Saigon, leaving hundreds of panicked
> South Vietnamese immediately behind and an entire region to
> the mercy of the communists. The scene was similar in Phnom
> Penh [Cambodia]. The torture and murder spree that followed left
> millions of corpses.[28]

And here's dear old Fox News, on July 26, 2007, reporters Sean Hannity and Alan Colmes, with their guest, actor Jon Voight. Voight says 'Right now, we're having a lot of people who don't know a whole lot of things crying for us pulling out of Iraq. This – there was a bloodbath when we pulled out of Vietnam, 2.5 million people in Cambodia and Vietnam – South Vietnam were slaughtered.' Alan Colmes's response, in its entirety: 'Yes, sir.' Hannity said nothing. The many devoted listeners of Fox News could only nod their heads knowingly.

In actuality, instead of a bloodbath of those who had collaborated with the enemy, the Vietnamese sent them to 're-education' camps, a more civilized treatment than in post-World War II Europe where many of those who had collaborated with the Germans were publicly paraded, shaven bald, humiliated in other ways, and/or hanged from the nearest tree. But some conservatives today would have you believe that the Vietnamese camps were virtually little Auschwitzes.[29]

Another historical reminder: since it's generally accepted that the United States lost the war in Vietnam, and since we were told back then that the war was a battle for our freedom, then the 'fight for our freedom' must have been unsuccessful, and we must be under the occupation of the North Vietnamese Army. Next time you're out on the street and you see a passing NVA patrol, please wave and tell them that I say hello.

Can anyone find a message hidden here?

The following quotations all come from the same article in the *Washington Post* of August 4, 2006 by Ann Scott Tyson concerning the Iraqi town of Hit:

> Residents are quick to argue that the American presence incites those attacks, and they blame the U.S. military rather than insurgents for turning their town into a combat zone. The Americans should pull out, they say, and let them solve their own problems.
>
> 'We want the same thing. I want to go home to my wife,' said an American soldier.
>
> 'Another U.S. officer put it more bluntly: "Nobody wants us here, so why are we here? That's the big question."'
>
> 'If we leave, all the attacks would stop, because we'd be gone.'
>
> 'The problem is with the Americans. They only bring problems,' said watermelon vendor Sefuab Ganiydum, 35. 'Closing the bridge, the curfew, the hospital. It's better for U.S. forces to leave the city.'
>
> 'What did we do to have all this suffering?' asked Ramsey Abdullah Hindi, 60, sitting outside a tea shop. Ignoring U.S. troops within earshot, he said Iraqis were justified to attack them. 'They have a right to fight against the Americans because of their religion and the bad treatment. We will stand until the last,' he said somberly.
>
> City officials, too, are adamant that U.S. troops leave Hit.

> 'I'm the guy doing the good stuff and I get shot at all the time!
> Nobody is pro-American in this city. They either tolerate us or
> all-out hate us,' said a US Marine major.
> 'If we do leave, the city will be a lot better and they'll build it a
> lot better.'

This just in: Bush has just read this article and says the hidden
message is that the United States is bringing freedom and democracy to Iraq.

Chutzpah of an imperial size

Do you remember the classic example of *chutzpah*? It's the young
man who kills his parents and then asks the judge for mercy
on the grounds that he's an orphan. The Bush administration's
updated version of that was starting a wholly illegal, immoral,
and devastating war and then dismissing all kinds of criticism
of its action on the grounds that 'we're at war.'

They used this excuse to defend warrantless spying, to defend
the imprisonment of people for years without charging them
with a crime, to abuse and torture them, to ignore the Geneva
Convention and other international treaties; they used it against
Democrats, accusing them of partisanship during 'a time of war';
they used it to justify the expansion of presidential powers and
the weakening of checks and balances. In short, they claimed
'We can do whatever we want about anything at all related to this
war, because we're at war.'

'War is war,' said Supreme Court Justice Antonin Scalia, 'and
it has never been the case that when you captured a combatant
you have to give them a jury trial in your civil courts. Give
me a break.'[30] Scalia, in his public talks, implies that prisoners
held in the far-flung American gulag were all 'captured on the
battlefield.'[31] But this is simply false. Very few of the poor souls
were captured on any kind of battlefield, few had even a gun in

their hand; most were just in the wrong place at the wrong time or were turned in by an informer for an American bounty or a personal grudge.

The American public, like all publics, requires only sufficient repetition from 'respectable' sources to learn how to play the game. In April 2006 many cities of Wisconsin held referendums on bringing the troops home from Iraq. Here's Jim Martin, 48, a handyman in Evansville. He thinks that his city shouldn't waste taxpayers' money running a referendum that means nothing. 'The fact of the matter remains, we're at war,' he said.[32] And here now is Chris Simcox, a leader in the Minuteman movement that patrols the Mexican border: 'If I catch you breaking into my country in the middle of the night and we're at war ... you're a potential enemy. I don't care if you're a busboy coming to wash dishes.'[33]

Dahlia Lithic of Slate.com summed up the legal arguments put forth by the Bush administration thus:

> The existing laws do not apply because this is a different kind of war. It's a different kind of war because the president says so. The president gets to say so because he is president. ... We follow the laws of war except to the extent that they do not apply to us. These prisoners have all the rights to which they are entitled by law, except to the extent that we have changed the law to limit their rights.[34]

Yet, George W. cut taxes heavily, something probably unprecedented while at war. Didn't he realize that we're at war?

Reconstruction, thy name is not the United States
(January 9, 2006)

In January 2006 the Bush administration announced that it did not intend to seek any new funds for Iraq reconstruction in the budget request going before Congress in February. When the last of the reconstruction budget is spent, US officials in Baghdad have made clear, other foreign donors and the fledgling Iraqi government will have to take up what authorities say is tens of billions of dollars of work yet to be done merely to bring reliable electricity, water and other services to Iraq's 26 million people.[35]

It should be noted that these services, including sanitation systems, were largely destroyed by US bombing – most of it rather deliberately – beginning in the first Gulf War: forty days and nights the bombing went on, demolishing everything that goes into the making of a modern society; followed by twelve years of merciless economic sanctions, accompanied by twelve years of often daily bombing supposedly to protect the so-called no-fly zones; finally the bombing, invasion and widespread devastation beginning in March 2003 and continuing even as you read this. 'The U.S. never intended to completely rebuild Iraq,' Brig. Gen. William McCoy, the Army Corps of Engineers commander overseeing the work, told reporters at a recent news conference. McCoy said: 'This was just supposed to be a jump-start.'[36] It's a remarkable pattern. The United States has a long record of bombing nations, reducing entire neighborhoods, and much of cities, to rubble, wrecking the infrastructure, ruining the lives of those the bombs didn't kill. And afterward doing shockingly little or literally nothing to repair the damage.

On January 27, 1973, in Paris, the United States signed the 'Agreement on Ending the War and Restoring Peace in Vietnam.' Among the principles to which the United States agreed was that stated in Article 21: 'In pursuance of its traditional [sic] policy, the United States will contribute to healing the wounds of war and to postwar reconstruction of the Democratic Republic of Vietnam [North Vietnam] and throughout Indochina.'

Five days later, President Nixon sent a message to the Prime Minister of North Vietnam in which he stipulated the following:

(1) The Government of the United States of America will contribute to postwar reconstruction in North Vietnam without any
political conditions. (2) Preliminary United States studies indicate
that the appropriate programs for the United States contribution
to postwar reconstruction will fall in the range of $3.25 billion of
grant aid over 5 years.

Nothing of the promised reconstruction aid was ever paid, or
ever will be.

During the same period, Laos and Cambodia were wasted by
US bombing as relentlessly as was Vietnam. After the Indochina
wars were over, these nations, too, qualified to become beneficia-
ries of America's 'traditional policy' of zero reconstruction.

Then came the American bombings of Grenada and Panama
in the 1980s. There goes our neighborhood. Hundreds of Pana-
manians petitioned the Washington-controlled Organization of
American States as well as American courts, all the way up to the
US Supreme Court, for 'just compensation' for the damage caused
by Operation Just Cause (this being the not-tongue-in-cheek name
given to the American invasion and bombing). They got just
nothing, the same amount the people of Grenada received.

In 1998, Washington, in its grand wisdom, fired more than a
dozen cruise missiles into a building in Sudan, which it claimed
was producing chemical and biological weapons. The completely
pulverized building was actually a major pharmaceuticals plant,
vital to the Sudanese people. The United States effectively admitted its mistake by releasing the assets of the plant's owner it had
frozen. Surely now it was compensation time. It appears that
nothing has ever been paid to the owner, who filed suit, or to
those injured in the bombing.[37]

The following year we had the case of Yugoslavia; seventy-
eight days of round-the-clock bombing, transforming an advanced
state into virtually a pre-industrial one; the reconstruction needs
were breathtaking. In all the years since Yugoslavian bridges fell

into the Danube, the country's factories and homes leveled, its roads made unusable, transportation torn apart ... the country has not received any funds for reconstruction from the architect and leading perpetrator of the bombing campaign, the United States.

The day after the above announcement about the US ending its reconstruction efforts in Iraq, it was reported that the United States is phasing out its commitment to reconstruction in Afghanistan as well.[38] This after several years of the usual launching of bombs and missiles on towns and villages, resulting in the usual wreckage and ruin.

The fairy tale behind the war
(December 6, 2005)

As it became apparent that the US war in Iraq was an embarrassing tragedy, there were lots of accusations going around between the Democrats and the Republicans, followed by counter-accusations, congressional investigations, demands for more investigations... Who said what? When did they say it? How did it contribute to the buildup for war?... intelligence failures, the administration should have known, we were misled, they lied, but the Democrats believed it also, voted for it... round and round it goes, back and forth, what passes for serious parliamentary debate in the US of A in the twenty-first century...

It's time once again to remind ourselves of the big lie, the biggest lie of all, the lie that makes this whole controversy rather irrelevant. For it didn't matter if Iraq had weapons of mass destruction, it didn't matter if the intelligence was right or wrong, or whether the Bush administration lied about the weapons, or who believed the lies and who didn't. All that mattered was the Bush administration's claim that Iraq was a threat to use the weapons against the United States, an imminent threat to wreak

great havoc upon America – 'Increasingly we believe the United
States will become the target of those [Iraqi nuclear] activities,'
declared Vice President Cheney six months before the invasion,
as but one example.[39]

Think about that. What possible reason could Saddam Hussein
have had for attacking the United States other than an irresistible desire for mass national suicide? 'Oh,' some people might
argue, 'he was so crazy, who knew what he might have done?'
But when it became obvious in late 2002 that the US was intent
upon invading Iraq, Saddam opened up the country to the UN
weapons inspectors much more than ever before, with virtually
full cooperation. This was not the behavior of a crazy person;
this was the behavior of a survivalist. He didn't even use those
weapons when he was invaded in 1991 when he certainly had
some of them. Moreover, we now know that Iraq had put out
peace feelers in early 2003 hoping to prevent the war.[40] They
were not crazy at all.

No, the United States didn't invade Iraq because of any threat
of an attack using WMD. Nor can it be argued that mere possession of such weapons – or the belief of same – was reason enough
to take action, for then the United States would have to invade
Russia, France, Israel et al.

The elephant in Saddam Hussein's courtroom
(November 10, 2005)

The trial of Saddam Hussein has begun. He is charged with the
deaths of more than 140 people who were executed after gunmen
fired on his motorcade in the predominantly Shiite Muslim town
of Dujail, north of Baghdad, in an attempt to assassinate him
in 1982. This appears to be the only crime he's being tried for.
Yet for a few years now we've been hearing about how Saddam
used chemical weapons against 'his own people' in the town

of Halabja in March 1988. (Actually, the people were Kurds, who could be regarded as Saddam's 'own people' only if the Seminoles were President Andrew Jackson's own people.) The Bush administration never tires of repeating that line to us. As recently as October 21, Karen Hughes, White House envoy for public diplomacy, told an audience in Indonesia that Saddam had 'used weapons of mass destruction against his own people. He had murdered hundreds of thousands of his own people using poison gas.' When challenged about the number, Hughes replied: 'It's something that our U.S. government has said a number of times in the past. It's information that was used very widely after his attack on the Kurds. I believe it was close to 300,000. That's something I said every day in the course of the campaign. That's information that we talked about a great deal in America.' The State Department later corrected Hughes, saying the number of victims in Halabja was about 5,000.[41] (This figure, too, may well have been inflated for political reasons; for at least the next six months following the Halabja attack one could find the casualty count being reported in major media as 'hundreds', even by Iran with whom Iraq was at war from 1981 to 1988; then, somehow, it ballooned to '5,000.'[42])

It should be noted, incidentally, that Abraham Lincoln did in fact kill his own people in the American Civil war, hundreds of thousands of them! Given the repeated administration emphasis of the Halabja event, one would think that it would be the charge used in the court against Saddam. Well, I can think of two reasons why the US would be reluctant to bring that matter to court. One, the evidence for the crime has always been somewhat questionable; for example, at one time an arm of the Pentagon issued a report suggesting that it was actually Iran which had used the poison gas in Halabja.[43] And two, the United States, in addition to providing Saddam abundant financial and intelligence support, supplied him with lots of materials to help Iraq achieve its chemical and biological weapons capability; it would be kind of awkward if Saddam's defense raised this issue in the court. But the United States has carefully orchestrated the trial to exclude any unwanted testimony, including the well-known fact that not long after the 1982 carnage Saddam is being charged with, in December 1983, Defense Secretary Donald Rumsfeld – perfectly well informed about the Iraqi regime's methods and the use of chemical weapons against Iranian troops – arrived in Baghdad, sent by Ronald Reagan with the objective of strengthening the relationship between the two countries.[44] There are photos and film available depicting the warm greetings extended to each other by Saddam and Rumsfeld.

War is peace, occupation is sovereignty
(October 17, 2005)

The town of Rawa in Northern Iraq is occupied. The United States has built an army outpost there to cut off the supply of foreign fighters purportedly entering Iraq from Syria. The Americans engage in house searches, knocking in doors, summary detentions, road blocks, air strikes, and other tactics highly upsetting to the people of Rawa. Recently, the commander of the outpost, Lt. Col. Mark Davis, addressed a crowd of 300 angry people. 'We're not going anywhere,' he told the murmuring citizens. 'Some of you are concerned about the attack helicopters and mortar fire from the base,' he said. 'I will tell you this: those are the sounds of peace.'[45] He could have said, making as much sense, that they were the sounds of sovereignty. Iraq is a sovereign nation, Washington assures us, particularly in these days of the constitutional referendum, although the vote will do nothing to empower the Iraqis to relieve their daily misery, serving only a public relations function for the United States. The votes, it should be noted, were counted on an American military base; and on the day of the referendum American warplanes and helicopters were busy killing some seventy people around the city of Ramadi.[46]

The British also insist that Iraq is a sovereign nation. Recently, hundreds of residents filled the streets in the southern city of Basra, shouting and pumping their fists in the air to condemn British forces for raiding a jail and freeing two British soldiers. Iraqi police had arrested the Britons, who were dressed as civilians, for allegedly firing their guns (at whom or what is not clear), and either trying to plant explosives or having explosives in their vehicle. British troops then assembled several armored vehicles, rammed them through the jailhouse wall, and freed the men, as helicopter gunships hovered above.[47]

An intriguing side question: we have here British soldiers dressed as civilians (at least one report said dressed as Arabs), driving around in a car with explosives, firing guns... Does this not feed into the frequent speculation that coalition forces have been to some extent part of the 'insurgency'? The same insurgency that's used as an excuse by the coalition to remain in Iraq?

AFGHANISTAN

Please tell me again... what is the war in Afghanistan about?
(February 3, 2012)

With the US war in Iraq supposedly having reached a good conclusion (or halfway decent... or better than nothing... or let's get the hell out of here while some of us are still in one piece and there are some Iraqis we haven't yet killed), the best and the brightest in our government and media turn their thoughts to what to do about Afghanistan. It appears that no one seems to remember, if they ever knew, that Afghanistan was not really about 9/11 or fighting terrorists (except the many the US has created by its invasion and occupation), but was about pipelines.

President Obama declared in August 2009:

> But we must never forget this is not a war of choice. This is a war of necessity. Those who attacked America on 9–11 are plotting to do so again. If left unchecked, the Taliban insurgency will mean an even larger safe haven from which al Qaeda would plot to kill more Americans.[1]

Never mind that out of the tens of thousands of people the United States and its NATO front have killed in Afghanistan not one has been identified as having had anything to do with the events of September 11, 2001.

Never mind that the 'plotting to attack America' in 2001 was carried out in Germany and Spain and the United States more than in Afghanistan. Why hasn't the United States attacked those countries?

Indeed, what actually was needed to plot to buy airline tickets and take flying lessons in the United States? A room with some chairs? What does 'an even larger safe haven' mean? A larger room with more chairs? Perhaps a blackboard? Terrorists intent upon attacking the United States can meet almost anywhere.

The only 'necessity' that drew the United States to Afghanistan was the desire to establish a military presence in this land that is next door to the Caspian Sea region of Central Asia – which reportedly contains the second largest proven reserves of petroleum and natural gas in the world – and build oil and gas pipelines from that region running through Afghanistan.

Afghanistan is well situated for oil and gas pipelines to serve much of South Asia, pipelines that can bypass those not-yet Washington clients Iran and Russia. If only the Taliban would not attack the lines. Here's Richard Boucher, US Assistant Secretary of State for South and Central Asian Affairs, in 2007: 'One of our goals is to stabilize Afghanistan, so it can become a conduit and a hub between South and Central Asia so that energy can flow to the south.'[2]

Since the 1980s all kinds of pipelines have been planned for the area, only to be delayed or canceled by one military, financial, or political problem or another. For example, the so-called TAPI pipeline (Turkmenistan–Afghanistan–Pakistan–India) had strong support from Washington, which was eager to block a competing pipeline that would bring gas to Pakistan and India from Iran. TAPI goes back to the late 1990s, when the Taliban government held talks with the California-based oil company Unocal Corporation. These talks were conducted with the full knowledge of the Clinton administration, and were undeterred by the extreme repression of Taliban society. Taliban officials even made trips to the United States for discussions.[3] Testifying before the House Subcommittee on Asia and the Pacific on February 12, 1998, Unocal representative John Maresca discussed the importance of the pipeline project and the increasing difficulties in dealing with the Taliban:

> The region's total oil reserves may well reach more than 60 billion barrels of oil. Some estimates are as high as 200 billion barrels ... From the outset, we have made it clear that construction of the pipeline we have proposed across Afghanistan could not begin until a recognized government is in place that has the confidence of governments, leaders, and our company.

When those talks stalled in July, 2001 the Bush administration threatened the Taliban with military reprisals if the government did not go along with American demands. The talks finally broke down for good the following month, a month before 9/11.

The United States has been serious indeed about the Caspian Sea and Persian Gulf oil and gas areas. Through one war or another beginning with the Gulf War of 1990–91, the US has managed to establish military bases in Saudi Arabia, Kuwait, Bahrain, Qatar, Oman, Afghanistan, Pakistan, Uzbekistan, Tajikistan, Kyrgyzstan, and Kazakhstan.

The war against the Taliban can't be 'won' short of killing everyone in Afghanistan. The United States may well try again to negotiate some form of pipeline security with the Taliban, then get out, and declare 'victory.' Barack Obama can surely deliver an eloquent victory speech from his teleprompter. It might include the words 'freedom' and 'democracy,' but certainly not 'pipeline.'

What it's about for Germany

The German president, Horst Koehler, resigned in June 2010 because he said something government officials are not supposed to say. He said that Germany was fighting in Afghanistan for economic reasons. No reference to democracy. Nothing about freedom. Not a word about Good Guys fighting Bad Guys. The word 'terrorism' was not mentioned at all. Neither was 'God.' On a trip to German troops in Afghanistan he had declared that a country such as Germany, dependent on exports and free trade, must be prepared to use military force. The country, he said, had to act 'to protect our interests, for example free trade routes, or to prevent regional instability which might certainly have a negative effect on our trade, jobs and earnings.'

'Koehler has said something openly that has been obvious from the beginning,' said the head of Germany's Left Party. 'German soldiers are risking life and limb in Afghanistan to defend the export interests of big economic interests.'[4] Other opposition politicians had called for Koehler to take back the remarks and accused him of damaging public acceptance of German military missions abroad.[5]

As T.S. Eliot famously observed: 'Humankind cannot bear very much reality.'

The myths of Afghanistan, past and present

On the Fourth of July, 2009 Senator Patrick Leahy declared he was optimistic that, unlike the Soviet forces that were driven from Afghanistan twenty years ago, US forces could succeed there. The Democrat from Vermont stated:

> The Russians were sent running as they should have been. We helped send them running. But they were there to conquer the country. We've made it very clear, and everybody I talk to within Afghanistan feels the same way: they know we're there to help and we're going to leave. We've made it very clear we are going to leave.

And it's going to be turned back to them. The ones that made the mistakes in the past are those that tried to conquer them.[6]

Leahy is a long-time liberal on foreign-policy issues, a champion of withholding US counter-narcotics assistance from foreign military units guilty of serious human-rights violations, and an outspoken critic of robbing terrorist suspects of their human and legal rights. Yet he was willing to send countless young Americans to a horrible death, or maimed survival. And for what? Every point he made in his statement was simply wrong.

The Russians were not in Afghanistan to conquer it. The Soviet Union had lived next door to the country for more than sixty years without any kind of invasion. It was only when the United States intervened in Afghanistan to replace a government friendly to Moscow with one militantly anti-communist that the Russians invaded to do battle with the US-supported Islamic jihadists; precisely what the United States would have done to prevent a communist government in Canada or Mexico.

As to the US leaving... utterly meaningless propaganda until it happens. Ask the people of South Korea – fifty-six years of American occupation and still counting; ask the people of Japan – sixty-four years. It's not even correct to say that the Russians were sent running. That was essentially Russian president Mikhail Gorbachev's decision, and it was more of a political decision than a military one. Gorbachev's fondest ambition was to turn the Soviet Union into a West European-style social democracy, and he fervently wished for the approval of those European leaders, virtually all of whom were Cold War anti-communists and opposed the Soviet intervention into Afghanistan.

It's also rather difficult for the United States to claim that it's in Afghanistan to help the people there when one considers all the harm and suffering it has already inflicted upon those utterly downtrodden people for more than thirty years.

The eternal struggle
between the good guys and the bad guys

The United States and its wholly owned subsidiary NATO regularly drop bombs on Afghanistan which kill varying amounts of terrorists (or 'terrorists,' also known as civilians, also known as women and children). They do this rather often, against people utterly defenseless against aerial attack.

US/NATO spokespersons tell us that these unfortunate accidents happen because the enemy is deliberately putting civilians in harm's way to provoke a backlash against the foreign forces. We are told at times that the enemy had located themselves in the same building as the victims, using them as 'human shields.'[7] Therefore, it would seem, the enemy somehow knows in advance that a particular building is about to be bombed and they rush a bunch of civilians to the spot before the bombs begin to fall. Or it's a place where civilians normally live and, finding out that the building is about to be bombed, the enemy rushes a group of their own people to the place so they can die with the civilians. Or, what appears to be much more likely, the enemy doesn't know of the bombing in advance, but then the civilians would have to always be there – that is, they *live* there; they may even be the wives and children of the enemy. Is there no limit to the evil cleverness and the clever evilness of this foe?

Western officials also tell us that the enemy deliberately attacks from civilian areas, even hoping to draw fire to drive a wedge between average Afghans and international troops.[8] Presumably the insurgents are attacking nearby Western military installations and troop concentrations. This raises the question: why are the Western forces building installations and/or concentrating troops near civilian areas, deliberately putting civilians in harm's way?

US/NATO military leaders argue that any comparison of casualties caused by Western forces and by the Taliban is fundamentally unfair because there is a clear moral distinction to be made between accidental deaths resulting from combat operations and deliberate killings of innocents by militants. 'No [Western] soldier ever wakes up in the morning with the intention of harming any Afghan citizen,' said Major John Thomas, a spokesman for the NATO-led International Security Assistance Force. 'If that does inadvertently happen, it is deeply, deeply regretted.'[9] Is that not comforting language? Can any right-thinking, sensitive person fail to see who the good guys are?

During its many bombings, from Vietnam to Iraq, Washington has repeatedly told the world that the resulting civilian deaths were accidental and very much 'regretted.' But if you go out and drop powerful bombs over a populated area, and then learn that there have been a number of 'unintended' casualties, and then the next day go out and drop more bombs and learn again that there were 'unintended' casualties, and then the next day you go out and bomb again... at what point do you lose the right to say that the deaths were 'unintended'?

During the US/NATO seventy-eight-day bombing of Serbia in 1999, which killed many civilians, a Belgrade office building – which housed political parties, television and radio stations, a hundred private companies, and more – was bombed. But before the missiles were fired into this building, NATO planners spelled out the risks: 'Casualty Estimate 50–100 Government/Party employees. Unintended Civ Casualty Est: 250 – Apts in expected blast radius.'[10] The planners were saying that about 250 civilians living in nearby apartment buildings could be expected to perish in the bombing, in addition to 50 to 100 government and political party employees, likewise innocent of any crime calling for execution. So what do we have here? We have grown men telling each other: We'll do A, and we think that B may well be the result. But even if B does in fact result, we're saying beforehand – as we'll insist afterward – that it was *unintended*.

It was actually worse than this. As I've detailed elsewhere, the main purpose of the Serbian bombings – admitted to by NATO officials – was to make life so difficult for the public that support of the government of Slobodan Milosevic would be undermined.[11] This, in fact, is the classic definition of 'terrorism', as used by the FBI, the CIA, and the United Nations: the use or threat of violence against a civilian population to induce the government to change certain policies.

The women: their last great chance

In their need to defend the US occupation of Afghanistan, many Americans have cited the severe oppression of women in that desperate land and would have us believe that the United States is the last great hope of those poor women. However, in the 1980s the United States played an indispensable role in the overthrow of a secular and relatively progressive Afghan government, one which endeavored to grant women much more freedom than they'll ever have under the current government, more perhaps than ever again. Here are some excerpts from a 1986 US Army manual on Afghanistan discussing the policies of this government concerning women: 'provisions of complete freedom of choice of marriage partner, and fixation of the minimum age at marriage at 16 for women and 18 for men'; 'abolished forced marriages'; 'bring [women] out of seclusion, and initiate social programs'; 'extensive literacy programs, especially for women'; 'putting girls and boys in the same classroom'; 'concerned with changing gender roles and giving women a more active role in politics.'[12]

The overthrow of this government paved the way for the coming to power of an Islamic fundamentalist regime, soon in the hands of the awful Taliban. And why did the United States in its infinite wisdom choose to do such a thing? Mainly because the Afghan government was allied with the Soviet Union and

Washington wanted to draw the Russians into a hopeless military quagmire. The women of Afghanistan will never know how the campaign to raise them to the status of full human beings would have turned out, but this, some might argue, is but a small price to pay for a marvelous Cold War victory.

5

IRAN

A designer monster: Mahmoud Ahmadinejad
(December 17, 2006)

Iranian president Mahmoud Ahmadinejad is a man seemingly custom-made for any American administration in its endless quest for enemies with whom to scare Congress, the American people, and the world, in order to justify the cost and questionable behavior of the empire. We've been told, repeatedly, that Ahmadinejad has declared that he wants to 'wipe Israel off the map'; that he claims the Holocaust never happened; that he held a conference in Iran for 'Holocaust deniers'; and that his government passed a law requiring Jews to wear a yellow insignia, à la Nazis. On top of all that, we are told, he's aiming to build nuclear bombs, one of which would surely be aimed at Israel. What decent person would not be alarmed by such a man?

However, as with all such designer monsters made bigger than life during the Cold War and since by Washington, the truth about Ahmadinejad is a bit more complicated. According to people who know Farsi, the Iranian leader has never said anything about 'wiping Israel off the map.' In his October 29, 2005 speech, when he reportedly first made the remark, the word 'map' does not even appear. According to the translation of Juan

IRAN   89

Cole, American professor of Modern Middle East and South
Asian History, Ahmadinejad said that 'the regime occupying
Jerusalem must vanish from the page of time.' His remark, said
Cole, 'does not imply military action or killing anyone at all,'
which presumably is what would make the remark threatening.[1]

At the December 2006 conference, Ahmadinejad declared: 'The
Zionist regime will be wiped out soon, the same way the Soviet
Union was, and humanity will achieve freedom.'[2] Obviously, the
man is not calling for any kind of violent attack upon Israel, for
the dissolution of the Soviet Union took place peacefully.

As for the Holocaust myth, I have yet to read or hear words
from Ahmadinejad's mouth saying simply and clearly and unequivocally that he thinks that what we know as the Holocaust
never happened. Indeed, it would be difficult to find *any* so-called
'Holocaust-denier' who actually, ever, umm, y'know... *denies
the Holocaust*. (Yes, I'm sure you can find at least one nutcase
somewhere.)

The Iranian president has commented about the peculiarity
of a Holocaust which took place in Europe resulting in a state
for the Jews in the Middle East instead of in Europe. Why are
the Palestinians paying a price for a German crime? he asks.
He also wonders about the accuracy of the number of Jews – 6
million – killed in the Holocaust, as have many other people of all
political stripes, including Holocaust survivors like author Primo
Levi. (The much publicized World War I atrocities which turned
out to be false made the public very skeptical of the Holocaust
claims for a long time.)

In a talk at Columbia University, September 24, 2007, Ahmadinejad said: 'I'm not saying that it [the Holocaust] didn't happen at
all. This is not the judgment that I'm passing here.'[3] That should
have put the matter to rest. But of course it didn't. Two days later,
September 26, a bill (H.R. 3675) was introduced in Congress 'To
prohibit Federal grants to or contracts with Columbia University',

to punish the school for inviting Ahmadinejad to speak. (Don't you just love the way members of Congress love freedom of speech?) The bill's first 'finding' states that 'Iranian President Mahmoud Ahmadinejad has called for the destruction of the State of Israel, a critical ally of the United States.' That same day, television comedian Jay Leno had great fun ridiculing Ahmadinejad for denying that the Holocaust ever happened 'despite all the eye-witness accounts.'

The conference in Tehran ('Review of the Holocaust: Global Vision') gave a platform to various points of view, including six members of Jews United Against Zionism, at least two of whom were rabbis. One was Ahron Cohen, from London, who declared: 'There is no doubt whatsoever, that during World War II there developed a terrible and catastrophic policy and action of genocide perpetrated by Nazi Germany against the Jewish People.' He also said that 'the Zionists make a great issue of the Holocaust in order to further their illegitimate philosophy and aims,' indicating as well that the figure of 6 million Jewish victims is debatable. The other rabbi was Moshe David Weiss, who told the delegates: 'We don't want to deny the killing of Jews in World War II, but Zionists have given much higher figures for how many people were killed. They have used the Holocaust as a device to justify their oppression [of the Palestinians].' His group rejects the creation of Israel on the grounds that it violates Jewish religious law in that a Jewish state can't exist until the return of the Messiah.[4]

Another speaker was Shiraz Dossa, professor of political science at St Francis Xavier University in Canada. In an interview after the conference, he described himself as an anti-imperialist and an admirer of Noam Chomsky, and said that he 'was invited because of my expertise as a scholar in the German-Jewish area, as well as my studies in the Holocaust.... I have nothing to do with Holocaust denial, not at all.' His talk was 'about the war on terrorism, and how the Holocaust plays into it. Other people [at the conference] have their own points of view, but that [Holocaust denial] is not my point of view. ... There was no pressure at all to say anything, and people there had different views.'[5] Clearly, the conference – which the White House called 'an affront to the entire civilized world'[6] – was not set up to be simply a forum for people to deny that the Holocaust ever took place at all.

As to the yellow star story – that was a complete fabrication by a prominent Iranian-American neoconservative, Amir Taheri. There are further egregious examples of Ahmadinejad's policies and words being twisted out of shape in the Western media, making him look like a danger to all that's holy and decent. Political science professor Virginia Tilley has written a good account of this. 'Why is Mr. Ahmadinejad being so systematically misquoted and demonized?' Tilley asks. 'Need we ask? If the world believes that Iran is preparing to attack Israel, then the US or Israel can claim justification in attacking Iran first. On that agenda, the disinformation campaign about Mr Ahmadinejad's statements has been bonded at the hip to a second set of lies: promoting Iran's (nonexistent) nuclear weapon programme.'[7]

Time magazine, in its 2006 year-ending issue, chose not to select its usual 'Person of the Year' and instead chose 'You,' the Internet user. Managing editor Richard Stengel said that if it came down to one individual it probably would have been Mahmoud Ahmadinejad, but that 'It just felt to me a little off selecting him.'[8] In previous years Time's 'Person of the Year' has included Joseph Stalin and Adolf Hitler.

One closing thought: if Ahmadinejad is anywhere near the *bête noire* anti-Semite he's portrayed as, why hasn't Iran at least started its holocaust by killing or throwing into concentration camps its own Jews, an estimated 30,000 in number? These are Iranian Jews who have representation in parliament and who have

been free for many years to emigrate to Israel but have chosen
not to do so.

What you need to succeed is sincerity, and if you can fake sincerity you've got it made (Old Hollywood axiom)

A few months ago I told the American people that I did not trade
arms for hostages. My heart and my best intentions still tell me
that is true, but the facts and evidence tell me it is not. (President
Ronald Reagan, 1987[9])

On April 23, 2012, speaking at the Holocaust Memorial Museum
in Washington, DC, President Barack Obama told his assembled
audience that, as president, 'I've done my utmost ... to prevent
and end atrocities.' Do the facts and evidence tell him that his
words are not true?

Well, let's see... There are the multiple atrocities carried out
in Iraq by American forces under President Obama. There are
the multiple atrocities carried out in Afghanistan by American
forces under Obama. There are the multiple atrocities carried
out in Pakistan by American forces under Obama. There are
the multiple atrocities carried out in Libya by American/NATO
forces under Obama. There are also the hundreds (thousands
by now?) of American drone attacks against people and homes
in Somalia and in Yemen (including against American citizens
in the latter). Might the friends and families of these victims
regard the murder of their loved ones and the loss of their homes
as atrocities?

Ronald Reagan was pre-Alzheimer's when he uttered the above.
What excuse can be made for Barack Obama?

The president then continued in the same fashion by saying
'We possess many tools... and using these tools over the past
three years, I believe – I know – that we have saved countless lives.'
Obama pointed out that this includes Libya, where the United

States, in conjunction with NATO, took part in seven months of almost daily bombing missions. We may never learn from the new pro-NATO Libyan government how many the bombs killed, or the extent of the damage to homes and infrastructure. But the president of the United States assured his Holocaust Museum audience that 'today, the Libyan people are forging their own future, and the world can take pride in the innocent lives that we saved.'

Language is an invention that makes it possible for a person to deny what he is doing even as he does it.

Mr. Obama closed with these stirring words; 'It can be tempting to throw up our hands and resign ourselves to man's endless capacity for cruelty. It's tempting sometimes to believe that there is nothing we can do.' But Barack Obama is not one of those doubters. He knows there is something he can do about man's endless capacity for cruelty. He can add to it. Greatly. And yet I am certain that, with exceedingly few exceptions, those in his Holocaust audience left with no doubt that this was a man wholly deserving of his Nobel Peace Prize.

And future American history books may well certify the president's words as factual, his motivation sincere, for his talk indeed possessed the quality needed for schoolbooks.

The Israeli-American-Iranian-Holocaust-NobelPeacePrize circus

Everyone now knows it. In 2005 Mahmoud Ahmadinejad threatened violence against Israel, to 'wipe Israel off the map.' Who can count the number of times it has been repeated in every kind of media, in every country of the world, without questioning the accuracy of what was reported? A 2012 Lexis–Nexis search of 'All News (English)' for <Iran and Israel and 'off the map'> for the previous seven years produced the message: 'This search has been interrupted because it will return more than 3000 results.'

Now, finally, we have the following exchange from the radio–television simulcast, *Democracy Now!*, of April 19, 2012:

A top Israeli official has acknowledged that Iranian President Mahmoud Ahmadinejad never said that Iran seeks to 'wipe Israel off the face of the map.' The falsely translated statement has been widely attributed to Ahmadinejad and used repeatedly by U.S. and Israeli government officials to back military action and sanctions against Iran. But speaking to Teymoor Nabili of the network *Al Jazeera*, Israeli Deputy Prime Minister Dan Meridor admitted Ahmadinejad had been misquoted.

TEYMOOR NABILI: As we know, Ahmadinejad didn't say that he plans to exterminate Israel, nor did he say that Iran policy is to exterminate Israel. Ahmadinejad's position and Iran's position always has been, and they've made this – they've said this as many times as Ahmadinejad has criticized Israel, he has said as many times that he has no plans to attack Israel. ...

DAN MERIDOR: Well, I have to disagree, with all due respect. You speak of Ahmadinejad. I speak of Khamenei, Ahmadinejad, Rafsanjani, Shamkhani. I give the names of all these people. They all come, basically ideologically, religiously, with the statement that Israel is an unnatural creature, it will not survive. They didn't say, 'We'll wipe it out,' you're right. But 'It will not survive, it is a cancerous tumor that should be removed,' was said just two weeks ago again.

TEYMOOR NABILI: 'Well, I'm glad you've acknowledged that they didn't say they will wipe it out.'

So that's that. Right? Of course not. Fox News, NPR, CNN, NBC et al. will likely continue to claim that Ahmadinejad threatened violence against Israel, threatened to 'wipe it off the map.' And that's only Ahmadinejad the Israeli Killer. There's still Ahmadinejad the Holocaust Denier, which we've seen has no basis in reality.

Let us now listen to Elie Wiesel, the simplistic, reactionary man who's built a career around being a Holocaust survivor, introducing President Obama at the Holocaust Museum for the talk referred to above, some five days after the statement made by Dan Meridor:

> How is it that the Holocaust's No. 1 denier, Ahmadinejad, is still a president? He who threatens to use nuclear weapons – to use nuclear weapons – to destroy the Jewish state. Have we not learned? We must. We must know that when evil has power, it is almost too late.

'Nuclear weapons' is of course adding a new myth on the back of the old myths.

Wiesel, like Obama, is a winner of the Nobel Peace Prize. As is Henry Kissinger and Menachim Begin. And several other such war-loving beauties. Tom Lehrer, the marvelous political songwriter of the 1950s and 1960s, once observed: 'Political satire became obsolete when Henry Kissinger was awarded the Nobel Peace Prize.' When will that monumental farce of a prize be put to sleep?

For the record, let it be noted that on March 4, 2002, speaking before the American Israel Public Affairs Committee (AIPAC), Obama said: 'Let's begin with a basic truth that you all understand: No Israeli government can tolerate a nuclear weapon in the hands of a regime that denies the Holocaust, threatens to wipe Israel off the map, and sponsors terrorist groups committed to Israel's destruction.'[10]

The Lord High Almighty Pooh-Bah of threats, the Grand Ayatollah of nuclear menace
(February 3, 2012)

As we all know only too well, the United States and Israel would hate to see Iran possessing nuclear weapons. Being 'the only nuclear power in the Middle East' is a great card for Israel to have in its hand. But – in the real, non-propaganda world – is USrael actually fearful of an attack from a nuclear-armed Iran? In case you've forgotten...

In 2007, in a closed discussion, Israeli Foreign Minister Tzipi Livni said that in her opinion 'Iranian nuclear weapons do not pose an existential threat to Israel.' She 'also criticized the exaggerated use that [Israeli] Prime Minister Ehud Olmert is making of the issue of the Iranian bomb, claiming that he is attempting to rally the public around him by playing on its most basic fears.'[11]

2009: 'A senior Israeli official in Washington' asserted that 'Iran would be unlikely to use its missiles in an attack [against Israel] because of the certainty of retaliation.'[12]

In 2010 the *Sunday Times* (January 10) reported that Brigadier-General Uzi Eilam, war hero, pillar of the Israeli defense establishment, and former director general of Israel's Atomic Energy Commission, 'believes it will probably take Iran seven years to make nuclear weapons.'

January 2012, US Secretary of Defense Leon Panetta told a television audience: 'Are they [Iran] trying to develop a nuclear weapon? No, but we know that they trying to develop a nuclear capability.'[13]

A week later we could read in the *New York Times* (January 15) that 'three leading Israeli security experts – the Mossad chief, Tamir Pardo, a former Mossad chief, Efraim Halevy, and a former military chief of staff, Dan Halutz – all recently declared that a nuclear Iran would not pose an existential threat to Israel.'

Then, a few days afterward, Israeli Defense Minister Ehud Barak, in an interview with Israeli Army Radio (January 18), had this exchange:

QUESTION: Is it Israel's judgment that Iran has not yet decided to turn its nuclear potential into weapons of mass destruction?

BARAK: People ask whether Iran is determined to break out from the control [inspection] regime right now ... in an attempt to obtain nuclear weapons or an operable installation as quickly as possible. Apparently that is not the case.

Lastly, we have the US Director of National Intelligence, James Clapper, in a report to Congress: 'We do not know, however, if Iran will eventually decide to build nuclear weapons. ... There are 'certain things [the Iranians] have not done' that would be necessary to build a warhead.[14]

Admissions like the above – and there are others – are never put into headlines by the American mass media; indeed, they are only very lightly reported at all; and sometimes distorted. On the Public Broadcasting System (PBS *News Hour*, January 9), the non-commercial network much beloved by American liberals, the Panetta quotation above was reported as: 'But we know that they're trying to develop a nuclear capability, and that's what concerns us.' Flagrantly omitted were the preceding words: 'Are they trying to develop a nuclear weapon? No...'[15]

One of Israel's leading military historians, Martin van Creveld, was interviewed by *Playboy* magazine in June 2007.

PLAYBOY: Can the World live with a nuclear Iran?

VAN CREVELD: The U.S. has lived with a nuclear Soviet Union and a nuclear China, so why not a nuclear Iran? I've researched how the U.S. opposed nuclear proliferation in the past, and each time a country was about to proliferate, the U.S. expressed its opposition in terms of why this other country was very dangerous and didn't deserve to have nuclear weapons. Americans believe they're the only people who deserve to have nuclear weapons, because they are good and democratic and they like Mother and apple pie and the flag. But Americans are the only ones who have used them. ... We are in no danger at all of having an Iranian nuclear weapon dropped on us. We cannot say so too openly, however, because we have a history of using any threat in order to get weapons ...

thanks to the Iranian threat, we are getting weapons from the U.S. and Germany.

And throughout these years, regularly, Israeli and American officials have been assuring us that Iran is World Nuclear Threat Number One, that we can't relax our guard against them, that there should be no limit to the ultra-tough sanctions we impose upon the Iranian people and their government. Repeated murder and attempted murder of Iranian nuclear scientists, sabotage of Iranian nuclear equipment with computer viruses, the sale of faulty parts and raw materials, unexplained plane crashes, explosions at Iranian facilities ... Who can be behind all this but USrael? How do we know? It's called 'plain common sense.' Or do you think it was Costa Rica? Or perhaps South Africa? Or maybe Thailand?

Defense Secretary Panetta recently commented succinctly on one of the assassinations of an Iranian scientist: 'That's not what the United States does.'[16] Does anyone know Leon Panetta's email address? I'd like to send him my list of United States assassination plots. More than fifty foreign leaders were targeted over the years, many successfully.[17]

Not long ago, Iraq and Iran were regarded by USrael as the most significant threats to Israeli Middle East hegemony. Thus was born the myth of Iraqi Weapons of Mass Destruction, and the United States proceeded to turn Iraq into a basket case. That left Iran, and thus was born the myth of the Iranian Nuclear Threat. As it began to sink in that Iran was not really that much of a nuclear threat, or that this 'threat' was becoming too difficult to sell to the rest of the world, USrael decided that, at a minimum, it wanted regime change. The next step may be to block Iran's lifeline – oil sales using the Strait of Hormuz. Ergo the recent US and EU naval buildup near the Persian Gulf, an act of war trying to goad Iran into firing the first shot. If Iran tries to counter this blockade it could be the signal for another US Basket Case, the fourth in a decade, with the devastated people of Libya and Afghanistan, along with Iraq, currently enjoying America's unique gift of freedom and democracy.

On January 11, the *Washington Post* reported: 'In addition to influencing Iranian leaders directly, [a US intelligence official] says another option here is that [sanctions] will create hate and discontent at the street level so that the Iranian leaders realize that they need to change their ways.' How utterly charming, these tactics and goals for the twenty-first century by the leader of the 'Free World.' (Is that expression still used?)

The neoconservative thinking (and Barack Obama can be regarded as often being a fellow traveler of such) is even more charming than that. Consider Danielle Pletka, vice president for foreign and defense policy studies at America's most prominent neocon think tank, American Enterprise Institute:

> The biggest problem for the United States is not Iran getting a nuclear weapon and testing it, it's Iran getting a nuclear weapon and not using it. Because the second that they have one and they don't do anything bad, all of the naysayers are going to come back and say, 'See, we told you Iran is a responsible power. We told you Iran wasn't getting nuclear weapons in order to use them immediately.' ... And they will eventually define Iran with nuclear weapons as not a problem.[18]

What are we to make of that and all the other quotations above? I think it gets back to my opening statement: being 'the only nuclear power in the Middle East' is a great card for Israel to have in its hand. Is USrael willing to go to war to hold on to that card?

Arab leaders: Arab people

One of the most common threads running through the WikiLeaks papers is Washington's manic obsession with Iran. In country after country the United States exerts unceasing pressure on the government to tighten the noose around Iran's neck, to make the American sanctions as extensive and as painful as can be, to inflate the alleged Iranian nuclear threat, to discourage normal contact as if Iran were a leper.

'Fear of "different world" if Iran gets nuclear weapons. Embassy cables reveal how US relentlessly cajoles and bullies governments not to give succour to Tehran,' read a *Guardian* headline on November 28, 2010. And we're told that Arab governments support the United States in this endeavor, that fear of Iran is widespread. John Kerry, the Democratic head of the Senate Foreign Relations Committee, jumped on this bandwagon. 'Things that I have heard from the mouths of King Abdullah [of Saudi Arabia] and Hosni Mubarak [Egyptian president] and others are now quite public,' he said. He went on to say there was a 'consensus on Iran' (*Guardian*, December 2). If all this is to have real meaning, the implication must be that the Arab people feel this way, and not just their dictator leaders. So let us look at some numbers.

The annual 'Arab Public Opinion Poll' was conducted in summer 2010 by Zogby International and the University of Maryland, in Egypt, Jordan, Lebanon, Morocco, Saudi Arabia, and the United Arab Emirates. A sample of the results:

- 'If Iran acquires nuclear weapons, which of the following is the likely outcome for the Middle East region?' More positive 57 percent, Would not matter 20 percent, More negative 21 percent.
- Among those who believe that Iran seeks nuclear weapons, 70 percent believe that Iran has the right to its nuclear program.
- 'In a world where there is only one superpower, which of the following countries would you prefer to be that superpower?' France 35 percent, China 16 percent, Germany 13 percent,

Britain 9 percent, Russia 8 percent, United States 7 percent,
Pakistan 6 percent.
- 'Name two countries that you think pose the biggest threat to
  you.' Israel 88 percent, US 77 percent, Algeria 10 percent, Iran
  10 percent, UK 8 percent, China 3 percent, Syria 1 percent.
- 'Which world leader (outside your own country) do you admire
  most?' (partial list) Recep Erdogan [Turkey] 20 percent, Hugo
  Chavez 13 percent, Mahmoud Ahmadinejad 12 percent, Hassan
  Nasrallah [Hezbollah/Lebanon] 9 percent, Osama bin Laden
  6 percent, Saddam Hussein 2 percent (Barack Obama not
  mentioned).[19]

Another peace scare. Boy, that was close.
(December 11, 2007)

In 2007, the US intelligence community's new National Intelligence
Estimate (NIE) – 'Iran: Nuclear Intentions and Capabilities' – made
a point of saying up front (in bold type): 'This NIE does *not* [stress
in original] assume that Iran intends to acquire nuclear weapons.'
The report goes on to state: 'We judge with high confidence that
in fall 2003, Tehran halted its nuclear weapons program.'

Isn't that good news, that Iran isn't about to attack the United
States or Israel with nuclear weapons? Surely everyone is thrilled
that the horror and suffering that such an attack – not to mention
an American or Israeli retaliation or pre-emptive attack – would
bring to this old world. Let's consider some of the happy reactions
from American leaders.

Senate Republicans are planning to call for a congressional
commission to investigate the NIE's conclusion that Iran discon-
tinued its nuclear weapons program in 2003.[20]

National Security Adviser, Stephen J. Hadley, said that the
report 'tells us that the risk of Iran acquiring a nuclear weapon
remains a very serious problem.'[21]

Defense Secretary Robert Gates 'argued forcefully at a Persian Gulf security conference … that U.S. intelligence indicates Iran could restart its secret nuclear weapons program "at any time" and remains a major threat to the region.'[22]

John R. Bolton, President Bush's former ambassador to the United Nations and pit bull of the neoconservatives, dismissed the report with: 'I've never based my view on this week's intelligence.'[23]

And Bush himself added:

> Look, Iran was dangerous, Iran *is* dangerous, and Iran will be dangerous if they have the knowledge necessary to make a nuclear weapon. The NIE says that Iran had a hidden – a covert nuclear weapons program. That's what it said. What's to say they couldn't start another covert nuclear weapons program? … Nothing has changed in this NIE that says, 'Okay, why don't we just stop worrying about it?' Quite the contrary. I think the NIE makes it clear that Iran needs to be taken seriously. My opinion hasn't changed.[24]

Hmmm. Well, maybe the reaction was more positive in Israel. Here's a report from Uri Avnery, a leading Israeli columnist:

> The earth shook. Our political and military leaders were all in shock. The headlines screamed with rage. … Shouldn't we be overjoyed? Shouldn't the masses in Israel be dancing in the streets? After all, we have been saved! … Lo and behold – no bomb and no any-minute-now. The wicked Ahmadinejad can threaten us as much as he wants – he just has not got the means to harm us. Isn't that a reason for celebration? So why does this feel like a national disaster?[25]

We have to keep this in mind: America, like Israel, cherishes its enemies. Without enemies, the United States appears to be a nation without moral purpose and direction. The various managers of the National Security State need enemies to protect their jobs, to justify their swollen budgets, to aggrandize their work, to give themselves a mission, to send truckloads of taxpayer money to the corporations for whom the managers will go to work after leaving government service. They understand the need for enemies only too well, even painfully. Here is US Col. Dennis Long, speaking in 1992, just after the end of the Cold War, when he was director of 'total armor force readiness' at Fort Knox:

> For 50 years, we equipped our football team, practiced five days a week and never played a game. We had a clear enemy with demonstrable qualities, and we had scouted them out. [Now] we will have to practice day in and day out without knowing anything about the other team. We won't have his playbook, we won't know where the stadium is, or how many guys he will have on the field. That is very distressing to the military establishment, especially when you are trying to justify the existence of your organization and your systems.[26]

In any event, all of the above is completely irrelevant if Iran has no intention of attacking the United States or Israel, which would be the case even if they currently possessed a large stockpile of nuclear weapons.

Intentional misunderstanding
(November 6, 2007)

> International misunderstanding is almost wholly voluntary: it is that contradiction in terms, intentional misunderstanding – a contradiction, because in order to misunderstand deliberately, you must at least suspect, if not actually understand what you intend to misunderstand. (Enoch Powell, British MP, 1983[27])

In October 2007, Israeli Foreign Minister Tzipi Livni told assembled world leaders at the United Nations that the time had come to take action against Iran:

> None disagrees that Iran denies the Holocaust and speaks openly of its desire to wipe a member state – mine – off the map. And

none disagrees that, in violation of Security Council resolutions, it is actively pursuing the means to achieve this end. Too many see the danger but walk idly by – hoping that someone else will take care of it. ... It is time for the United Nations, and the states of the world, to live up to their promise of never again. To say enough is enough, to act now and to defend their basic values.[28]

Yet, as mentioned before, we were informed by *Haaretz* (frequently described as 'the *New York Times* of Israel') that the same Foreign Minister Tzipi Livni had said a few months earlier, in a series of closed discussions, that in her opinion 'Iranian nuclear weapons do not pose an existential threat to Israel.' *Haaretz* reported that 'Livni also criticized the exaggerated use that [Israeli] Prime Minister Ehud Olmert is making of the issue of the Iranian bomb, claiming that he is attempting to rally the public around him by playing on its most basic fears.'[29] What are we to make of such a self-contradiction, such perfect hypocrisy?

And here is Fareed Zakaria, editor of *Newsweek International*:

> The one time we seriously negotiated with Tehran was in the closing days of the war in Afghanistan [early 1990s], in order to create a new political order in the country. Bush's representative to the Bonn conference, James Dobbins, says that 'the Iranians were very professional, straightforward, reliable and helpful. They were also critical to our success. They persuaded the Northern Alliance [Afghan foes of the Taliban] to make the final concessions that we asked for.' Dobbins says the Iranians made overtures to have better relations with the United States through him and others in 2001 and later, but got no reply. Even after the Axis of Evil speech, he recalls, they offered to cooperate in Afghanistan. Dobbins took the proposal to a principals meeting in Washington only to have it met with dead silence. The then-Secretary of Defense Donald Rumsfeld, he says, 'looked down and rustled his papers.' No reply was ever sent back to the Iranians. Why bother? They're mad.[30]

Dobbins has further written:

The original version of the Bonn agreement ... neglected to mention either democracy or the war on terrorism. It was the Iranian representative who spotted these omissions and successfully urged that the newly emerging Afghan government be required to commit to both.[31]

Only weeks after Hamid Karzai was sworn in as interim leader in Afghanistan, President Bush listed Iran among the 'axis of evil' – surprising payback for Tehran's help in Bonn. A year later, shortly after the invasion of Iraq, all bilateral contacts with Tehran were suspended. Since then, confrontation over Iran's nuclear program has intensified.[32]

Shortly after the US invasion of Iraq in 2003, Iran made another approach to Washington, via the Swiss ambassador, who sent a fax to the State Department. The *Washington Post* described it as 'a proposal from Iran for a broad dialogue with the United States, and the fax suggested everything was on the table – including full cooperation on nuclear programs, acceptance of Israel and the termination of Iranian support for Palestinian militant groups.' The Bush administration 'belittled the initiative. Instead, they formally complained to the Swiss ambassador who had sent the fax.' Richard Haass, head of policy planning at the State Department at the time and now president of the Council on Foreign Relations, said the Iranian approach was swiftly rejected because in the administration 'the bias was toward a policy of regime change.'[33]

So there we have it. The Israelis know it, the Americans know it. Iran is not any kind of military threat. Before the invasion of Iraq I posed the question: What possible reason would Saddam Hussein have for attacking the United States or Israel other than an irresistible desire for mass national suicide? He had no reason, and neither do the Iranians.

GEORGE W. BUSH

'Come out of the White House with your hands up!'
(May 21, 2006)

'I used to be called brother, John, Daddy, uncle, friend,' John Allen Muhammad said at his trial in Maryland this month. 'Now I'm called evil.' Muhammad, formerly known as 'the DC Sniper,' was on trial for six slayings in Maryland in 2002. Already sentenced to die in Virginia for several other murders, he insisted that he was innocent despite the evidence against him – including DNA, fingerprints, and ballistics analysis of a rifle found in his car.[1]

Bereft of any real political power, I'm reduced to day-dreaming... a courtroom in some liberated part of the world, in the not-too-distant future, a tribunal... a defendant testifying... 'I used to be called brother, George, son, Daddy, uncle, friend, Dubya, governor, president. Now I'm called war criminal,' he says sadly, insisting on his innocence despite the overwhelming evidence presented against him.

Can the man ever take to heart or mind the realization that America's immune system is trying to get rid of him? Probably not. No more than his accomplice can.

In 2004, Vice President Dick Cheney visited Yankee Stadium for a baseball game. During the singing of 'God Bless America' in the seventh inning, an image of Cheney was shown on the scoreboard.

It was greeted with so much booing that the Yankees quickly removed the image.[2] Yet last month the vice president showed up at the home opener for the Washington Nationals to throw out the first pitch. The *Washington Post* reported that he 'drew boisterous boos from the moment he stepped on the field until he jogged off. The derisive greeting was surprisingly loud and long, given the bipartisan nature of our national pastime, and drowned out a smattering of applause reported from the upper decks.'[3]

It will be interesting to see if Cheney shows up again before a large crowd in a venue which has not been carefully chosen to insure that only right-thinking folks will be present. Even that might not help. Twice in the last few months, a public talk of Donald Rumsfeld has been interrupted by people in the audience calling him a war criminal and accusing him of lying to get the United States into war. This happened in a meeting room at the very respectable National Press Club in Washington and again at a forum at the equally respectable Southern Center for International Policy in Atlanta.

In Chile, in November 2005, as former dictator Augusto Pinochet moved closer to being tried for the deaths of thousands, he declared to a judge: 'I lament those losses and suffer for them. God does things, and he will forgive me if I committed some excesses, which I don't believe I did.'[4]

Dubya couldn't have said it better. Let's hope that one day we can compel him to stand before a judge, not one appointed by him.

After the war-crimes trial we'll need a second tribunal for shameless lying, gross insults to our intelligence, and just plain weird stupidity and stupid weirdness

George W. Bush, speaking on March 29, 2006 to the Freedom House organization in Washington:

We're a country of deep compassion. We care. One of the great things about America, one of the beauties of our country, is that when we see a young, innocent child blown up by an IED [improvised explosive device], we cry. We don't care what the child's religion may be, or where that child may live, we cry. It upsets us. The enemy knows that, and they're willing to kill to shake our confidence.[5]

In the words of Voltaire: 'Those who can make you believe absurdities can make you commit atrocities.'

If you sometimes think that the dumbness, lies, hypocrisy, cynicism, cruelty, and arrogance could never have been as bad as now...

Here is President George H.W. Bush, in a speech to the US Air Force Academy, May 29, 1991:

Nowhere are the dangers of weapons of proliferation more urgent than in the Middle East. After consulting with governments inside the region and elsewhere about how to slow and then reverse the buildup of unnecessary and destabilizing weapons, I am today proposing a Middle East arms control initiative. It features supplier guidelines on conventional arms exports; barriers to exports that contribute to weapons of mass destruction; a freeze now, and later a ban on surface-to-surface missiles in the region; and a ban on production of nuclear weapons material.

The next day (that is to say the VERY next day, May 30, 1991), Secretary of Defense Dick Cheney announced that the United States would give Israel $65 million worth of US fighter planes and underwrite most of a new Israeli missile program.[6]

In that same speech, Bush, Sr. declared: 'Our service men and women in the Gulf, weary from months in the desert, now help suffering Kurds.' The truth was that since the Gulf War fighting had ceased in February, the United States had been doing its best to suppress the Kurdish revolt against the rule of Saddam

Hussein, a revolt which the Bush administration had openly encouraged for Kurds and Shiites in Washington's perennial professed role of democratic liberator; but when the heat of the moment had cooled down, the prospect of a Kurdish autonomous area next to US ally Turkey and/or an Iraq–Iran–Shiite coalition next to the Saudi allies made successful revolts appear unpalatable to the United States. Accordingly, the Kurds and Shiites were left to their [not very nice] fates. But hey, that's business.

Seconds later in his talk, Daddy Bush succeeded in pushing the following words past his lips: 'We do not dictate the courses nations follow.'

Civil liberties holds an important place in the heart of the Bush administration's rhetoric

'This is a limited program designed to prevent attacks on the United States of America and, I repeat, limited,' said President George W. Bush in 2006 about the National Security Agency's domestic spying on Americans without a court order.[7] Let's give the devil his due. It's easy to put down the domestic spying program, but the fact is that the president is right, it is indeed limited. It's limited to those who are being spied upon. No one – I repeat, no one – who is not being spied upon is being spied upon.

Thomas Jefferson said that the price of freedom is eternal vigilance. But he of course was talking about citizens watching the government, not the reverse.

A marriage made in heaven... or in Albania

Former White House counsel Harriet Miers once called George W. Bush the most brilliant man she has ever known.[8] She's now no longer alone in her bizarre little padded cell. On June 10,

2007 during the president's visit to Albania – arguably the most backward country in all of Europe, today as well as when it was a Soviet satellite – the joyous townspeople of Fushe Kruje yelled 'Bushie! Bushie!' and Albania's prime minister gushed over the 'greatest and most distinguished guest we have ever had in all times.'

This was reported by *Washington Post* columnist Eugene Robinson, and prompted a letter from a reader, which said in part: 'Regarding Eugene Robinson's June 12 op-ed.... It was inevitable that somebody would sneer at the Albanian reception of President Bush ... [Robinson] patronizingly writing of "a wonderful reverse-Borat moment".... U.S. support for Albania following the collapse of communism explains Albanian gratitude to the United States.'[9]

Ah yes, the wonderful collapse of Communism and the even more wonderful birth of democracy, freedom, capitalism... and much increased poverty and deprivation in the former Soviet dominion. What actually happened is that the first election in 'Free Albania,' in March 1991, resulted in an overwhelming endorsement of the Communists. And what did the United States then do? Of course it proceeded to undertake a campaign to overthrow this very same elected government. The previous year in neighboring Bulgaria, another former Soviet satellite, the Communists also won the election. And the United States overthrew them as well.[10] These were the first of the post-Cold War, non-violent, overthrows of governments of the former Soviet Union and its satellites directed and financed by the United States.[11]

7

CONDOLEEZZA RICE

Is the bullshit not enough to murder your brain?

Secretary of State Condoleezza Rice, testifying on April 5, 2006 before the Senate Foreign Relations Committee about a US–India nuclear pact:

> India's society is open and free. It is transparent and stable. It is multiethnic. It is a multi-religious democracy that is characterized by individual freedom and the rule of law. It is a country with which we share common values. ... India is a rising global power that we believe can be a pillar of stability in a rapidly changing Asia. In other words, in short, India is a natural partner for the United States.

And here is a State Department human rights report – released the very same day – that had this to say about India:

> The Government generally respected the rights of its citizens and continued efforts to curb human rights abuses, although numerous serious problems remained. These included extrajudicial killings, disappearances, custodial deaths, excessive use of force, arbitrary arrests, torture, poor prison conditions, and extended pretrial detention, especially related to combating insurgencies in Jammu and Kashmir. Societal violence and discrimination against women, trafficking of women and children for forced prostitution and labor, and female feticide and infanticide remained concerns. Poor

enforcement of laws, widespread corruption, a lack of account-
ability, and the severely overburdened court system weakened the
delivery of justice.

The Dragon Lady gets hers, a bit

We dissenters, we fringe people in America, we beggars, we do
not get many occasions for public vindication and satisfaction in
the mainstream political arena. The 'bad guys' always seem to
come out ahead, and unscathed. Thus did I take some pleasure
on January 18, 2005 to hear Condoleezza Rice verbally slapped
around by Senator Barbara Boxer at the Senate hearings on Rice's
nomination to be Secretary of State. Boxer documented in detail
several of the very serious lies and contradictions that Rice had
engaged in, in her attempts to justify the Iraq War; nothing that we
dissenters had not reported in countless places some time ago, but
confronting the Dragon Lady to her face was something else.

And now Rice's voice was clearly strained as she asked that she
be questioned 'without impugning my credibility or my integrity.'
She proceeded to defend her past remarks and in the process
rewrote yet more history – saying that the no-fly zones, used by
the US and Britain to bomb Iraq repeatedly over the years, had
been authorized by the UN. Not so; it was a joint private creation
of Washington and London. And then she said that the US had
good reason to fear Saddam Hussein because we knew that he
had a biological weapons capability, failing to mention that we
knew about that because we had given him that capability in the
1980s.

I had the thought that if these further statements of Rice were
challenged by the senators, along with the many other questionable statements she made in discussing Cuba, Haiti and Venezuela
(she said that she could not think of anything positive to say about
the Chávez government), the Dragon Lady might just crack a bit.

I pictured Humphrey Bogart in *The Caine Mutiny*, when, under intense questioning by a Navy board of inquiry, he suddenly takes out a pair of metal balls from his pocket and begins to nervously and obsessively play with them. And that was the end of Captain Queeg.

Well, a poor, ungratified dissenter can dream, can he not?

There's no business like show business (2010)

She played Mozart's Piano Concerto in D minor.
And accompanied the one and only Aretha Franklin.
A gala benefit performance in Philadelphia.
At the home of the Philadelphia Orchestra.
Before 8,000 people.
And they loved it.
How many of them knew that the pianist was a genuine,
   unindicted war criminal?
Guilty of crimes against humanity.
Defender of torture.
With much blood on her pianist hands.
Whose style in office for years could be characterized as
   hypocrisy, disinformation, and outright lying.
But what did the audience care?
This is America.
Home of the Good Guys.
She was fighting against the Bad Guys.
And we all know that the show must go on.
So let's hear it, folks... Let's have a real all-American hand...
Let's hear it for our own darling virtuoso... The Sweetheart
of Baghdad... Miss Condoleezza Rice!

HUMAN RIGHTS, CIVIL LIBERTIES, AND TORTURE

The stain on humankind that does not go away
(June 8, 2007)

A report in the March 2007 issue of *Archives of General Psychiatry*, a journal of the American Medical Association, based on interviews of hundreds of survivors of the 1990s' conflicts in the former Yugoslavia, concludes that

> aggressive interrogation techniques or detention procedures involving deprivation of basic needs, exposure to adverse environmental conditions, forced stress positions, hooding or blindfolding, isolation, restriction of movement, forced nudity, threats, humiliating treatment and other psychological manipulations do not appear to be substantially different from physical torture in terms of the extent of mental suffering they cause, the underlying mechanisms of traumatic stress, and their long-term traumatic effects.

The report adds that these findings do not support the distinction between torture and 'other cruel, inhuman and degrading treatment' (an expression taken from the Universal Declaration of Human Rights, 1948, often used in international human rights conventions and declarations). Although these conventions prohibit both types of acts, the report points out that 'such a distinction nevertheless reinforces the misconception that cruel, inhuman and degrading treatment causes lesser harm and might therefore be permissible under exceptional circumstances.'[1]

These conclusions directly counter the frequent declarations by George W. Bush, the Pentagon et al. that 'We don't torture.' They would have the world believe that aggressive psychological torture isn't really torture; although they of course have often employed the physical kind as well, to a degree leading on a number of occasions to a prisoner's death. (Justice Andrew Collins of the British High Court: 'America's idea of what is torture is not the same as ours and does not appear to coincide with that of most civilized nations.'[2])

The conclusions of the journal's report do not, however, counter the argument of those like Harvard Law School professor Alan Dershowitz, who loves to pose the classic question: 'What if a bomb has been set to go off, which will kill many people, and only your prisoner knows where it's located. Is it okay to torture him to elicit the information?'

Humankind has been struggling for centuries to tame its worst behaviors; ridding itself of the affliction of torture is high on that list. Finally, a historic first step was taken by the United Nations General Assembly in 1984 with the drafting of the 'Convention Against Torture and Other Cruel, Inhuman or Degrading Treatment or Punishment' (which came into force in 1987, was ratified by the United States in 1994). Article 2, section 2 of the Convention states: 'No exceptional circumstances whatsoever, whether a state of war or a threat of war, internal political instability or any other public emergency, may be invoked as a justification of torture.'

Such marvelously clear, unambiguous and principled language, to set a single standard for a world that makes it increasingly difficult to feel proud of humanity. We cannot slide back. If torture is broached as a possibility, it will become a reality. If today it's deemed acceptable to torture the person who has the vital information, tomorrow it will be acceptable to torture his colleague, or his wife or child, who – it's suspected – may know almost as much. Would we allow slavery to resume for just a short while to serve some 'national emergency' or some other 'higher purpose'?

'I would personally rather die than have anyone tortured to save my life': the words of Craig Murray, former British ambassador to Uzbekistan, who lost his job after he publicly condemned the Uzbek regime in 2003 for its systematic use of torture.[3]

If you open the window of torture, even just a crack, the cold air of the Dark Ages will fill the whole room.

Being serious about torture – or not
(March 4, 2009)

In Cambodia they're once again endeavoring to hold trials to bring some former senior Khmer Rouge officials to justice for their 1975–79 war crimes and crimes against humanity. The current defendant in a United Nations-organized trial, Kaing Guek Eav, who was the head of a Khmer Rouge torture center, has confessed to atrocities, but insists he was acting under orders.[4] As we all know, this is the defense that the Nuremberg Tribunal rejected for the Nazi defendants. Everyone knows that, right? No one places any weight on such a defense any longer, right? We make jokes about Nazis declaring: 'I was only following orders!' Except that both the Bush and Obama administrations have spoken in favor of it. Here's the head of the CIA, Leon Panetta:

> What I have expressed as a concern, as has the president, is that those who operated under the rules that were provided by the Attorney General in the interpretation of the law [concerning torture] and followed those rules ought not to be penalized. And ... I would not support, obviously, an investigation or a prosecution of those individuals. I think they did their job.[5]

Operating under the rules... following the rules... doing their job... are all of course the same as following orders.

The UN Convention Against Torture, which has been ratified by the United States, states quite clearly: 'An order from a superior officer or a public authority may not be invoked as a justification of torture.' The Torture Convention enacts a prohibition against torture that is a cornerstone of international law and a principle on a par with the prohibition against slavery and genocide.

Of course, those *giving* the orders are no less guilty. On the very day of Obama's inauguration, the United Nations Special Rapporteur on torture invoked the Convention in calling on the United States to pursue former president George W. Bush and defense secretary Donald Rumsfeld for torture and bad treatment of Guantánamo prisoners.[6]

On several occasions, President Obama has indicated his reluctance to pursue war crimes charges against Bush officials, by expressing a view such as: 'I don't believe that anybody is above the law. On the other hand I also have a belief that we need to look forward as opposed to looking backwards.' This is the same excuse Cambodian Prime Minister Hun Sen has given for not punishing Khmer Rouge leaders. In December 1998 he asserted: 'We should dig a hole and bury the past and look ahead to the 21st century with a clean slate.'[7] Hun Sen has been in power all the years since then, and no Khmer Rouge leader has been convicted for their role in the historic mass murder.

And by not indicting, or even investigating, Bush officials, Obama is indeed saying that they're above the law. Like the Khmer Rouge officials have been. Michael Ratner, a professor at Columbia Law School and president of the Center for Constitutional Rights, said prosecuting Bush officials is necessary to set future anti-torture policy.

The only way to prevent this from happening again is to make sure that those who were responsible for the torture program pay the price for it. I don't see how we regain our moral stature by allowing those who were intimately involved in the torture programs to simply walk off the stage and lead lives where they are not held accountable.[8]

One reason for the non-prosecution may be that serious trials of the many Bush officials who contributed to the torture policies might reveal the various forms of Democratic Party non-opposition and collaboration.

It should also be noted that the United States supported Pol Pot (who died in April 1998) and the Khmer Rouge for several years after they were ousted from power by the Vietnamese in 1979. This support began under Jimmy Carter and his national security adviser, Zbigniew Brzezinski, and continued under Ronald Reagan.[9] A lingering bitterness by American cold warriors toward Vietnam, the small nation which monumental US power had not been able to defeat, and its perceived closeness to the Soviet Union, appears to be the only explanation for this policy. Humiliation runs deep when you're a superpower.

Neither should it be forgotten in this complex cautionary tale that the Khmer Rouge in all likelihood would never have come to power, nor even made a serious attempt to do so, if not for the massive American 'carpet bombing' of Cambodia in 1969–70 and the US-supported overthrow of Prince Sihanouk in 1970 and his replacement by a man closely tied to the United States.[10] Thank you Richard Nixon and Henry Kissinger. Well done, lads.

By the way, if you're not already turned off by many of Obama's appointments, listen to how James Jones opened his talk at the Munich Conference on Security Policy on February 8, 2009: 'Thank you for that wonderful tribute to Henry Kissinger yesterday. Congratulations. As the most recent National Security Advisor of the United States, I take my daily orders from Dr. Kissinger.'[11]

Lastly, Spain's High Court recently announced it would launch a war crimes investigation into an Israeli ex-defense minister and six other top security officials for their role in a 2002 attack that killed a Hamas commander and fourteen civilians in Gaza.[12] Spain has for some time been the world's leading practitioner of 'universal jurisdiction' for human-rights violations, such as their indictment of Chilean dictator Augusto Pinochet a decade ago. The Israeli case involved the dropping of a bomb on the home of the Hamas leader; most of those killed were children. The United States does this very same thing every other day in Afghanistan or Pakistan. Given the refusal of American presidents to invoke even their 'national jurisdiction' over American officials-cum-war criminals, we can only hope that someone reminds the Spanish authorities of a few names, like Bush, Cheney, Rumsfeld, Powell, Rice, Feith, Perle, Yoo, and a few others with a piece missing, a piece that's shaped like a social conscience. There isn't even a need to rely on international law alone, for there's an American law against war crimes, passed by a Republican-dominated Congress in 1996.[13]

The noted Israeli columnist Uri Avnery, writing about the Israeli case, tried to capture the spirit of Israeli society that produces such war criminals and war crimes. He observed:

> This system indoctrinates its pupils with a violent tribal cult, totally ethnocentric, which sees in the whole of world history nothing but an endless story of Jewish victimhood. This is a religion of a Chosen People, indifferent to others, a religion without compassion for anyone who is not Jewish, which glorifies the God-decreed genocide described in the Biblical book of Joshua.[14]

It would take very little substitution to apply this statement to the United States – like 'American' for 'Jewish' and 'American exceptionalism' for 'a Chosen People.'

The two nations have something else of importance in common: the major problem in establishing both the United States and Israel as nations was what to do with the indigenous people. They chose the same solution. Kill 'em. Without legality. Without mercy.

Not your father's kind of torture
(December 6, 2005)

We've been raised to associate torture with acts such as the German and Japanese practices on prisoners during World War II, the Salem witch trials, the Spanish Inquisition, and what we've seen in torture museums, Hollywood films, and our comic books ... bodies stretched out on racks; locked into devices which press metal points into the victim's flesh and twist muscles and bones into agonizingly painful positions; red-hot pincers burning off flesh; the tearing out of fingernails; thumbscrews to crush fingers and toes; eyes gouged out ... while the torturer's assistant, a hunchback named Igor, looks on, salivating with sadistic glee.

To the extent that Cheney, Bush, Gonzales, and the rest of the torture apologists and deniers think about it at all, these are the kinds of images they'd like us to associate with torture, which, they hope, will show that what the US does is not torture. But who decided, and where is it written, that the historical torture methods, both real and imagined, comprise the *sine qua non* definition of torture? No one who has gone through the American dungeons in Iraq, Afghanistan, Guantánamo Bay, or spent time at any of the many secret CIA facilities, and no American who would be subjected to the same, would have any hesitation calling what they experienced 'torture.' Merely reading some of the stories is enough to convince a person with any sensitivity. (Yes, to answer your question, that would exclude Cheney, Bush and Gonzales.) I've put together a long and graphic list of the techniques employed – from sleep deprivation, the use of dogs, drowning simulation, and lying naked on a sheet of ice, to electric shock, anal assault with various implements, being kept in highly stressful positions for hours on end, and ninety-nine other ways to totally humiliate a human being; many of which the Nazis, Japanese et al. could have learned from.[15]

Interestingly, the United States granted immunity to a number of the German and Japanese torturers after the war in exchange for information about their torture methods.

Does the Obama administration use torture?
(April 6, 2012)

Another claim the Obamabots are fond of making to defend their man is that he has abolished torture. That sounds very nice, but there's no good reason to accept it at face value. Shortly after Obama's inauguration, both he and Leon Panetta, the new director of the CIA, explicitly stated that 'rendition' was not being ended. As the *Los Angeles Times* reported: 'Under executive orders issued by Obama recently, the CIA still has authority to carry out what are known as renditions, secret abductions and transfers of prisoners to countries that cooperate with the United States.'[16]

The English translation of 'cooperate' is 'torture.' Rendition is equal to torture. There was no other reason to take prisoners to Lithuania, Poland, Romania, Egypt, Jordan, Kenya, Somalia, Kosovo, or the Indian Ocean island of Diego Garcia, to name some of the known torture centers frequented by America's national security team. Kosovo and Diego Garcia – both of which house very large and secretive American military bases – if not some of the other locations, may well still be open for torture business. The same goes for Guantánamo. Moreover, the executive order concerning torture, issued on January 22, 2009 ('Executive Order 13491 – Ensuring Lawful Interrogations') leaves loopholes, such as being applicable only 'in any armed conflict.' Thus, torture by Americans outside environments of 'armed conflict,' which is where much torture in the world happens anyway, is not prohibited. What about, for example, torture in a 'counter-terrorism' environment?

One of Mr Obama's orders required the CIA to use only the interrogation methods outlined in a revised *Army Field Manual*. However, using the *Army Field Manual* as a guide to prisoner treatment and interrogation still allows solitary confinement, perceptual or sensory deprivation, sleep deprivation, the induction of fear and hopelessness, mind-altering drugs, environmental manipulation such as temperature and perhaps noise, and possibly stress positions and sensory overload.

After Panetta was questioned by a Senate panel, the *New York Times* wrote that he had

> left open the possibility that the agency could seek permission to use interrogation methods more aggressive than the limited menu that President Obama authorized under new rules ... Mr. Panetta also said the agency would continue the Bush administration practice of 'rendition' – picking terrorism suspects off the street and sending them to a third country. But he said the agency would refuse to deliver a suspect into the hands of a country known for torture or other actions 'that violate our human values.'[17]

He gave no examples of such a place.

Johnny got his gun
(January 2007)

In the past year Iran has issued several warnings to the United States about the consequences of an American or Israeli attack. One statement, issued in November 2006 by a high-ranking Iranian military official, declared: 'If America attacks Iran, its 200,000 troops and 33 bases in the region will be extremely vulnerable, and both American politicians and military commanders are aware of it.'[18] Iran apparently believes that American leaders would be so deeply distressed by the prospect of their young men and women being endangered and possibly killed that they would forswear any reckless attacks on Iran. As if American leaders have been deeply stabbed by pain about throwing youthful American bodies into the bottomless snakepit called Iraq, or the other one which goes by the name Afghanistan, or were restrained by fear of retaliation or by moral qualms while feeding 58,000 young lives to the Vietnam beast. As if American leaders, like all world leaders, have ever had such concerns.

Let's have a short look at some modern American history, which may be instructive in this regard. A report of the US Congress in 1994 informed us that

> Approximately 60,000 military personnel were used as human subjects in the 1940s to test two chemical agents, mustard gas and lewisite [blister gas]. Most of these subjects were not informed of the nature of the experiments and never received medical followup after their participation in the research. Additionally, some of these human subjects were threatened with imprisonment at Fort Leavenworth if they discussed these experiments with anyone, including their wives, parents, and family doctors. For decades, the Pentagon denied that the research had taken place, resulting in decades of suffering for many veterans who became ill after the secret testing.[19]

In the decades between the 1940s and 1990s, we find a remarkable variety of government programs, either formally, or in effect, using soldiers as guinea pigs: marched to nuclear explosion sites, with pilots sent through the mushroom clouds; subjected to chemical and biological weapons experiments; radiation experiments; behavior modification experiments that washed their brains with LSD; widespread exposure to the highly toxic dioxin of Agent Orange in Korea and Vietnam ... literally millions of experimental subjects, seldom given a choice or adequate information, often with disastrous effects to their physical and/or mental health, rarely with proper medical care or even monitoring.[20]

In the 1990s, many thousands of American soldiers came home from the Gulf War with unusual, debilitating ailments. Exposure to harmful chemical or biological agents was suspected, but the Pentagon denied that this had occurred. Years went by while the veterans suffered terribly: neurological problems, chronic fatigue, skin problems, scarred lungs, memory loss, muscle and joint pain, severe headaches, personality changes, passing out, and much more. Eventually, the Pentagon, inch by inch, was forced to move away from its denials and admit that, yes, chemical weapon depots had been bombed; then, yes, there probably were releases of deadly poisons; then, yes, American soldiers were indeed in the vicinity of these poisonous releases, 400 soldiers; then, it might have been 5,000; then, 'a very large number', probably more than 15,000; then, finally, a precise number – 20,867; then, 'The Pentagon announced that a long-awaited computer model estimates that nearly 100,000 US soldiers could have been exposed to trace amounts of sarin gas.'[21]

If the Pentagon had been much more forthcoming from the outset about what it knew all along about these various substances and weapons, the soldiers might have had a proper diagnosis early on and received appropriate care sooner. The cost in terms of human suffering is incalculable.

Soldiers have also been forced to take vaccines against anthrax and nerve gas not approved by the US Food and Drug Administration as safe and effective; and punished, sometimes treated like criminals, if they refused. (During World War II, soldiers were forced to take a yellow fever vaccine, with the result that some 330,000 of them were infected with the hepatitis B virus.[22])

And through all the recent wars, countless American soldiers have been put in close proximity to the radioactive dust of exploded depleted uranium-tipped shells and missiles on the battlefield; depleted uranium has been associated with a long list of rare and terrible illnesses and birth defects. The widespread dissemination of depleted uranium by American warfare – from Serbia to Afghanistan to Iraq – should be an international scandal and crisis, like AIDS, and would be in a world not so intimidated by the United States.

The catalog of Pentagon abuses of American soldiers goes on. Troops serving in Iraq or their families have reported purchasing with their own funds bullet-proof vests, better armor for their vehicles, medical supplies, and global positioning devices, all for their own safety, which were not provided by the army... Continuous complaints by servicewomen of sexual assault and rape at the hands of their male counterparts are routinely played down or ignored by the military brass... Numerous injured and disabled vets from all wars have to engage in an ongoing struggle to get the medical care they were promised... Read 'Army Acts to Curb Abuses of Injured Recruits' (*New York Times*, May 12, 2006) for accounts of the callous, bordering on sadistic, treatment of soldiers in bases in the United States... repeated tours of duty, which fracture family life and increase the chance not only of death or injury but of post-traumatic stress disorder (PTSD).[23]

National Public Radio's *All Things Considered*, on December 4, 2006 and other days, ran a series on army mistreatment of soldiers home from Iraq and suffering serious PTSD. At Colorado's Fort Carson these afflicted soldiers are receiving a variety of abuse and punishment much more than the help they need, as officers harass and punish them for being emotionally 'weak.'

Keep the above in mind the next time you hear a president or a general speaking on Memorial Day about 'honor' and 'duty' and about how much we 'owe to the brave young men and women who have made the ultimate sacrifice in the cause of freedom and democracy.' These officials have scarcely any more concern for the hapless American servicemen than they do for the foreigners they kill as in a video game. And read *Johnny Got His Gun* by Dalton Trumbo.

The moral progression of mankind

> When it comes to supporting the rights of Jews, there is no greater
> leader than the Third Reich, and we show that by holding people
> accountable when they violate the rights of our Jewish citizens.
> We show that by supporting the advance of religious and ethnic
> tolerance and supporting those Jewish people in countries where
> their human rights are denied or violated, like Austria. (Joseph
> Goebbels, German Minister of Propaganda, March 6, 1941)

> When it comes to human rights, there is no greater leader than
> the United States of America, and we show that by holding people
> accountable when they break the law or violate human rights. We
> show that by supporting the advance of freedom and democracy
> and supporting those in countries that are having their human
> rights denied or violated, like North Korea. (Scott McClellan,
> White House spokesman, December 2, 2005)

Can you guess which of these statements I've made up?

A drone attack, coming soon
to a country (or city) near you?

On January 13, 2006 the United States of America, in its shocking
and awesome wisdom, saw fit to fly an unmanned Predator aircraft
over a remote village in the sovereign nation of Pakistan and fire a
Hellfire missile into a residential compound in an attempt to kill
some 'bad guys.' Several houses were incinerated, eighteen people
were killed, including an unknown number of 'bad guys'; reports
since then give every indication that the unknown number is as
low as zero, al-Qaeda second-in-command Ayman al-Zawahiri,
the principal target, not being among them. Outrage is still being
expressed in Pakistan. In the United States the reaction in the
Senate typified the American outrage.

'We apologize, but I can't tell you that we wouldn't do the same
thing again,' said Senator John McCain of Arizona.

'It's a regrettable situation, but what else are we supposed to do?' asked Senator Evan Bayh of Indiana.

'My information is that this strike was clearly justified by the intelligence,' said Senator Trent Lott of Mississippi.[24]

Similar US attacks using such drones and missiles have angered citizens and political leaders in Afghanistan, Iraq, and Yemen. It has not been uncommon for the destruction to be so complete that it is impossible to establish who was killed, or even how many people. Amnesty International has lodged complaints with the Busheviks following each suspected Predator strike. A UN report in the wake of the 2002 strike in Yemen called it 'an alarming precedent [and] a clear case of extrajudicial killing' in violation of international laws and treaties.[25]

Can it be imagined that American officials would fire a missile into a house in Paris or London or Ottawa because they suspected that high-ranking al-Qaeda members were present there? Even if the US knew of their presence for an absolute fact, and was not just acting on speculation, as in the Predator cases mentioned above? Well, they most likely would not attack, but can we put anything past Swaggering–Superarrogant–Superpower–Cowboys-on-steroids? After all, they've already done it to their own – a US drone attack killed two American citizens in Yemen in 2011, and on May 13, 1985, a bomb dropped by a police helicopter over Philadelphia, Pennsylvania burned down an entire block, some sixty homes destroyed, eleven dead, including several small children. The police, the mayor's office, and the FBI were all involved in this effort to evict an organization called MOVE from the house they lived in.

The victims in Philadelphia were all black of course. So let's rephrase the question: can it be imagined that American officials would fire a missile into a residential area of Beverly Hills or the Upper East Side of Manhattan? Stay tuned.

The right to exercise one's mind
(December 6, 2005)

The Supreme Court announced in 2005 it would review a Pennsylvania case concerning prisons denying dangerous prisoners access to most reading material, television, and radio. These prisoners are permitted to read only religious and legal materials and paperback books from the prison library. A three-judge federal appeals court that struck the policy down did so over the dissent of Judge Samuel A. Alito, Jr, President Bush's nominee for the Supreme Court.

"'On their face,'" Alito wrote, "these regulations are reasonably related to the legitimate penological goal of curbing prison misconduct" – because prisoners would be deterred from misbehaving by the prospect of being sent to a place where they have to do without TV and magazines.'[26]

Never mind Alito's views on abortion, civil liberties, or gay rights, which have preoccupied those evaluating his fitness for the high court. But consider the deep-seated, plain, simple meanness of the man in wishing to deprive prisoners of mental stimulation through their long nights and years behind bars. Why doesn't he advocate that these prisoners be deprived of food? Surely that would be an even greater deterrent against misbehavior.

Since I gave up hope, I feel better
(May 1, 2008)

> More than any time in history, mankind now faces a crossroads.
> One path leads to despair and utter hopelessness, the other to
> total extinction. Let us pray that we have the wisdom to choose
> correctly. (Woody Allen)

Food riots, in dozens of countries, in the twenty-first century. Is this what we envisioned during the post-World War II, moon-landing twentieth century as humankind's glorious future?

American writer Henry Miller (1891–1980) once asserted that the role of the artist was to 'inoculate the world with disillusionment.' So just in case you, for whatever odd reason, still cling to the belief/hope that the United States can be a positive force in ending or slowing down the new jump in world hunger, here are some disillusioning facts of life.

On December 14, 1981 a resolution was proposed in the United Nations General Assembly which declared that 'education, work, health care, proper nourishment, national development are human rights.' Notice the 'proper nourishment.' The resolution was approved by a vote of 135:1. The United States cast the only 'No' vote.

A year later, on December 18, 1982, an identical resolution was proposed in the General Assembly. It was approved by a vote of 131:1. The United States again cast the only 'No' vote.

The following year, December 16, 1983, the resolution was again put forward, a common practice at the United Nations. This time it was approved by a vote of 132:1. There's no need to tell you who cast the sole 'No' vote.

These votes took place under the Reagan administration.

Under the Clinton administration, in 1996, a United Nations-sponsored World Food Summit affirmed the 'right of everyone to have access to safe and nutritious food.' The United States took issue with this, insisting that it does not recognize a 'right to food.' Washington instead championed free trade as the key to ending the poverty at the root of hunger, and expressed fears that recognition of a 'right to food' could lead to lawsuits from poor nations seeking aid and special trade provisions.[27]

The situation did not improve under the administration of George W. Bush. In 2002, in Rome, world leaders at another UN-sponsored World Food Summit again approved a declaration that everyone had the right to 'safe and nutritious food.' The United States continued to oppose the clause, again fearing it would leave them open to future legal claims by famine-stricken countries.[28]

Moreover, those defending the US opposition to a Human Right to Food (HRF) have been motivated by the fact that it is not protected by the US Constitution; that it is associated with un-American and socialist political systems; that the American way is self-reliance; that freedom from want is an invention of President Franklin Roosevelt; that food anxiety is an energizing challenge that can mobilize the needy to surmount their distressing circumstances; that taking on HRF obligations would be too expensive.[29]

WIKILEAKS

WikiLeaks, the United States, Sweden, and Devil's Island

DECEMBER 16, 2010: I'm standing in the snow in front of the White House. Standing with Veterans for Peace.

I'm only a veteran of standing in front of the White House; the first time was February 1965, handing out flyers against the war in Vietnam. I was working for the State Department at the time and my biggest fear was that someone from that noble institution would pass by and recognize me. Five years later I was still protesting Vietnam, although long gone from the State Department. Then came Cambodia. And Laos. Soon Nicaragua and El Salvador. Then Panama was the new great threat to America, to freedom and democracy and all things holy and decent, so it had to be bombed without mercy. This was followed by the first war against the people of Iraq, and the bombing of Yugoslavia. Then the land of Afghanistan had rained down upon it depleted uranium, napalm, phosphorous bombs, and other witches' brews and weapons of the chemical dust; then Iraq again. And I've skipped a few. I think I hold the record for picketing the White House the most times by a right-handed batter.

And through it all, the good, hard-working, righteous people of America have believed mightily that their country always means well; some even believe to this day that we never started a war, certainly nothing deserving of the appellation 'war of aggression.'

On that same snowy day Julian Assange of WikiLeaks was freed from prison in London and told reporters that he was more concerned that the United States might try to extradite him than he was about being extradited to Sweden, where he faced 'sexual' charges.[1]

That's a fear many political and drug prisoners in various countries have expressed in recent years. The United States is the new Devil's Island of the Western world. From the mid-nineteenth to the mid-twentieth century, political prisoners were shipped to that godforsaken strip of French land off the eastern coast of South America. One of the current residents of the new Devil's Island is Bradley Manning, the former US intelligence analyst suspected of leaking diplomatic cables to WikiLeaks. Manning faces virtual life in prison if found guilty, of something. Without being tried or convicted of anything, he is allowed only very minimal contact with the outside world; or with people, daylight, or news; among the things he is denied are a pillow, sheets, and exercise; his sleep is restricted and frequently interrupted. See Glenn Greenwald's discussion of how Manning's treatment constitutes torture.[2]

A friend of the young soldier says that many people are reluctant to talk about Manning's deteriorating physical and mental condition because of government harassment, including surveillance, seizure of their computer without a warrant, and even attempted bribes. 'This has had such an intimidating effect that many are afraid to speak out on his behalf.'[3] A developer of the transparency software used by WikiLeaks was detained for several hours last summer by federal agents at a Newark, New Jersey airport, where he was questioned about his connection to WikiLeaks and Assange as well as his opinions about the wars in Afghanistan and Iraq.[4]

This is but a tiny incident from the near-century buildup of the American police state, from the Red Scare of the 1920s to the McCarthyism of the 1950s to the crackdown against Central American protesters in the 1980s... elevated by the War on Drugs... now multiplied by the War on Terror. It's not the worst police state in history, not even the worst police state in the world today, but nonetheless it is a police state, and certainly the most pervasive police state ever – a *Washington Post* study revealed that there are 4,058 separate federal, state and local 'counterterrorism' organizations spread across the United States, each with its own responsibilities and jurisdictions.[5] The police of America, of many types, generally get what and who they want. If the United States gets its hands on Julian Assange, under any legal pretext, fear for him; it might be the end of his life as a free person; the actual facts of what he's done or the actual wording of US laws will not matter; hell hath no fury like an empire scorned.

John Burns, chief foreign correspondent for the *New York Times*, after interviewing Assange, stated: 'He is profoundly of the conviction that the United States is a force for evil in the world, that it's destructive of democracy.'[6] Can anyone who believes that be entitled to a full measure of human rights on Devil's Island?

The WikiLeaks documents have added to the steady, gradual erosion of people's belief in the US government's good intentions, which is necessary to overcome a lifetime of indoctrination. Many more individuals over the years would have been standing in front of the White House if they had had access to the plethora of information that floods people today; which is not to say that we would have succeeded in stopping any of the wars – that's a question of to what extent the United States is a democracy.

One further consequence of Assange's predicament may be to put an end to the widespread belief that Sweden, or the Swedish government, is peaceful, progressive, neutral, and independent.

Stockholm's behavior in this matter and others has been as American-poodle-like as London's, as it lined itself up with an Assange accuser who has been associated with right-wing anti-Castro Cubans, who are of course US-government-supported. This is the same Sweden that for some time in recent years was working with the CIA on its torture-rendition flights and has about 500 soldiers in Afghanistan. Sweden is the world's largest per capita arms exporter, and for years has taken part in US/NATO military exercises, some within its own territory. The left should get themselves a new nation to admire. Try Cuba.

There's also the old stereotype held by Americans of Scandinavians practicing a sophisticated and tolerant attitude toward sex, an image that was initiated, or enhanced, by the celebrated 1967 Swedish film *I Am Curious (Yellow)*, which had been banned for a while in the United States. And now what do we have? Sweden sending Interpol on an international hunt for a man who apparently upset two women, perhaps for no more than sleeping with them both in the same week.

And while they're at it, American progressives should also lose their quaint belief that the BBC is somehow a liberal broadcaster. Americans are such suckers for British accents. John Humphrys, the presenter of the BBC *Today* program, asked Assange: 'Are you a sexual predator?' Assange said the suggestion was 'ridiculous,' adding: 'Of course not.' Humphrys then asked Assange how many woman he had slept with.[7] Would even Fox News have descended to that level? I wish Assange had been raised in the streets of Brooklyn, as I was. He would then have known precisely how to reply to such a question: 'You mean including your mother?'

Another group of people who should learn a lesson from all this are the knee-reflex conspiracists. Several of them have already written me snide letters informing me of my naiveté in not realizing that Israel is actually behind the release of the WikiLeaks documents; which is why, they inform me, nothing about Israel is mentioned. I had to inform them that I had already seen a few documents putting Israel in a bad light. I've since seen others, and Assange, in an interview with Al Jazeera on December 23, 2010 stated that only a meager number of files related to Israel had been published so far because the publications in the West that were given exclusive rights to publish the secret documents were reluctant to publish much sensitive information about Israel. (Imagine the flak Germany's *Der Spiegel* would get hit with.) 'There are 3,700 files related to Israel and the source of 2,700 files is Israel,' said Assange. 'In the next six months we intend to publish more files.'[8]

Naturally, several other individuals have informed me that it's the CIA that is actually behind the document release.

The saga of Bradley Manning, Julian Assange, and WikiLeaks, to be put to ballad and film (March 5, 2012)

> Defense lawyers say Manning was clearly a troubled young soldier whom the Army should never have deployed to Iraq or given access to classified material while he was stationed there ... They say he was in emotional turmoil, partly because he was a gay soldier at a time when homosexuals were barred from serving openly in the U.S. armed forces.[9]

It's unfortunate and disturbing that Bradley Manning's attorneys have chosen to consistently base his legal defense upon the premise that personal problems and shortcomings are what motivated the young man to turn over hundreds of thousands of classified government files to WikiLeaks. They should not be presenting him that way any more than Bradley should be tried as a criminal or traitor. He should be hailed as a national hero. Yes, even when the lawyers are talking to the military mind. May as well try to penetrate that mind and find the freest and best person living there. Bradley also wears a military uniform.

Here are Manning's own words from an online chat:

> If you had free reign [*sic*] over classified networks ... and you saw incredible things, awful things ... things that belonged in the public domain, and not on some server stored in a dark room in Washington DC ... what would you do? ... God knows what happens now. Hopefully worldwide discussion, debates, and reforms. ... I want people to see the truth ... because without information, you cannot make informed decisions as a public.

Is the world to believe that these are the words of a disturbed and irrational person? Do not the Nuremberg Tribunal and the Geneva Conventions speak of a higher duty than blind loyalty to one's government, a duty to report the war crimes of that government?

Below is a listing of some of the things revealed in the State Department cables and Defense Department files and videos. For exposing such embarrassing and less-than-honorable behavior, Bradley Manning of the United States Army and Julian Assange of WikiLeaks may spend most of their remaining days in a modern dungeon, much of it while undergoing that particular form of torture known as 'solitary confinement.' Indeed, it has been suggested that the mistreatment of Manning has been for the purpose of making him testify against and implicate Assange. Dozens of members of the American media and public officials have called for Julian Assange's execution or assassination. Under the new National Defense Authorization Act, Assange could well be kidnapped or assassinated. What century are we living in? What world?

It was after seeing American war crimes such as those depicted in the video *Collateral Murder* and documented in the 'Iraq War Logs,' made public by Manning and WikiLeaks, that the Iraqis refused to exempt US forces from prosecution for future crimes. The video depicts an American helicopter indiscriminately murdering several non-combatants in addition to two Reuters

journalists, and the wounding of two small children, while the
helicopter pilots cheer the attacks in a Baghdad suburb like it was
the Army–Navy game in Philadelphia.

The insistence of the Iraqi government on legal jurisdiction
over American soldiers for violations of Iraqi law – something the
United States rarely, if ever, accepts in any of the many countries
where its military is stationed – forced the Obama administration
to pull virtually all American troops from the country.

If Manning had committed war crimes in Iraq instead of exposing them, he would be a free man today, like the numerous
American soldiers guilty of truly loathsome crimes in cities such
as Haditha and Fallujah.

Besides playing a role in writing *finis* to the awful Iraq War,
the WikiLeaks disclosures helped to spark the Arab Spring,
beginning in Tunisia.

When people in Tunisia read or heard of US embassy cables
revealing the extensive corruption and decadence of the extended
ruling family there – one long and detailed cable being titled 'Corruption in Tunisia: What's Yours is Mine' – how Washington's
support of Tunisian President Ben Ali was not really strong,
and that the US would not support the regime in the event of a
popular uprising, they took to the streets.

Here is a sample of some of the other WikiLeaks revelations
based on the embassy cables that have made the people of the
world wiser:

- In 2009 Japanese diplomat Yukiya Amano became the new
  head of the International Atomic Energy Agency, which plays
  the leading role in the investigation of whether Iran is devel-
  oping nuclear weapons or is working only on peaceful civilian nuclear energy projects. A US embassy cable of October
  2009 said Amano 'took pains to emphasize his support for
  U.S. strategic objectives for the Agency. Amano reminded the

[American] ambassador on several occasions that ... he was solidly in the U.S. court on every key strategic decision, from high-level personnel appointments to the handling of Iran's alleged nuclear weapons program.'

- Russia refuted US claims that Iran has missiles that could target Europe.
- The British government's official inquiry into how it got involved in the Iraq War was deeply compromised by the government's pledge to protect the Bush administration in the course of the inquiry.
- A discussion between Yemeni President Ali Abdullah Saleh and American General David H. Petraeus in which Saleh indicated he would cover up the US role in missile strikes against al-Qaeda's affiliate in Yemen. 'We'll continue saying the bombs are ours, not yours,' Saleh told Petraeus.
- The US embassy in Madrid had serious points of friction with the Spanish government and civil society: (a) trying to get the criminal case dropped against three US soldiers accused of killing a Spanish television cameraman in Baghdad during a 2003 unprovoked US tank shelling of the hotel where he and other journalists were staying; (b) torture cases brought by a Spanish NGO against six senior Bush administration officials, including former attorney general Alberto Gonzales; (c) a Spanish government investigation into the torture of Spanish subjects held at Guantánamo; (d) a probe by a Spanish court into the use of Spanish bases and airfields for American extraordinary rendition (= torture) flights; (e) continual criticism of the Iraq War by Spanish Prime Minister José Luis Rodríguez Zapatero, who eventually withdrew Spanish troops.
- State Department officials at the United Nations, as well as US diplomats in various embassies, were assigned to gather as much of the following information as possible about UN officials, including Secretary General Ban Ki Moon, permanent

WIKILEAKS 139

Security Council representatives, senior UN staff, and foreign diplomats: email and website addresses, Internet user names and passwords, personal encryption keys, credit card numbers, frequent flyer account numbers, work schedules, and biometric data. US diplomats at the embassy in Asunción, Paraguay, were asked to obtain dates, times, and telephone numbers of calls received and placed by foreign diplomats from China, Iran, and the Latin American leftist states of Cuba, Venezuela, and Bolivia. US diplomats in Romania, Hungary, and Slovenia were instructed to provide biometric information on 'current and emerging leaders and advisers.' The UN directive also specifically asked for 'biometric information on ranking North Korean diplomats.' A cable to embassies in the Great Lakes region of Africa said biometric data included DNA, as well as iris scans and fingerprints.

- A special 'Iran observer' in the Azerbaijan capital of Baku reported on a dispute that played out during a meeting of Iran's Supreme National Security Council. An enraged Revolutionary Guard Chief of Staff, Mohammed Ali Jafari, allegedly got into a heated argument with Iranian president Mahmoud Ahmadinejad and slapped him in the face because the generally conservative president had, surprisingly, advocated freedom of the press.

- The State Department, virtually alone in the Western hemisphere, did not unequivocally condemn a June 28, 2009 military coup in Honduras, even though an embassy cable declared: 'there is no doubt that the military, Supreme Court and National Congress conspired on June 28 in what constituted an illegal and unconstitutional coup against the Executive Branch.' [US support for the coup government has been unwavering ever since.]

- [There has been much US criticism of Ecuador's President Rafael Correa for his hostile behavior toward the mass media, but a March 31, 2009 State Department cable stated:] 'There is more than a grain of truth to Correa's observation that the Ecuadorian media play a political role, in this case the role of the opposition. Many media outlet owners come from the elite business class that feels threatened by Correa's reform agenda, and defend their own economic interests via their outlets.'

- The leadership of the Swedish Social Democratic Party visited the US embassy in Stockholm and asked for advice on how best to sell the war in Afghanistan to a skeptical Swedish public, asking if the US could arrange for a member of the Afghan government to visit Sweden and talk up NATO's humanitarian efforts on behalf of Afghan children, and so forth.

- The US pushed to influence Swedish wiretapping laws so communication passing through Sweden could be intercepted. [The American interest was clear: reportedly 80 percent of all the Internet traffic from Russia travels through Sweden.]

- Herman Van Rompuy, president of the European Council, told US embassy officials in Brussels in January 2010 that no one in Europe believed in Afghanistan anymore. He said Europe was going along in deference to the United States and that there must be results in 2010, or 'Afghanistan is over for Europe.'

- Iraqi officials saw Saudi Arabia, not Iran, as the biggest threat to the integrity and cohesion of their fledgling democratic state. The Iraqi leaders were keen to assure their American patrons that they could easily 'manage' the Iranians, who wanted stability; but that the Saudis wanted a 'weak and fractured' Iraq, and were even 'fomenting terrorism that would destabilize the government.' The Saudi King, moreover, wanted a US military strike on Iran.

- Saudi Arabia in 2007 threatened to pull out of a Texas oil refinery investment unless the US government intervened to stop Saudi Aramco from being sued in US courts for alleged oil price fixing. The deputy Saudi oil minister said that he wanted the US to grant Saudi Arabia sovereign immunity from lawsuits.

- Saudi donors were the chief financiers of Sunni militant groups like al-Qaeda, the Afghan Taliban, and Lashkar-e-Taiba, which carried out the 2008 Mumbai attacks.
- Pfizer, the world's largest pharmaceuticals company, hired investigators to unearth evidence of corruption against the Nigerian attorney general in order to persuade him to drop legal action over a controversial 1996 drug trial involving children with meningitis.
- Oil giant Shell claimed to have 'inserted staff' and fully infiltrated Nigeria's government.
- The United States overturned a ban on training the Indonesian Kopassus army special forces – despite the Kopassus's long history of arbitrary detention, torture, and murder – after the Indonesian president threatened to derail President Obama's trip to the country in November 2010.
- The Obama administration renewed military ties with Indonesia in spite of serious concerns expressed by American diplomats about the Indonesian military's activities in the province of West Papua, expressing fears that the Indonesian government's neglect, rampant corruption, and human rights abuses were stoking unrest in the region.
- US officials collaborated with Lebanon's defense minister to spy on, and allow Israel to potentially attack, Hezbollah in the weeks that preceded a violent May 2008 military confrontation in Beirut.
- Gabon president Omar Bongo allegedly pocketed millions in embezzled funds from central African states, channeling some of it to French political parties in support of Nicolas Sarkozy.
- Cables from the US embassy in Caracas in 2006 asked the US secretary of state to warn President Hugo Chávez against a

Venezuelan military intervention to defend the Cuban revolution in the eventuality of an American invasion after Castro's death.

- The United States was concerned that the leftist Latin American television network Telesur, headquartered in Venezuela, would collaborate with Al Jazeera of Qatar, whose coverage of the Iraq War had gotten under the skin of the Bush administration.
- The Vatican told the United States it wanted to undermine the influence of Venezuelan president Hugo Chávez in Latin America because of concerns about the deterioration of Catholic power there. It feared that Chávez was seriously damaging relations between the Catholic Church and the state by identifying the Church hierarchy in Venezuela as part of the privileged class.
- The Holy See welcomed President Obama's new outreach to Cuba and hoped for further steps soon, perhaps to include prison visits for the wives of the Cuban Five [arrested in the US]. Better US–Cuba ties would deprive Hugo Chávez of one of his favorite screeds and could help restrain him in the region.
- In 2010, UK Prime Minister Gordon Brown raised with Secretary of State Hillary Clinton the question of visas for two wives of members of the 'Cuban Five.' 'Brown requested that the wives (who have previously been refused visas to visit the U.S.) be granted visas so that they could visit their husbands in prison. ... Our subsequent queries to Number 10 indicate that Brown made this request as a result of a commitment that he had made to UK trade unionists, who form part of the Labour Party's core constituency. Now that the request has been made, Brown does not intend to pursue this matter further. There is no USG action required.'
- UK officials concealed from Parliament how the US was allowed to bring cluster bombs onto British soil in defiance of a treaty banning the housing of such weapons.

- A cable was sent by an official at the US Interests Section in Havana in July 2006, during the runup to the Non-Aligned Movement conference. He noted that he was actively looking for 'human interest stories and other news that shatters the myth of Cuban medical prowess.' [Presumably to be used to weaken support for Cuba among the member nations at the conference.]

- Most of the men sent to Guantánamo prison were innocent people or low-level operatives; many of the innocent individuals were sold to the US for bounty.

- DynCorp, a powerful American defense contracting firm that claims almost $2 billion per year in revenue from US tax dollars, threw a 'boy-play' party for Afghan police recruits. [Yes, it's what you think.]

- Even though the Bush and Obama administrations repeatedly maintained publicly that there was no official count of civilian casualties, the Iraq and Afghanistan War Logs showed that this claim was untrue.

- A 2009 US cable said that police brutality in Egypt against common criminals was routine and pervasive, the police using force to extract confessions from criminals on a daily basis.

- Known Egyptian torturers received training at the FBI Academy in Quantico, Virginia.

- The United States put great pressure on the Haitian government not to go ahead with various projects, with no regard for the welfare of the Haitian people. A 2005 cable stressed continued US insistence that all efforts must be made to keep former president Jean-Bertrand Aristide, whom the United States had overthrown the previous year, from returning to Haiti or influencing the political process. In 2006, Washington's target was President René Préval for his agreeing to a deal with Venezuela to join Caracas's Caribbean oil alliance PetroCaribe, under which Haiti would buy oil from Venezuela, paying only 60 percent up-front with the remainder payable over twenty-five years at 1 percent interest. And in 2009, the State Department backed American corporate opposition to an increase in the minimum wage for Haitian workers, the poorest paid in the Western hemisphere.

- The United States used threats, spying, and more to try to get its way at the crucial 2009 climate conference in Copenhagen.
- Mahmoud Abbas, president of the Palestinian National Authority, and head of the Fatah movement, turned to Israel for help in attacking Hamas in Gaza in 2007.
- The British government trained a Bangladeshi paramilitary force condemned by human rights organizations as a 'government death squad.'
- A US military order directed American forces not to investigate cases of torture of detainees by Iraqis.
- The US was involved in the Australian government's 2006 campaign to oust Solomon Islands Prime Minister Manasseh Sogavare.
- US diplomats pressured the German government to stifle the prosecution of CIA operatives who abducted and tortured Khalid El-Masri, a German citizen. [El-Masri was kidnapped by the CIA while on vacation in Macedonia on December 31, 2003. He was flown to a torture center in Afghanistan, where he was beaten, starved, and anally assaulted. The US government released him on a hilltop in Albania five months later without money or the means to go home.]
- 2005 cable re 'widespread severe torture' by India. The International Committee of the Red Cross reported: 'The continued ill-treatment of detainees, despite longstanding ICRC–GOI [Government of India] dialogue, have led the ICRC to conclude that New Delhi condones torture.' Washington was briefed on this matter by the ICRC years ago. [American leaders, including the present ones, continued to speak warmly of 'the world's

largest democracy'; as if torture and one of the worst rates of poverty and child malnutrition in the world do not contradict the very idea of democracy.]

- Since at least 2006 the United States has been funding political opposition groups in Syria, including a satellite television channel that beams anti-government programming into the country.

10

CONSPIRACIES

**Once is an accident; twice is a coincidence;
three times is a conspiracy**

> All science would be superfluous if the outward appearance and
> the essence of things directly coincided. (Karl Marx, *Das Kapital*,
> Vol. III)

I believe in conspiracies. So do all of you. American and world
history are full of conspiracies. Watergate was a conspiracy.
The cover-up of Watergate was a conspiracy. So was Enron.
And Iran–Contra. The October Surprise really took place. For
a full year, George W. Bush and Dick Cheney conspired to
invade Iraq while continually denying that they had made any
such decision. The Japanese conspired to attack Pearl Harbor
while negotiating with Washington to find peaceful solutions to
the issues separating the two governments. There are numerous people sitting in prison at this very moment in the United
States for having been convicted of 'conspiracy' to commit this
or that crime.

However, it doesn't follow that all conspiracy theories are
created equal, all to be taken seriously. Many people send me
emails about perceived conspiracies which I don't place much
weight on. Here are a few examples.

If they try to access my website a few times and keep getting an error message, they ask me if the FBI or Homeland Security or America Online has finally gotten around to shutting me down.

If they send me an email and it's returned to them, for whatever reason, they wonder if AOL is blocking their particular mail or perhaps blocking all my mail.

If they fail to receive a copy of my monthly *Anti-Empire Report*, they wonder if AOL or some government agency is blocking it.

If they come upon a news item on the Internet which exposes really bad behavior of the powers-that-be, they point out how 'the mainstream media is completely ignoring this,' even though I may already have read it in the *Washington Post* or the *New York Times*. To make the claim that the mainstream media is completely ignoring a particular news item, one would need to have access to the full version of a service like Lexis–Nexis and know how to use it expertly. Google often won't suffice if the news item has not appeared on the website of any mainstream media even though it may be in print or have been broadcast, although the creation of Google News has improved chances of finding an item.

No matter how many times I'm critical of Israel, no matter how many years I've gone without issuing a single favorable word about Israeli policies towards the Palestinians, if I happen to discuss a number of US interventions but don't make any mention of how Israel is the driving force behind [most? almost all? all?] of these interventions, then I'm a closet Zionist.

With every new audiotape or videotape from Osama bin Laden my correspondents were sure to inform me that the man was really dead and that the tape was a CIA fabrication. In January 2006, when bin Laden, on an audiotape, recommended that Americans read my book *Rogue State*, the mainstream media were eager to interview me. But a number of my correspondents were quick to inform me and the entire Internet that the tape was phony, implying that I was being naive to believe it. When I ask them why the CIA would want to publicize and increase the book sales of a writer like myself, who has been exposing the intelligence agency's crimes his entire writing life, I get no answer that's worth remembering, often not even understandable.

'Why do you bother criticizing Bush (or Obama)? He's not the real power. He's just a puppet,' they say to me. The real power behind the throne, I've been told, is/was Dick Cheney/ David Rockefeller/the Federal Reserve/the Council on Foreign Relations/the Bilderberger Group/the Trilateral Commission/ Bohemian Grove, and so on. Why, I wonder, are the annual meetings of the Bilderberger Group et al. thought to be so vital to their members and so indicative of their power? To the extent that the Bilderbergerites have access to those in power and are able to influence them, they have this access and power all year long, whether or not they gather together in a once-a-year closed meeting. I think their meetings are primarily a social thing. Money and power like to enjoy cocktails with money and power.

Finally, there's September 11, 2001. Among those in the '9/11 Truth Movement' I am a sinner because I don't champion the idea that it was an 'inside job,' although I don't dismiss this idea categorically. I think it more likely that the Bush administration had received intelligence that something was about to happen involving airplanes, perhaps took it to mean an old-fashioned hijacking with political demands, and then let it happen, to make use of it politically, as they certainly did.

When I say that I don't think that 9/11 was an 'inside job,' it's not because I believe that men like Dick Cheney, George W. Bush, Donald Rumsfeld et al. were not morally depraved enough to carry out such a monstrous act; these men consciously and directly instigated the Iraqi and Afghanistan horrors which have cost many more American lives than were lost on 9/11, not to mention more than a million Iraqis and Afghans who dearly wanted to remain among the living. In the Gulf War of 1991, Cheney and other American leaders purposely destroyed electricity-generating plants, water-pumping systems, and sewerage systems in Iraq, then imposed sanctions upon the country making the repair of the infrastructure extremely difficult. Then, after twelve years, when the Iraqi people had performed the heroic task of getting these systems working fairly well again, the US bombers came back to inflict devastating damage to them all once more. My books and many others document one major crime against humanity after another by our America once so dear and cherished.

So it's not the moral question that makes me doubt the inside-job scenario. It's the logistics of it all – the incredible complexity of arranging it all so that it would work and not be wholly and transparently unbelievable. That and the gross overkill – they didn't need to destroy *all* those buildings and planes and people. One of the twin towers killing more than a thousand would certainly have been enough to sell the War on Terror, the Patriot Act, Homeland Security, and the new American Police State. The American people are not such a hard sell. They really yearn to be true believers. Look how so many of them worship Obama despite his waging one war after another.

To win over people like me, the 9/11 truth people need to present a scenario that makes the logistics reasonably plausible. They might start by trying to answer questions like the following. Did planes actually hit the towers and the Pentagon and crash in Pennsylvania? Were these the same four United Airline and American Airline planes that took off from Boston and Newark? At the time of collision, were they being piloted by people or by remote control? If by people, who were these people? What happened to all the passengers?

Also, why did building 7 collapse? If it was purposely de-molished – why? All the reasons I've read so far I find not very credible. As to the films of the towers and building 7 collapsing, which make it appear that this had to be the result of controlled demolitions – I agree, it does indeed look that way. But what do *I* know? I'm no expert. It's not like I've seen, in person or on film, numerous examples of buildings collapsing due to controlled demolition and numerous other examples of buildings collapsing due to planes crashing into them, so I could make an intelligent distinction. We are told by the 9/11 truth people that no building constructed like the towers has ever collapsed due to fire. But how about fire plus a full-size, loaded airplane smashing into it? How many examples of that do we have?

But there's at least one argument those who support the official version use against the skeptics that I would question. It's the argument that if the government planned the operation there would have to have been many people in on the plot, and surely by now one of them would have talked and the mainstream media would have reported their stories. But in fact a number of firemen, the buildings' janitor, and others have testified to hearing many explosions in the towers some time after the planes crashed, supporting the theory of planted explosives. But scarce little of this has made it to the mainstream media. Similarly, following the JFK assassination at least two men came forward afterward and identified themselves as being one of the three 'tramps' on the grassy knoll in Dallas. So what happened? The mainstream media ignored them both. I know of them only because the tabloid press ran their stories. One of the men was the father of actor Woody Harrelson.

But I do wish you guys in the 9/11 Truth Movement luck; if you succeed in proving that it was an inside job, that would do more to topple the empire than anything I have ever written.

Lockerbie: don't believe anything until it's been officially denied

Abdelbaset Ali Mohmed al-Megrahi was a Libyan who spent eight years in a Scottish prison charged with the bombing of PanAm flight 103 over Lockerbie, Scotland in December 1988, which took the lives of 270 people. Many of those who investigated the case, including several in prominent establishment legal positions, argued for years that the evidence against Megrahi was exceedingly thin and unpersuasive. At one point a court in Scotland appeared to agree and ordered a new appeal for Megrahi. But then Megrahi was released back to Libya because of terminal cancer, from which he died in 2012.

Briefly, the key international political facts are these. For well over a year after the bombing, the US and the UK insisted that Iran, Syria, and a Palestinian group, the PFLP–GC, had been behind the bombing, allegedly done at the behest of Iran as revenge for the US shooting down of an Iranian passenger plane over the Persian Gulf on July 3, 1988, which claimed 290 lives. (An act the US called an accident, but which came about because of deliberate American intrusion into the Iran–Iraq war on the side of Iraq.)

Then the buildup to the US invasion of Iraq came along in 1990 (how quickly do nations change from allies to enemies on the empire's chessboard) and the support of Iran and Syria was desired for the operation. Suddenly, in October 1990, the US declared that it was Libya – the Arab state least supportive of the US buildup to the Gulf War and the sanctions imposed against Iraq – that was behind the bombing after all. Megrahi and another Libyan were fingered.

The PFLP–GC was headquartered in, financed by, and closely supported by Syria. The support for the scenario described above was, and remains, impressive, as the following sample indicates: In April 1989, the FBI leaked the news that it had tentatively identified the person who unwittingly carried the bomb aboard the plane. His name was Khalid Jaafar, a 21–year-old Lebanese American. The report said that the bomb had been planted in Jaafar's suitcase by a member of the PFLP–GC.

In May, the State Department stated that the CIA was 'confident' of the Iran/Syria/PFLP–GC account of events. Then *The Times* in London reported that 'security officials from Britain, the United States and West Germany were "totally satisfied" that it was the PFLP–GC' behind the crime. In December 1989, Scottish investigators announced that they had 'hard evidence' of the involvement of the PFLP–GC in the bombing. A National Security Agency electronic intercept disclosed that Ali Akbar Mohtashemi, Iranian interior minister, had paid Palestinian terrorists $10 million dollars to gain revenge for the downed Iranian airplane. Israeli intelligence also intercepted a communication between Mohtashemi and the Iranian embassy in Beirut 'indicating that Iran paid for the Lockerbie bombing.'

For many more details about this case, which cast even greater doubt upon the official version of Libyan guilt, with full documentation, see killinghope.org/bblum6/panam.htm ('I am absolutely astounded, astonished,' said the Scottish law professor who was the architect of the trial. 'I was extremely reluctant to believe that any Scottish judge would convict anyone, even a Libyan, on the basis of such evidence.')

And, by the way, Libya under Gaddafi never confessed to having carried out the act. They only took 'responsibility,' in the hope of getting various sanctions against them ended.

The conspiracy to trivialize conspiracy theories

During the Cold War when Washington was confronted with a charge of covert American misbehavior abroad, it was common to imply that the Russkies or some other nefarious commies were behind the spread of such tales; this was usually enough to discredit the story in the mind of any right-thinking American. Since that period, the standard defense against uncomfortable accusations and questions has been a variation of 'Oh, that sounds like a conspiracy theory' (chuckle, chuckle). Every White House press secretary learns that before his first day on the job.

Ironically, Pierre Salinger, press secretary to presidents Kennedy and Johnson, was himself on the receiving end of this practice. When he died on October 16, 2004, the *Washington Post* obituary included this: 'His journalistic reputation was besmirched in the 1990s, however, after his insistence that two major airline crashes were not what they seemed. He said that the 1988 explosion of Pan Am Flight 103 over Lockerbie, Scotland was a Drug Enforcement Agency operation that went wrong – a theory for which no evidence materialized.'[1] (There is, in fact, much more evidence in support of the incidental DEA role than of the Libyan role.)

'Conspiracy' researcher and author Jonathan Vankin has observed:

> Journalists like to think of themselves as a skeptical lot. This is a flawed self-image. The thickest pack of American journalists are all too credulous when dealing with government officials, technical experts, and other official sources. They save their vaunted 'skepticism' for ideas that feel unfamiliar to them. Conspiracy theories are treated with the most rigorous skepticism.
>
> Conspiracy theories *should* be approached skeptically. But there's no fairness. Skepticism should apply equally to official and unofficial information.[2]

11

YUGOSLAVIA

The international left still in bitter dispute

The events in the former Yugoslavia in the 1990s were very contentious at the time and remain so today; contentious not only between the usual supporters and foes of American imperialism, but among those on the left. There has been hardly any issue in modern times that has divided the international left as much as this one; arguments about the US/NATO 'humanitarian intervention' still pop up as a result of current events; the overthrow of the Libyan government in 2011 is the latest example – was it carried out to rescue the Libyan people from a terrible tyrant, or was it to remove Muammar Gaddafi because of his long history of not catering to the Western powers as they are accustomed to being catered to? The same question applies to Serbian leader Slobodan Milosevic, who had refused to fall happily under the dominion of the US/NATO/European Union/World Bank/IMF/WTO world government. The quasi-socialist Serbian state was regarded as Europe's last 'communist' holdout. Moreover, post-Cold War, NATO needed to demonstrate a *raison d'être* if it was to remain alive as Washington's enforcement thug.

One of the key issues in contention has been Kosovo. The prolonged US/NATO bombing of the former Yugoslavia in 1999, the world was assured, was in response to the 'ethnic cleansing' being carried out by the Serbian government against their ancient province of Kosovo. Numerous intelligent, well-meaning people remain convinced that the bombing took place *after* the mass forced deportation of ethnic Albanians from Kosovo was well under way; which is to say that the bombing was launched *in response to and to stop* this 'ethnic cleansing.' In actuality, the systematic forced deportations of large numbers of people from Kosovo did not begin until a few days *after* the bombing began, and was clearly a reaction to it, born of extreme anger and powerlessness on the part of the Serb leaders. This is easily verified by looking at a daily newspaper for the few days before the bombing began, the night of March 23/24, and the few days after. Or simply look at the *New York Times* of March 26, page 1, which reads: 'with the NATO bombing already begun, a deepening sense of fear took hold in Pristina [Kosovo's main city] that the Serbs would *now* vent their rage against ethnic Albanian civilians in retaliation' (emphasis added). Only on March 27 do we find the first reference to a 'forced march' or anything of that sort. But the propaganda version is already set in marble.

Victors' justice and impunity
(August 5, 2008)

So, former Bosnian Serb leader Radovan Karadzic has finally been apprehended. He's slated to appear before the International Criminal Tribunal for the Former Yugoslavia (ICTY) in The Hague, Netherlands, charged with war crimes, genocide, and crimes against humanity.

The ICTY was created by the United Nations in 1993. Its full name is 'The International Tribunal for the Prosecution of Persons Responsible for Serious Violations of International Humanitarian Law Committed in the Territory of the Former

Yugoslavia since 1991'. Notice the 'who' – 'Persons Responsible for Serious Violations of International Humanitarian Law.' Notice the 'where' – 'Territory of the Former Yugoslavia.' This is all spelled out in the statute of the Tribunal.[1]

In 1999, NATO (primarily the United States) bombed the Yugoslav republic of Serbia for seventy-eight consecutive days, ruining the economy, the ecology, power supply, bridges, apartment buildings, transportation, infrastructure, churches, schools, pushing the country many years back in its development, killing hundreds or thousands of people, traumatizing countless children, who'll be reacting unhappily to certain sounds and sights for perhaps the remainder of their days; the most ferocious sustained bombing of a nation in the history of the world, at least up to that time. Nobody has ever suggested that Serbia had attacked or was preparing to attack a member state of NATO, and that is the only event which justifies a reaction under the NATO treaty.

The ICTY has already held one high-level trial in an attempt to convince the world of the justice of the NATO bombing – former Yugoslav president Slobodan Milosevic, who died in his Hague prison while trying to defend himself against charges that remain unproven. Radovan Karadzic is next. When will the Western leaders behind the bombing of Serbia be tried for war crimes, as called for by the Tribunal's own statute, as noted above?

Shortly after the bombing began in March, 1999, professionals in international law from Canada, the United Kingdom, Greece, and the United States began to file complaints with the ICTY charging leaders of NATO countries with 'grave violations of international humanitarian law,' including:

> wilful killing, wilfully causing great suffering and serious injury to body and health, employment of poisonous weapons and other weapons to cause unnecessary suffering, wanton destruction of cities, towns and villages, unlawful attacks on civilian objects, devastation not necessitated by military objectives, attacks on

undefended buildings and dwellings, destruction and wilful damage done to institutions dedicated to religion, charity and education, the arts and sciences.

The Canadian suit named sixty-eight leaders, including William Clinton, Madeleine Albright, William Cohen, Tony Blair, Canadian prime minister Jean Chrétien, and NATO officials Javier Solana, Wesley Clark, and Jamie Shea. The complaint also alleged 'open violation' of the United Nations Charter, the NATO treaty itself, the Geneva Conventions, and the Principles of International Law Recognized by the International Military Tribunal at Nuremberg.

The complainants' briefs pointed out that the prosecution of those named by them was 'not only a requirement of law, it is a requirement of justice to the victims and of deterrence to powerful countries such as those in NATO who, in their military might and in their control over the media, are lacking in any other natural restraint such as might deter less powerful countries.' Charging the war's victors, not only its losers, it was argued, would be a watershed in international criminal law.

In a letter to Louise Arbour, the court's chief prosecutor, Michael Mandel, a professor of law in Toronto and the initiator of the Canadian suit, stated:

Unfortunately, as you know, many doubts have already been raised about the impartiality of your Tribunal. In the early days of the conflict, after a formal and, in our view, justified complaint against NATO leaders had been laid before it by members of the Faculty of Law of Belgrade University, you appeared at a press conference with one of the accused, British Foreign Secretary Robin Cook, who made a great show of handing you a dossier of Serbian war crimes. In early May, you appeared at another press conference with US Secretary of State Madeleine Albright, by that time herself the subject of two formal complaints of war crimes over the targeting of civilians in Yugoslavia.[2]

Arbour herself made little attempt to hide the pro-NATO bias she wore beneath her robe. She trusted NATO to be its own police, judge, jury, and prison guard. Here are her words:

> I am obviously not commenting on any allegations of violations of international humanitarian law supposedly perpetrated by nationals of NATO countries. I accept the assurances given by NATO leaders that they intend to conduct their operations in the Federal Republic of Yugoslavia in full compliance with international humanitarian law.[3]

The ICTY on its website tells us: 'By holding individuals accountable regardless of their position, the ICTY's work has dismantled the tradition of impunity for war crimes and other serious violations of international law, particularly by individuals who held the most senior positions.'[4] US/NATO leaders, however, have immunity not only for the 1999 bombings of Serbia, but the many bombings of Bosnia in the period 1993–95, including the use of depleted uranium. 'Dismantling the tradition of impunity' indeed.

Arbour was succeeded in 1999 as the ICTY's chief prosecutor by Carla Del Ponte, a Swiss diplomat. In accordance with her official duties, she looked into possible war crimes of all the participants in the conflicts of the 1990s surrounding the breakup of Yugoslavia and the NATO bombing of Serbia and its province of Kosovo, where ethnic Albanians were trying to secede. In late December 1999, in an interview with the London *Observer*, Del Ponte was asked if she was prepared to press criminal charges against NATO personnel (and not just against the former Yugoslav republics). She replied: 'If I am not willing to do that, I am not in the right place. I must give up my mission.'

The Tribunal then announced that it had completed a study of possible NATO crimes, declaring: 'It is very important for this tribunal to assert its authority over any and all authorities to the armed conflict within the former Yugoslavia.' Was this a sign from heaven that the new millennium (2000 was but a week away) was going to be one of more equal international justice? Could this really be?

No, it couldn't. From official quarters, military and civilian, of the United States and Canada, came disbelief, shock, anger, denials ... 'appalling' ... 'unjustified'. Del Ponte got the message. Her office quickly issued a statement: 'NATO is not under investigation by the Office of the Prosecutor of the International Criminal Tribunal for the former Yugoslavia. There is no formal inquiry into the actions of NATO during the conflict in Kosovo.[5]

Del Ponte remained in her position until the end of 2007, leaving to become the Swiss ambassador to Argentina; at the same time writing a book about her time with the Tribunal, *The Hunt: Me and War Criminals*. The book created something of a scandal in Europe, for in it she revealed how the Kosovo Liberation Army (KLA) abducted hundreds of Serbs in 1999, and took them to Kosovo's fellow Muslims in Albania where they were killed, their kidneys and other body parts then removed and sold for transplant in other countries.

The KLA for years before and since has been engaging in other charming activities, such as heavy trafficking in drugs, trafficking in women, various acts of terrorism, and carrying out ethnic cleansing of Serbs who have had the bad fortune to be in Kosovo because it has long been their home.[6] Between 1998 and 2002, the KLA appeared at times on the State Department terrorism list; at first because of its tactic of targeting innocent Serb civilians in order to provoke retaliation from Serb troops; later because mujahideen mercenaries from various Islamic countries, including some groups tied to al-Qaeda, were fighting alongside the KLA, as they were in Bosnia with the Bosnian Muslims during the 1990s' Yugoslav civil wars. The KLA remained on the terrorist list until the United States decided to make them an ally, partly due to the existence of a major American military base in Kosovo,

Camp Bondsteel. (It's remarkable, is it not, how these American bases pop up all around the world?) In November 2005, following a visit there, Alvaro Gil-Robles, the human rights envoy of the Council of Europe, described the camp as a 'smaller version of Guantánamo.'[7]

On February 17, 2008, in a move of highly questionable international legality, the KLA declared the independence of Kosovo from Serbia. The next day the United States recognized this new 'nation,' thus affirming the unilateral declaration of independence of a part of another country's territory. The new country has as its prime minister a gentleman named Hashim Thaci, described in Del Ponte's book as the brain behind the abductions of Serbs and the sale of their organs. The new gangster state of Kosovo is supported by Washington and other Western powers who can't forgive Serbia–Yugoslavia–Milosevic for not wanting to wholeheartedly embrace the NATO/US/European Union triumvirate, which recognizes no higher power, United Nations or other. The independent state of Kosovo is regarded as reliably pro-West, a state that will serve as a militarized outpost for the triumvirate.

In her book, Del Ponte asserts that there was sufficient evidence for prosecution of Kosovo Albanians involved in war crimes, but the investigation 'was nipped in the bud,' focusing instead on 'the crimes committed by Serbia.' She claims that she could do nothing because it was next to impossible to collect evidence in Kosovo, which was swarming with criminals, in and out of the government. Witnesses were intimidated, and even judges in The Hague were afraid of the Kosovo Albanians.[8]

'12

LIBYA

Arguing Libya

On July 9, 2011 I took part in a demonstration in front of the White House, the theme of which was 'Stop Bombing Libya.' The last time I had taken part in a protest against US bombing of a foreign country which the White House was selling as a 'humanitarian intervention,' as they did in Libya, was in 1999 during the prolonged bombing of Serbia. At that time I went to a couple of such demonstrations and both times I was virtually the only American there. The rest, maybe two dozen, were almost all Serbs. 'Humanitarian intervention' is a great selling device for imperialism, particularly in the American market. Americans are desperate to renew their precious faith that the United States means well, that we are still 'the good guys.'

This time there were about a hundred taking part in the protest. I don't know if any were Libyans, but there was a new element – almost half of the protesters were black, marching with signs saying: 'Stop Bombing Africa.'

There was another new element: people supporting the bombing of Libya, facing us from their side of Pennsylvania Avenue about 40 feet away. They were made up largely of Libyans, probably living in the area, who had only praise and love for the United

States and NATO. Their theme was that Gaddafi was so bad that they would support anything to get rid of him, even daily bombing of their homeland, which eventually exceeded Serbia's seventy-eight days. I of course crossed the road and got into arguments with some of them. I kept asking: 'I hate that man there [pointing to the White House] just as much as you hate Gaddafi. Do you think I should therefore support the bombing of Washington? Destroying the beautiful monuments and buildings of this city, as well as killing people?'

None of the Libyans even tried to answer my question. They only repeated their anti-Gaddafi vitriol. 'You don't understand. We have to get rid of Gaddafi. He's very brutal.' (See the CNN video of the July 1 mammoth pro-Gaddafi rally in Tripoli for an indication that these Libyans' views were far from universal at home: www.mathaba.net/news/?x=627196?rss)

'But you at least get free education and medical care,' I pointed out. 'That's a lot more than we get here. And Libya has the highest standard of living in the entire region, at least it did before the NATO and US bombing. If Gaddafi is brutal, what do you call all the other leaders of the region, whom Washington has long supported?' One retorted that there had been free education under the king, whom Gaddafi had overthrown. I was skeptical of this but I didn't know for sure that it was incorrect, so I replied: 'So what? Gaddafi at least didn't get rid of the free education like leaders in Britain and Europe did in recent years.'

A police officer suddenly appeared and forced me to return to my side of the road. I'm sure if pressed for an explanation, the officer would have justified this as a means of preventing violence from breaking out. But there was never any danger of that at all; another example of the American police-state mentality – order and control come before civil liberties, before anything.

Most Americans overhearing my argument with the Libyans would probably have interjected something like: 'Well, no matter how much you hate the president you can still get rid of him with an election. The Libyans can't do that.' And I would have come back with: 'Right. I have the freedom to replace George W. Bush with Barack H. Obama. Oh joy. As long as our elections are overwhelmingly determined by money, nothing of any significance will change.'

It doesn't matter to them if it's untrue. It's a higher truth.
(November 1, 2011)

'We came, we saw, he died.' The words of US Secretary of State, Hillary Clinton, giggling, as she spoke of the depraved murder of Muammar Gaddafi.

Imagine Osama bin Laden or some other Islamic leader speaking of 9/11: 'We came, we saw, 3,000 died... ha-ha.'

Clinton and her partners-in-crime in NATO can also have a good laugh at how they deceived the world. The destruction of Libya, the reduction of a modern welfare state to piles of rubble, to ghost towns, the murder of perhaps thousands ... this tragedy was the culmination of a series of falsehoods spread by the Libyan rebels, the Western powers, and Qatar (through its television station, Al Jazeera) – from the declared imminence of a 'bloodbath' in rebel-held Benghazi if the West didn't intervene to stories of government helicopter gunships and airplanes spraying gunfire onto large numbers of civilians to tales of Viagra-induced mass rapes by Gaddafi's army. (This last fable was proclaimed at the United Nations by the American ambassador, as if young soldiers were in need of Viagra!)[1]

The *New York Times* (March 22, 2011) observed: 'The rebels feel no loyalty to the truth in shaping their propaganda, claiming nonexistent battlefield victories, asserting they were still fighting in a key city days after it fell to Qaddafi forces, and making vastly inflated claims of his barbaric behavior.'

The *Los Angeles Times* (April 7, 2011) added this about the rebels' media operation:

> It's not exactly fair and balanced media. In fact, as [its editor] helpfully pointed out, there are four inviolate rules of coverage on the two rebel radio stations, TV station and newspaper:
>
> • No pro-[Gaddafi] reportage or commentary.
> • No mention of a civil war. (The Libyan people, east and west, are unified in a war against a totalitarian regime.)
> • No discussion of tribes or tribalism. (There is only one tribe: Libya.)
> • No references to Al Qaeda or Islamic extremism. (That's [Gaddafi's] propaganda.)

The Libyan government undoubtedly spouted its share of misinformation as well, but it was the rebels' trail of lies, of both omission and commission, which was used by the UN Security Council to justify its vote for 'humanitarian intervention'; followed in Act Three by unrelenting NATO/US bombs and drone missiles, day after day, week after week, month after month; you can't get much more humanitarian than that. If the people of Libya prior to the NATO/US bombardment had been offered a referendum on the aerial attacks, can it be imagined that they would have endorsed it?

In fact, it appears rather likely that a majority of Libyans supported Gaddafi. How else could the government have held off the most powerful military forces in the world for more than seven months? Before NATO and the US laid waste to the land, Libya had the highest life expectancy, lowest infant mortality, and highest UN Human Development Index in Africa. During the first few months of the civil war, giant rallies were held in support of the Libyan leader.[2]

If Gaddafi had been less oppressive of his political opposition over the years and had made some gestures of accommodation to them during the Arab Spring, the benevolent side of his regime might still be keeping him in power, although the world has plentiful evidence making it plain that the Western powers are not particularly concerned about political oppression except to use as an excuse for intervention when they want to; indeed, government files seized in Tripoli during the fighting show that the CIA and British intelligence worked with the Libyan government in tracking down dissidents, turning them over to Libya, and taking part in interrogations.[3]

In any event, many of the rebels had a religious motive for opposing the government and played dominant roles within the rebel army; previously a number of them had fought against the United States in Afghanistan and Iraq.[4] The new Libyan regime promptly announced that Islamic *sharia* law would be the 'basic source' of legislation, and laws that contradict 'the teachings of Islam' would be nullified. There would also be a reinstitution of polygamy; the Muslim holy book, the Quran, allows men up to four wives.[5]

Thus, just as in Afghanistan in the 1980-90s, the United States has supported Islamic militants fighting against a secular government. The US also fought on the same side as the Islamic militants in Bosnia, Kosovo, and Syria. The American government has imprisoned many people as 'terrorists' in the United States for a lot less than supporting al-Qaeda types.

What began in Libya as 'normal' civil war violence from both sides – repeated before and since by the governments of Egypt, Tunisia, Yemen, Bahrain, and Syria without any Western military intervention (the US continues to arm the Bahrain and Yemen regimes) – was transformed by the Western propaganda machine into a serious Gaddafi *genocide* of innocent Libyans. Addressing the validity of this key issue is another video, *Humanitarian War in Libya: There Is No Evidence.*[6] The main feature of the film is an interview with Soliman Bouchuiguir, secretary general, and one of the founders in 1989, of the Libyan League for Human

Rights, perhaps the leading Libyan dissident group, in exile in Switzerland. Bouchuiguir is asked several times if he can document various charges made against the Libyan leader. Where is the proof of the many rapes? The many other alleged atrocities? The more than 6,000 civilians alleged killed by Gaddafi's planes? Again and again Bouchuiguir cites the National Transitional Council as the source. Yes, that's the rebels who carried out the civil war in conjunction with the NATO/US forces. At other times Bouchuiguir speaks of 'eyewitnesses': 'little girls, boys who were there, whose families we know personally.' After a while he declares that 'there is no way' to document these things. This is probably true to some extent, but why, then, the UN Security Council resolution for a military intervention in Libya? Why almost eight months of bombing?

Bouchuiguir also mentions his organization's working with the National Endowment for Democracy in its effort against Gaddafi, and one has to wonder if the man has any idea that the NED was founded to be a front for the CIA.

Another source of charges against Gaddafi and his sons has been the International Criminal Court. The Court's chief prosecutor, Luis Moreno-Ocampo, is shown in the film *Humanitarian War in Libya* at a news conference discussing the same question of proof of the charges. He refers to an ICC document of seventy-seven pages which he says contains the evidence. The film displays the document's table of contents, which shows that pages 17-71 are not available to the public; these pages, apparently the ones containing the testimony and evidence, are marked as 'redacted.' In an appendix, the ICC report lists its news sources; these include Fox News, CNN, the CIA, Soliman Bouchuiguir, and the Libyan League for Human Rights. Earlier, the film had presented Bouchuiguir citing the ICC as one of his sources. The documentation is thus a closed circle.

Historical footnote: 'Aerial bombing of civilians was pioneered by the Italians in Libya exactly a century ago, 1911, perfected by the British in Iraq in 1920 and used by the French in 1925 to level whole quarters of Syrian cities. Home demolitions, collective punishment, summary execution, detention without trial, routine torture – these were the weapons of Europe's takeover' in the Mideast.[7]

Unending American hostility
(July 1, 2011)

If I could publicly ask our beloved president Barack Obama one question, it would be this: 'Mr President, in your short time in office you've waged war against six countries – Iraq, Afghanistan, Pakistan, Somalia, Yemen, and Libya. This makes me wonder something. With all due respect: what is wrong with you?'

The American media has done its best to dismiss or ignore Libyan charges that NATO/US missiles have been killing civilians (the people they're supposedly protecting), at least up until the recent bombing 'error' that was too blatant to be covered up. But who in the mainstream media has questioned the NATO/US charges that Libya was targeting and 'massacring' Libyan civilians a few months ago, which, we've been told, is the reason for the Western powers' attacks? Don't look to Al Jazeera for such questioning. The government of Qatar, which owns the station, has a deep-seated animosity toward Libyan leader Muammar Gaddafi and was itself a leading purveyor of the Libyan 'massacre' stories, as well as playing a military role itself in the war against Tripoli. Al Jazeera's reporting on the subject has been remarkably slanted.

Alain Juppé, foreign minister of France, which has been the leading force behind the attacks on Libya, spoke at the Brookings Institution in Washington on June 7, 2011. After his talk he was asked a question from the audience by local activist Ken Meyercord:

> An American observer of events in Libya has commented: 'The evidence was not persuasive that a large-scale massacre or genocide was either likely or imminent.' That comment was made by Richard Haass, President of our Council on Foreign Relations. If Mr. Haass is right, and he's a fairly knowledgeable fellow, then what NATO has done in Libya is attack a country that wasn't threatening anyone; in other words, aggression. Are you at all concerned that as NATO deals more and more death and destruction on the people of Libya that the International Criminal Court may decide that you and your friends in the Naked Aggression Treaty Organization should be prosecuted rather than Mr. Gaddafi?

Monsieur Juppé then stated, without attribution, somebody's estimate that 15,000 Libyan civilians had been killed by pro-Gaddafi forces. To which Mr. Meyercord replied: 'So where are the 15,000 bodies?' M. Juppé failed to respond to this, although in the tumult caused by the first question it was not certain that he had heard the second one.[8]

It should be noted that, as of June 30, 2011 NATO had flown 13,184 air missions (sorties) over Libya, 4,963 of which are described as strike sorties.[9]

If any foreign power fired missiles at the United States, would Barack Obama regard that as an act of war? If the US firing many hundreds of missiles at Libya is not an act of war, as Obama insists (to avoid having to declare war as required by US law), then the deaths resulting from the missile attacks are murder. That's it. It's either war or murder. To the extent there's a difference between the two.

It should be further noted that since Gaddafi came to power in 1969 there has virtually never been a sustained period when the United States has been prepared to treat him and the many positive changes he's instituted in Libya and Africa with any respect.[10]

A word from the man the world's mightiest military power spent years trying to kill

The following is an excerpt from *Recollections of My Life*, written by Col. Muammar Gaddafi, April 8, 2011:

Now, I am under attack by the biggest force in military history, my little African son, Obama wants to kill me, to take away the freedom of our country, to take away our free housing, our free medicine, our free education, our free food, and replace it with American style thievery, called 'capitalism,' but all of us in the Third World know what that means, it means corporations run the countries, run the world, and the people suffer, so, there is no alternative for me, I must make my stand, and if Allah wishes, I shall die by following his path, the path that has made our country rich with farmland, with food and health, and even allowed us to help our African and Arab brothers and sisters to work here with us ... I do not wish to die, but if it comes to that, to save this land, my people, all the thousands who are all my children, then so be it. ... In the West, some have called me 'mad', 'crazy'. They know the truth but continue to lie, they know that our land is independent and free, not in the colonial grip.

13

LATIN AMERICA

The crime of GWS – governing while socialist
(December 11, 2007)

In Chile, during the 1964 presidential election campaign, in which Salvador Allende, a Marxist, was running against two other major candidates much to his right, one radio spot featured the sound of a machine gun, followed by a woman's cry: 'They have killed my child – the communists.' The announcer then added in impassioned tones: 'Communism offers only blood and pain. For this not to happen in Chile, we must elect Eduardo Frei president.'[1] Frei was the candidate of the Christian Democratic Party, the majority of whose campaign costs were underwritten by the CIA, according to the US Senate.[2] One anti-Allende campaign poster which appeared in the thousands showed children with a hammer and sickle stamped on their foreheads.[3]

The scare campaign played up to the fact that women in Chile, as elsewhere in Latin America, are traditionally more religious than men, more susceptible to being alarmed by the specter of 'godless, atheist communism'.

Allende lost. He won the men's vote by 67,000 over Frei (in Chile men and women vote separately), but among the women Frei came out ahead by 469,000 – testimony, once again, to the remarkable ease with which the minds of the masses can be manipulated, in any and all societies.

In Venezuela, during the 2007 campaign concerning the constitutional reforms put forth by Hugo Chávez, the opposition played to the same emotional themes of motherhood and 'communist' oppression. (Quite possibly because of similar CIA advice.) 'I voted for Chávez for President, but not now. Because they told me that if the reform passes, they're going to take my son, because he will belong to the state,' said a woman, Gladys Castro, interviewed in Venezuela before the vote for a report by Venezuelanalysis.com, an English-language news service published by North Americans in Caracas. The report added:

> Gladys is not the only one to believe the false rumors she's heard. Thousands of Venezuelans, many of them Chávez supporters, have bought the exaggerations and lies about Venezuela's Constitutional Reform that have been circulating across the country for months. Just a few weeks ago, however, the disinformation campaign ratcheted up various notches as opposition groups and anti-reform coalitions placed large ads in major Venezuelan papers. The most outrageous was ... [a] two-page spread in the country's largest circulation newspaper, *Últimas Noticias*, which claimed about the Constitutional Reform: 'If you are a Mother, YOU LOSE! Because you will lose your house, your family and your children. Children will belong to the state.'

This particular ad was placed by a Venezuelan business organization, Cámara Industrial de Carabobo, which has among its members dozens of subsidiaries of the largest US corporations operating in Venezuela.[4]

It's widely believed that US hostility toward Chávez arises from Washington's desire to grab Venezuela's oil. However, in the post-World War II period, in Latin America alone, the US has had a similar contentious policy toward progressive governments and movements in Guatemala, El Salvador, Nicaragua, Honduras,

Grenada, the Dominican Republic, Chile, Brazil, Argentina, Cuba, and Bolivia. What these governments and movements all had in common was that they were or are leftist; it's nothing to do with oil. For more than half a century Washington has been trying to block the rise of any government in Latin America that threatens to offer a viable alternative to the capitalist model. Venezuela of course fits perfectly into that scenario, oil or no oil. This ideology was the essence of the Cold War all over the world.

Chávez's ideological crime is multiplied by his being completely independent of Washington, using his oil wealth to become a powerful force in Latin America, inspiring and aiding other independent-minded governments in the region, like Cuba, Bolivia, Nicaragua, and Ecuador, as well as carrying on close relations with the likes of China, Russia, and Iran. The man does not show proper understanding that he's living in the Yankees' back yard; indeed, in the Yankee's world. The Yankee empire grew to its present size and power precisely because it did not tolerate men like Salvador Allende and Hugo Chávez and their quaint socialist customs. Despite its best efforts, the CIA was unable to prevent Allende from becoming Chile's president in 1970. When subsequent parliamentary elections made it apparent to the Agency and their Chilean conservative allies that they would not be able to oust the left from power legally, they instigated a successful military coup, in 1973, during which Allende died.

In a 1970 memo to President Nixon, Henry Kissinger wrote: 'The example of a successful elected Marxist government in Chile would surely have an impact on – and even precedent value for – other parts of the world, especially in Italy; the imitative spread of similar phenomena elsewhere would in turn significantly affect the world balance and our own position in it.'

Chávez has spoken publicly about his being assassinated, and his government has several times uncovered what they perceived to be planned assassination attempts, from both domestic and foreign sources. In addition to the case of Salvador Allende, the cases of Jaime Roldós, president of Ecuador, and Omar Torrijos, military leader of Panama, have to be considered. Both were reformers who refused to allow their countries to become client states of Washington or American corporations. Both were firm supporters of the radical Sandinista revolution in Nicaragua; both banned an American missionary group, the Summer Institute of Linguistics – long suspected of CIA ties – because of suspicious political behavior; both died in mysterious plane crashes during the Reagan administration in 1981, Torrijos's plane exploding in midair.[5] Torrijos had earlier been marked for assassination by Richard Nixon.[6]

In contrast to the cases of Roldós and Torrijos, over the years, the United States has gotten along just fine with brutal dictators, mass murderers, torturers, and leaders who did nothing to relieve the poverty of their populations – Augusto Pinochet, Pol Pot, the Greek Junta, Ferdinand Marcos, Suharto, Duvalier, Mobutu, the Brazilian Junta, Somoza, Saddam Hussein, South African apartheid leaders, Portuguese fascists, and so on, all terrible guys, all seriously supported by Washington for an extended period; for none made it a regular habit, if ever, publicly to express strong disrespect for American leaders or their policies.

What if NBC cheered on a military coup against Bush?
(June 8, 2007)

During the Cold War, if an American journalist or visitor to the Soviet Union reported seeing churches full of people, this was taken as a sign that the people were rejecting and escaping from communism. If the churches were empty, this clearly was proof of the suppression of religion. If consumer goods were scarce, this was seen as a failure of the communist system. If consumer goods appeared to be more plentiful, this gave rise to speculation about was happening in the Soviet Union that was prompting the authorities to try to buy off the citizenry.[7]

I'm reminded of this kind of thinking concerning Venezuela. The conservative anti-communist American mind sees things pertaining to Washington's newest *bête noire* in the worst possible light. If Chávez makes education more widely available to the masses of poor people, it's probably for the purpose of indoctrinating them. If Chávez invites a large number of Cuban doctors to Venezuela to treat the poor, it's a sign of a new and growing communist conspiracy in Latin America, which includes Evo Morales, president of Bolivia. If Chávez wins repeated democratic elections... here's the former US Secretary of Defense Donald Rumsfeld: 'I mean, we've got Chávez in Venezuela with a lot of oil money. He's a person who was elected legally just as Adolf Hitler was elected legally and then consolidated power and now is, of course, working closely with Fidel Castro and Mr. Morales and others.'[8]

The latest manifestation of this mindset is the condemnation of the Venezuelan government's refusal to renew the license of RCTV, a private television station. This has been denounced by the American government and media, and all other right-thinking people, as suppression of free speech, even though they all know very well that the main reason, the *sine qua non*, for the refusal of the license renewal has to do with RCTV's unqualified support for the 2002 coup that briefly overthrew Chávez. If there was a successful military coup in the United States and a particular television station applauded the overthrow of the president (and the dissolving of Congress and the Supreme Court, as well as the suspension of the Constitution), and if then the coup was reversed by other military forces accompanied by mass demonstrations, and the same television station did not report any of this while it was happening to avoid giving support to the counter-coup, and instead kept reporting that the president had voluntarily resigned... how long would it be before the US government, back in power, shut down the station, arrested its executives, charging them under half a dozen terrorist laws, and throwing them into shackles and orange jumpsuits never to be seen again? How long? Five minutes? The Venezuelan government waited five years, until the station's license was due for renewal. And none of the executives has been arrested. And RCTV is still free to broadcast via cable and satellite. Is there a country in the entire world that would be as lenient?[9]

It can be said that the media in Venezuela are a lot more free than in the United States. How many daily newspapers or television networks in the United States are unequivocally opposed to US foreign policy? How many of them in the entire United States have earned the label 'opposition media'? Maybe Fox News when a Democrat is in the White House. Venezuela has lots of opposition media.

Venezuela: hell hath no fury like an empire scorned

In 2007, Hugo Chávez lost a complicated and extensive reform referendum, which included removing term limits for the presidency, but he then proposed a more limited reform in 2009 to eliminate just term limits for all elected offices and he won. The American media and the opposition in Venezuela have made it sound as if Chávez was going to be guaranteed office for as long as he wanted; a veritable dictatorship. But in fact there was nothing at all automatic about the process – Chávez would have to be elected each time. It's not unusual for a nation to have no term limit for its highest office. France, Germany, and the United Kingdom, if not most of Europe and much of the rest of the world, do not have such a limit. The United States did not have a term limit on the office of the president during the nation's first 162 years, until the ratification of the 22nd Amendment in 1951. Were all American presidents prior to that time dictators?

In 2005, when Colombian President Alvaro Uribe succeeded in getting term limits lifted, the US mainstream media took scant notice. President Bush subsequently honored Uribe with the American Presidential Medal of Freedom. But in the period leading up to the February 15, 2007 referendum in Venezuela, the American media were competing with each other over who could paint Chávez and the Venezuelan constitutional process in the most critical and ominous terms. Typical was an op-ed in the *Washington Post* the day before the vote, which was headlined: 'Closing in on Hugo Chávez.' Its opening sentence read: 'The beginning of the end is setting in for Hugo Chávez.'[10]

For several years, the campaign to malign Chávez has at times included issues of Israel and anti-Semitism. The isolated vandalism of a Caracas synagogue on January 30, 2009 fed into this campaign. Synagogues are of course vandalized occasionally in the United States and many European countries, but no one ascribes this to a government policy driven by anti-Semitism. With Chávez they do. In the American media, the lead-up to the Venezuelan vote was never far removed from the alleged 'Jewish' issue.

'Despite the government's efforts to put the [synagogue] controversy to rest,' the *New York Times* wrote a few days before the referendum vote, 'a sense of dread still lingers among Venezuela's 12,000 to 14,000 Jews.'[11]

A day earlier, a *Washington Post* editorial was entitled 'Mr. Chávez vs. the Jews – With George W. Bush gone, Venezuela's strongman has found new enemies.'[12] Shortly before, a *Post* headline had informed us 'Jews in S. America Increasingly Uneasy – Government and Media Seen Fostering Anti-Semitism in Venezuela, Elsewhere.'[13]

So commonplace did the Chávez–Jewish association become that a leading US progressive organization, Council on Hemispheric

Affairs (COHA) in Washington, DC, distributed an article that read more like the handiwork of a conservative group than a progressive one. I was prompted to write to them as follows:

Dear People,

I'm very sorry to say that I found your Venezuelan commentary by Larry Birns and David Rosenblum Felson to be remarkably lacking. The authors seem unable, or unwilling, to distinguish between being against Israeli policies from anti-Semitism. It's kind of late in the day for them to not have comprehended the difference. They are forced to fall back on a State Department statement to make their case. Is that not enough said?

They condemn Chávez likening Israel's occupation of Gaza to the Holocaust. But what if it's an apt comparison? They don't delve into this question at all.

They also condemn the use of the word 'Zionism', saying that 'in 9 times out of 10 involving the use of this word in fact smacks of anti-Semitism.' Really? Can they give a precise explanation of how one distinguishes between an anti-Semitic use of the word and a non-anti-Semitic use of it? That would be interesting.

The authors write that Venezuela's 'anti-Israeli initiative ... revealingly transcends the intensity of almost every Arabic nation or normal adversary of Israel.' Really. Since when are the totally gutless, dictator Arab nations the standard bearer for progressives? The ideal we should emulate. Egypt, Saudi Arabia, and Jordan are almost never seriously and harshly critical of Israeli policies toward the Palestinians. Therefore, Venezuela shouldn't be?

The authors state: 'In a Christmas Eve address to the nation, Chávez charged that, "Some minorities, descendants of the same ones who crucified Christ ... took all the world's wealth for themselves." Here, Chávez was not talking so much about Robin Hood, but rather unquestionably dipping into the lore of anti-Semitism.' Well, here's the full quotation: 'The world has enough for all, but it turns out that some minorities, descendants of the same ones who crucified Christ, descendants of the same ones who threw Bolivar out of here and also crucified him in their own way at Santa Marta there in Colombia ...' Hmm, were the Jews so active in nineteenth-century South America?

The ellipsis after the word 'Christ' indicates that the authors consciously and purposely omitted the words that would have given the lie to their premise. Truly astonishing.

(Note: The Reagan administration in 1983 flung charges of anti-Semitism against the Sandinista government of Nicaragua, led by Daniel Ortega, who became the head once again in 2007–12 and continuing.[14] Stay tuned. Daniel, watch out.)

The ideology of the ruling class in any society is one that tries to depict the existing social order as 'natural'
(February 3, 2007)

In 1972 I traveled by land from San Francisco to Chile, to observe and report on Salvador Allende's 'socialist experiment.' One of the lasting impressions of my journey through Latin America is of the strict class order of the societies I visited. There are probably very few places in the world where the dividing lines between the upper and middle classes, on the one hand, and the lower class, on the other, are more distinct and emotionally clung to, including Great Britain. In the Chilean capital of Santiago I went to look at a room in a house advertised by a woman. Because I was American she assumed that I was anti-Allende, the same assumption she'd have made if I had been European, for she wanted to believe that only 'Indians,' only poor dumb *indígenas* and their ilk, supported the government. She was pleased by the prospect of an American living in her home and was concerned that he might be getting the wrong impression about her country. 'All this chaos,' she assured me, 'it's not normal, it's not Chile.' When I relieved her of her misconception about me she was visibly confused and hurt, and I was a little uncomfortable as well, as if I had betrayed her trust. I made my departure quickly.

There's the classic Latin American story of the servant of a family of the oligarchy. He bought steak for his *patrón*'s dog, but his own family ate scraps. He took the dog to the vet, but couldn't take his own children to a doctor. And he complained not. In Chile, under Allende, there was a terribly nagging fear among the privileged classes that servants no longer knew their place. (In Sweden, for some years now, they have been able to examine children of a certain age – their height, weight, and various health measurements – and not be able to tell which social class the child is from; they have ended class warfare against children.)

In the 1980s, in Central America, servants rose up in much of the region against their betters, the latter of course being unconditionally supported with Yankee money, Yankee arms, even Yankee lives. At the end of that decade the *New York Times* offered some snapshots of El Salvador:

> Over canapes served by hovering waiters at a party, a guest said she was convinced that God had created two distinct classes of people: the rich and people to serve them. She described herself as charitable for allowing the poor to work as her servants. 'It's the best you can do,' she said.
>
> The woman's outspokenness was unusual, but her attitude is shared by a large segment of the Salvadoran upper class.
>
> The separation between classes is so rigid that even small expressions of kindness across the divide are viewed with suspicion. When an American, visiting an ice cream store, remarked that he was shopping for a birthday party for his maid's child, other store patrons immediately stopped talking and began staring at the American. Finally, an astonished woman in the check-out line spoke out. 'You must be kidding,' she said.[15]

The same polarization is taking place now in Venezuela as Hugo Chávez attempts to build a more egalitarian society. The Associated Press (January 29, 2007) presented some snapshots from Caracas. A man of European parents says that at his son's private Jewish school some parents are talking about how and when to leave the country. The man wants a passport for his

10-year-old son in case they need to leave for good. 'I think we're headed toward totalitarianism.' A middle-class retiree grimaces at what she sees coming: 'Within one year, complete communism. ... What he's forming is a dictatorship.' The fact that Chávez is himself part *indígena* and part black, and looks it, can well add to their animosity toward the man.

I wonder what such people think of George 'I am the decider' Bush and his repeated use of 'signing statements,' which effectively mean a law is what he says it is, no more, no less; plus his Patriot Act, his various assaults on the principle of habeas corpus, and his expanding surveillance state – to name some of the scary practices of his authoritarian rule. If Hugo Chávez tried to institute such measures into Venezuela the accusation of 'dictatorship' would have more meaning.

Chuck Kaufman, national co-coordinator of the Washington-based Nicaragua Network, was with a group which visited Venezuela last fall. Following is part of his report:

> Venezuela is politically polarized. We witnessed the extremes of this during a dinner with lawyer and author Eva Golinger. Some very drunk opposition supporters recognized Golinger as author of *The Chávez Code* and a strong Chávez partisan. Some of them surrounded our table and began screaming at Golinger and the delegation, calling us 'assassins,' 'Cubans,' and 'Argentines.' The verbal abuse went on for long minutes until waiters ejected the most out-of-control anti-Chávez woman. We were later told that she worked in the Attorney General's office, highlighting one of the many contradictions arising from the fact that Chávez's Bolivarian revolution came into power democratically through the ballot box rather than by force of arms. Armed revolutions generally sweep opponents out of government jobs and places of influence such as the media, but in Venezuela many in the opposition are still in the civil service and most of the media is virulently anti-Chávez.[16]

I admire Hugo Chávez and what he's trying to do in Venezuela, but I wish he wouldn't go out of his way to taunt the Bush administration, as he does frequently. Doesn't he know that he's dealing with a bunch of homicidal maniacs? Someone please tell him to cool it or he will endanger his social revolution.

Nicaragua: Operation Because We Can

Captain Ahab had his Moby Dick; Inspector Javert had his Jean Valjean; the United States has its Fidel Castro. But Washington also has its Daniel Ortega. For more than thirty years, the most powerful nation in the world has found it impossible to share the Western hemisphere with one of its poorest and weakest neighbors, Nicaragua, if the country's leader was not in love with capitalism.

From the moment the Sandinista revolutionaries overthrew the US-supported Somoza dictatorship in 1979, Washington was concerned about the rising up of that long-dreaded beast – 'another Cuba.' This was war. On the battlefield and in the voting booths. For almost ten years, the American proxy army, the Contras, carried out a particularly brutal insurgency against the Sandinista government and its supporters. In 1984, Washington tried its best to sabotage the elections, but failed to keep Sandinista leader Ortega from becoming president. And the war continued. In 1990, Washington's electoral tactic was to hammer home the simple and clear message to the people of Nicaragua: if you re-elect Ortega all the horrors of the civil war and America's economic hostility will continue. Just two months before the election, in December 1989, the United States invaded Panama for no apparent reason acceptable to international law, morality, or common sense (the United States naturally called it 'Operation Just Cause'). One likely reason it was carried out was to send a clear message to the people of Nicaragua that this is what they could expect, that the US–Contra war would continue and even escalate, if they re-elected the Sandinistas.

It worked; one cannot overestimate the power of fear, of murder, rape, and your house being burned down. Ortega lost, and Nicaragua returned to the rule of the free market, striving to roll back the progressive social and economic programs that had been undertaken by the Sandinistas. Within a few years widespread malnutrition, wholly inadequate access to health care and education, and other social ills, had once again become a daily fact of life for the people of Nicaragua.

Each presidential election since then has pitted perennial candidate Ortega against Washington's interference in the process in shamelessly blatant ways. Pressure has been regularly exerted on certain political parties to withdraw their candidates so as to avoid splitting the conservative vote against the Sandinistas. US ambassadors and visiting State Department officials publicly and explicitly campaign for anti-Sandinista candidates, threatening all kinds of economic and diplomatic punishment if Ortega wins, including difficulties with exports, visas, and vital family remittances by Nicaraguans living in the United States. In the 2001 election, shortly after the September 11 attacks, American officials tried their best to tie Ortega to terrorism, placing a full-page ad in the leading newspaper which declared, among other things, that 'Ortega has a relationship of more than thirty years with states and individuals who shelter and condone international terrorism.'[17] That same year a senior analyst in Nicaragua for the international pollsters Gallup was moved to declare: 'Never in my whole life have I seen a sitting ambassador get publicly involved in a sovereign country's electoral process, nor have I ever heard of it.'[18]

Additionally, the National Endowment for Democracy (NED) – which would like the world to believe that it's a private nongovernmental organization, when it's actually a creation and an agency of the US government – regularly furnishes large amounts of money and other aid to organizations in Nicaragua which are opposed to the Sandinistas. The International Republican

Institute (IRI), a long-time wing of NED, whose chairman is Arizona Senator John McCain, has also been active in Nicaragua creating the Movement for Nicaragua, which has helped organize marches against the Sandinistas. An IRI official in Nicaragua, speaking to a visiting American delegation in June, 2006, equated the relationship between Nicaragua and the United States to that of a son to a father. 'Children should not argue with their parents,' she said.

With the 2006 presidential election in mind, one senior US official wrote in a Nicaraguan newspaper the year before that should Ortega be elected, 'Nicaragua would sink like a stone.' In March 2006, Jeanne Kirkpatrick, the US ambassador to the UN under Reagan and a prime supporter of the Contras, came to visit. She met with members of all the major Sandinista opposition parties and declared her belief that democracy in Nicaragua 'is in danger' but that she had no doubt that the 'Sandinista dictatorship' would not return to power. The following month, the American ambassador in Managua, Paul Trivelli, who openly spoke of his disapproval of Ortega and the Sandinista party, sent a letter to the presidential candidates of conservative parties offering financial and technical help to unite them for the general election in November. The ambassador stated that he was responding to requests by Nicaraguan 'democratic parties' for US support in their mission to keep Daniel Ortega from a presidential victory. The visiting American delegation reported: 'In a somewhat opaque statement Trivelli said that if Ortega were to win, the concept of governments recognizing governments wouldn't exist anymore and it was a nineteenth-century concept anyway. The relationship would depend on what his government put in place.' One of the fears of the ambassador likely had to do with Ortega talking of renegotiating CAFTA, the trade agreement between the US and Central America, so dear to the hearts of corporate globalizationists.

Then, in June, US Deputy Secretary of State Robert Zoellick said it was necessary for the Organization of American States (OAS) to send a mission of electoral observation to Nicaragua 'as soon as possible' so as to 'prevent the old leaders of corruption and communism from attempting to remain in power' (though the Sandinistas had not occupied the presidency, only lower offices, since 1990).

The explicit or implicit message of American pronouncements concerning Nicaragua was often the warning that if the Sandinistas come back to power, the horrible war, so fresh in the memory of Nicaraguans, would return. The London *Independent* reported in September that 'One of the Ortega billboards in Nicaragua was spray-painted "We don't want another war". What it was saying was that if you vote for Ortega you are voting for a possible war with the US.'[19]

Per capita income in Nicaragua is $900 a year; some 70 per cent of the people live in poverty. It is worth noting that Nicaragua and Haiti are the two nations in the Western Hemisphere that the United States has intervened in the most, from the nineteenth century to the twenty-first, including long periods of occupation. And they are today the two poorest in the hemisphere, wretchedly so.

Yankee karma forces them to emigrate

The questions concerning immigration into the United States from south of the border go on year after year, with the same issues argued back and forth. What's the best way to block the flow into the country? How shall we punish those caught here illegally? Should we separate families, which happens when parents are deported but their American-born children remain? Should the police and various other institutions have the right to ask for proof of legal residence from anyone they suspect of being here illegally? Should we punish employers who hire illegal immigrants? Should we grant amnesty to at least some of the immigrants already here for years? On and on, round and round it goes, for decades. Every once in a while someone opposed to immigration will make it a point to declare that the United States does not have any moral obligation to take in these Latino immigrants.

But the counter-argument to the last is almost never mentioned: yes, the United States does have a moral obligation because so many of the immigrants are escaping situations in their homelands made hopeless by American interventions and policy since World War II. In Guatemala and Nicaragua, Washington overthrew progressive governments which were sincerely committed to fighting poverty. In El Salvador the US played a major role in suppressing a movement striving to install such a government, and to a lesser extent played such a role in Honduras. And in Mexico, although Washington has not intervened militarily since 1919, over the years the US has been providing training, arms, and surveillance technology to Mexico's police and armed forces to better their ability to suppress their own people's aspirations, as in Chiapas, and this has added to the influx of the impoverished to the United States. Moreover, Washington's North American Free Trade Agreement (NAFTA) has brought a flood of cheap, subsidized US agricultural products into Mexico and driven many Mexican farmers off the land.

The end result of all these policies has been an army of migrants heading north in search of a better life. It's not that these people prefer to live in the United States. They'd much rather remain with their families and friends, be able to speak their native language at all times, and avoid the hardships imposed on them by American police and right-wingers.

14

CUBA

The UN vote on the Cuban embargo: twenty years of defeat doesn't discourage the brave American leaders

For years American political leaders and media were fond of labeling Cuba an 'international pariah.' We don't hear that any more. Perhaps one reason is the annual vote in the United Nations General Assembly on the resolution which reads: 'Necessity of ending the economic, commercial and financial embargo imposed by the United States of America against Cuba.' This is how the vote has gone (not including abstentions):

	YES–NO	
1992	59–2	(US, Israel)
1993	88–4	(US, Israel, Albania, Paraguay)
1994	101–2	(US, Israel)
1995	117–3	(US, Israel, Uzbekistan)
1996	138–3	(US, Israel, Uzbekistan)
1997	143–3	(US, Israel, Uzbekistan)
1998	157–2	(US, Israel)
1999	155–2	(US, Israel)
2000	167–3	(US, Israel, Marshall Islands)
2001	167–3	(US, Israel, Marshall Islands)
2002	173–3	(US, Israel, Marshall Islands)
2003	179–3	(US, Israel, Marshall Islands)
2004	179–4	(US, Israel, Marshall Islands, Palau)
2005	182–4	(US, Israel, Marshall Islands, Palau)

2006	183–4	(US, Israel, Marshall Islands, Palau)
2007	184–4	(US, Israel, Marshall Islands, Palau)
2008	185–3	(US, Israel, Palau)
2009	187–3	(US, Israel, Palau)
2010	187–2	(US, Israel)
2011	186–2	(US, Israel)
2012	188–3	(US, Israel, Palau)

Each fall the UN vote is a welcome reminder that the world has not *completely* lost its senses and that the American empire does not *completely* control the opinion of other governments.

How it began. On April 6, 1960, Lester D. Mallory, US deputy assistant secretary of state for inter-American affairs, wrote in an internal memorandum: 'The majority of Cubans support Castro... The only foreseeable means of alienating internal support is through disenchantment and disaffection based on economic dissatisfaction and hardship. ... every possible means should be undertaken promptly to weaken the economic life of Cuba.' Mallory proposed 'a line of action which ... makes the greatest inroads in denying money and supplies to Cuba, to decrease monetary and real wages, to bring about hunger, desperation and overthrow of government.'[1] Later that year, the Eisenhower administration instituted the suffocating embargo against its eternally declared enemy.

Since the early days of the Cuban Revolution assorted anti-communists and capitalist true-believers around the world have been relentless in publicizing the failures, real and alleged, of life in Cuba; each perceived shortcoming is attributed to the perceived shortcomings of socialism – it's simply a system that can't work, we are told, given the nature of human beings, particularly in this modern, competitive, globalized, consumer-oriented world.

In response to many of these criticisms, defenders of Cuban society have regularly pointed out how the numerous draconian sanctions imposed by the United States since 1960 are largely responsible for most of the problems pointed out by the critics. The critics, in turn, say that this is just an excuse, one given by Cuban apologists for every failure of their socialist system. However, it would be very difficult for the critics to prove their point. The United States would have to drop all sanctions and then we'd have to wait long enough for Cuban society to recover much of what it has lost and demonstrate what its system can do when not under constant attack by the most powerful nation in the world.

The sanctions, expanded under the George W. Bush administration, both in number and in vindictiveness. Washington adopted sharper reprisals against those who do business with Cuba or establish relations with the country based on cultural or tourist exchanges; for example, the US Treasury froze the accounts in the United States of the Netherlands Caribbean Bank because it had an office in Cuba, and banned US firms and individuals from having any dealings with the Dutch bank.

In 2003, the US Treasury Department fined the Alliance of Baptists $34,000, charging that certain of its members and parishioners of other churches had engaged in tourism during a visit to Cuba for religious purposes; that is, they had spent money there. (As George W. once said: 'U.S. law forbids Americans to travel to Cuba for pleasure.'[2])

American courts and government agencies have helped US companies expropriate the famous Cuban cigar brand name Cohiba and the well-known rum Havana Club.

The Bush administration sent a note to American Internet service providers telling them not to deal with six specified countries, including Cuba.[3] This is one of several actions by Washington and American corporations over the years to restrict Internet availability in Cuba; yet Cuba's critics claim that problems with the Internet in Cuba are due to government suppression.

Cubans in the United States are limited to how much money they can send to their families in Cuba, a limit that Washington imposes only on Cubans and on no other nationals. Not even during the worst moments of the Cold War was there a general limit to the amount of money that people in the US could send to relatives living in the Soviet satellites in Eastern Europe.

In 1999, Cuba filed a suit against the United States for $181.1 billion in compensation for economic losses and loss of life during the first forty years of this aggression. The suit held Washington responsible for the death of 3,478 Cubans and the wounding and disabling of 2,099 others. In the years since, these figures have of course all increased. The sanctions, in numerous ways large and small, make acquiring many kinds of products and services from around the world much more difficult and expensive for Cuba, often impossible; frequently, they are things indispensable to Cuban medicine, transportation or industry; or they mean that Americans and Cubans can't attend professional conferences in each other's countries.

What the fate of the Cuban suit has been is a mystery. It was reportedly filed in the United Nations and was at one point in the hands of the UN's Counter-Terrorism Committee, a committee made up of all fifteen members of the Security Council, which of course includes the United States, and which may account for the inaction on the matter.

The preceding is but a small sample of the excruciating pain inflicted by the United States upon the body, soul, and economy of the Cuban people.

Cuba's sin, like Venezuela's, which the United States can not forgive, is to have created a society that can serve as a successful example of an alternative to the capitalist model, and, moreover, to have done so under the very nose of the United States. And despite all the hardships imposed on it by Washington, Cuba has indeed inspired countless peoples and governments all over the world.

(Is it of any significance, I wonder, that the two countries of the Western hemisphere whose governments the United States would most like to overthrow – Venezuela and Cuba – have the greatest national obsession with baseball outside of the United States?)

Long-time American writer about Cuba Karen Lee Wald has observed: 'The United States has more pens, pencils, candy, aspirin, etc. than most Cubans have. They, on the other hand, have better access to health services, education, sports, culture, childcare, services for the elderly, pride and dignity than most of us have within reach.'

In a 1996 address to the General Assembly, Cuban Vice President Carlos Lage stated: 'Each day in the world 200 million children sleep in the streets. Not one of them is Cuban.'

Is Cuba a dictatorship?

Why does the mainstream media routinely refer to Cuba as a dictatorship? Why do some people on the left occasionally do the same? I think that many of the latter do so in the belief that to say otherwise runs the risk of not being taken seriously, largely a vestige of the Cold War when Communists all over the world were ridiculed for following Moscow's party line. But what does Cuba do or lack that makes it a dictatorship? No 'free press'? Apart from the question of how free Western media are, if that's to be the standard, what would happen if Cuba announced that from now on anyone in the country could own any kind of media and print or broadcast whatever they want? How long would it be before CIA money – secret and unlimited CIA money financing all kinds of fronts in Cuba – would own or control most of the media worth owning or controlling?

Is Cuba a dictatorship because it arrests dissidents? Many thousands of anti-war, Occupy, and other protesters have been arrested in the United States in recent years, as in most periods in American history. Large numbers of them have been beaten by police and mistreated in other ways while incarcerated.

And remember: the United States is to the Cuban government what al-Qaeda is to the United States, only much more powerful and much closer. Since the Cuban Revolution, the United States and anti-Castro Cuban exiles in the US have inflicted upon Cuba greater damage and greater loss of life than what happened in New York and Washington on September 11, 2001. Thus, Cuban dissidents – who typically have had very close, indeed intimate, political and financial connections to American government officials, particularly in Havana through the US Interests Section – will fall under great suspicion by the Cuban government. Would the US government ignore a group of Americans receiving funds from al-Qaeda and engaging in repeated meetings with known members of that organization? In recent years the United States has arrested a great many people in the US and abroad solely on the basis of alleged ties to al-Qaeda, with a lot less evidence to go on than Cuba has had with its dissidents' ties to the United States. Virtually all of Cuba's 'political prisoners' are such dissidents. While others may call Cuba's security policies dictatorship, I call it basic self-defense.[4]

Is Washington's work with Cuban dissidents to be seen as a purely harmless undertaking? Not done for a purpose? How can Cuba not feel extremely threatened, even more than the usual threat of the past fifty or so years? How can they fail to take precautionary measures?

Is it 'free elections' that Cuba lacks? The country regularly has elections at municipal, regional, and national levels. Money plays virtually no role in these elections; neither does party politics, including the Communist Party, since candidates run as individuals. Again, what is the standard by which Cuban elections are to be judged? Most Americans, if they gave it any thought, might find it difficult to even imagine what a free and democratic election, without great concentrations of corporate money, would look like, or how it would operate. Would Ralph Nader finally be able to get on all fifty state ballots, take part in national television debates, and be able to match the two monopoly parties in media advertising? If that were the case, I think he'd probably win; and that's why it's not the case. Or perhaps what Cuba lacks is the US's marvelous 'electoral college' system, where the presidential candidate with the most votes is not necessarily the winner. If Americans really think this system is a good example of democracy, why don't they use it for local and state elections as well?

The Cuban elections, which observe universal suffrage and a secret ballot, are for seats in the Municipal Assemblies, the Provincial Assemblies, and the National Assembly. There is direct nomination of candidates by the citizenry, not by the Communist Party, which does not get involved in any stage of the electoral process. All candidates have the same public exposure, which is the publication and posting of a biography listing their qualities and history, in accessible and commonly visited places in the community. There is one deputy in the Municipal Assembly for each 20,000 of population. Candidates must receive over 50 percent of the vote to be elected, if not in the first round then in a runoff. The 609 members of the National Assembly elect the 31 members of the Council of State. The President of the Council of State is the head of state and head of government. Fidel Castro was repeatedly chosen for this position, purportedly because of his sterling qualities.

I don't know enough detail about the actual workings of the Cuban electoral system to point out the flaws and shortcomings of the above, which most likely exist in practice. But can it be more deadening to the intellect, the spirit, and one's idealism than the American electoral system? From the splashy staged nominating conventions to the interminable, boring, and insulting campaigns to the increasingly questionable voting and counting processes, all to select one or the other corporate representative... Are the Cubans ready for this? If they were to institute any kind of electoral system in which those candidates with the most money to spend had an advantage, what would keep the CIA from pouring in money-without-end to get its people into office?

Manure of the taurus
(May 2006)

The US Interests Section in Havana has been flashing electronic messages on its building for the benefit of Cubans passing by. One message said that *Forbes*, the weekly financial magazine, had named Fidel Castro the world's seventh-wealthiest head of state, with a fortune estimated at $900 million. This has shocked Cuban passers by,[5] as well it should in a socialist society that claims to have the fairest income distribution in the world. Are you not also shocked, dear readers?

What's that? You want to know exactly what *Forbes* based its rankings on? Well, as it turns out, two months before the Interests Section flashed its message, *Forbes* had already stated that the estimates were 'more art than science.' 'In the past,' wrote the magazine, 'we have relied on a percentage of Cuba's gross domestic product to estimate Fidel Castro's fortune. This year, we have used more traditional valuation methods, comparing state-owned assets Castro is assumed to control with comparable publicly traded companies.' The magazine gave as examples state-owned companies such as retail and pharmaceuticals businesses and a convention center.[6] So there you have it. It was based on nothing. Inasmuch as the American president 'controls' the US military, shall we assign the value of all the Defense Department assets to his personal wealth? And the British prime minister's personal wealth includes the BBC, does it not?

Another message flashed by the Interests Section is: 'In a free country you don't need permission to leave the country. Is Cuba a free country?' This too is an attempt to blow smoke in people's eyes. It implies that there's some sort of blanket government restriction or prohibition on travel abroad for Cubans, a limitation on their 'freedom.' However, the main barrier to overseas travel for most Cubans is financial; they simply can't afford it. If they have the money and a visa they can normally fly anywhere, but it's very difficult to obtain a visa from the United States unless you're part of the annual immigration quota (about 20,000 or so per year). However, if a Cuban risks his life by trying to cross the 90 miles of water on some kind of vessel and makes it safely to Florida he is then granted automatic residence because he's now a shining example of 'fleeing communist tyranny to gain American freedom.'

Cuba, being a poor country concerned with equality, tries to make sure that citizens complete their military service or their social service. Before emigrating abroad, trained professionals are supposed to give something back to the country for their free education, which includes medical school and all other schools. And Cuba, being unceasingly threatened by a well-known country to the north, must take precautions: certain people in the military and those who have worked in intelligence or have other sensitive information may also need permission to travel; this is something that is found to one extent or another all over the world.

Americans need permission to travel to Cuba. Is the United States a free country? And Washington makes it rather difficult for its citizens to obtain permission to travel to Cuba, particularly for any politically leftist reason. I have applied twice to the US Treasury Department, and been rejected twice.

Americans on the 'No-fly list' can't go anywhere.

All Americans need permission to leave the country. The permission slip – of which one must have a sufficient quantity

– is green and bears the picture of a US president or other famous American.

The Cuban punching bag *ad infinitum*

I could scarcely contain my surprise. A National Public Radio (NPR) newscaster was speaking on August 1, 2006 with an NPR correspondent who had just left a White House press conference and was reporting that the president, in response to a question, had stated that the United States had nothing whatsoever to do with Israeli policies in Lebanon and Gaza. The newscaster, Alex Chadwick, then asked the reporter: 'How do you know what to believe from the White House?'

Was this a sign of the long-awaited breath of skepticism blowing in the mainstream media? No, it wasn't. I've made the story up. What really happened was that the correspondent reported that the Cuban government had announced that Fidel Castro was going to have an operation and that his brother, Raúl Castro, would be replacing him temporarily. Chadwick then asked: 'How do you know what to believe in Cuba?'[7]

This also really happened: Jay Leno on his August 7, 2006 television program: 'There's news of a major medical crisis from Cuba concerning Fidel Castro. It looks like he's getting better.' Think of a US president battling a serious ailment and a broadcaster on Cuban TV making such a remark.

Why is the United States waging perpetual war against the Cuban people's health system?

In January 2011 the government of the United States of America, acting as middle-man disburser, saw fit to seize $4.207 million in funds allocated to Cuba by the United Nations Global Fund to Fight AIDS, Tuberculosis and Malaria for the first quarter of

2011. The UN Fund is a \$22 billion a year program that works to combat the three deadly pandemics in 150 countries.[8]

'This mean-spirited policy,' the Cuban government said, 'aims to undermine the quality of service provided to the Cuban population and to obstruct the provision of medical assistance in over 100 countries by 40,000 Cuban health workers.' Most of the funds are used to import expensive AIDS medication to Cuba, where antiretroviral treatment is provided free of charge to some 5,000 HIV patients.[9] Washington sees the Cuban health system and Havana's sharing of such as a means of Cuba winning friends and allies in the Third World, particularly Latin America; a situation sharply in conflict with long-standing US policy to isolate Cuba. The United States in recent years has attempted to counter the Cuban international success by dispatching the US Naval Ship *Comfort* to the region. With twelve operating rooms and a 1,000-bed hospital, the converted oil tanker has performed hundreds of thousands of free surgeries in Central and South America.

However, the *Comfort*'s port calls likely will not substantially enhance America's influence in the hemisphere. 'It's hard for the U.S. to compete with Cuba and Venezuela in this way,' said Peter Hakim, president of the Inter-American Dialogue, a pro-US policy-research group in Washington. 'It makes us look like we're trying to imitate them. Cuba's doctors aren't docked at port for a couple days, but are in the country for years.'[10]

As mentioned earlier, the 2011 disclosure by WikiLeaks of US State Department documents included this little item. A cable was sent by Michael Parmly from the US Interests Section in Havana in July 2006, during the runup to the Non-Aligned Movement conference. He notes that he is actively looking for 'human interest stories and other news that shatters the myth of Cuban medical prowess.'

Michael Moore refers to another WikiLeaks State Department cable: 'On January 31, 2008, a State Department official stationed in Havana took a made-up story and sent it back to his headquarters in Washington. Here's what they came up with:

> [The official] stated that Cuban authorities have banned Michael Moore's documentary, *Sicko*, as being subversive. Although the film's intent is to discredit the US healthcare system by highlighting the excellence of the Cuban system, the official said the Cuban regime knows the film is a myth and does not want to risk a popular backlash by showing to Cubans facilities that are clearly not available to the vast majority of them.

Moore points out an Associated Press story of June 16, 2007 (seven months prior to the cable) with the headline: 'Cuban health minister says Moore's *Sicko* shows "human values" of communist system.'

Moore adds that the people of Cuba were shown the film on national television on April 25, 2008. 'The Cubans embraced the film so much it became one of those rare American movies that received a theatrical distribution in Cuba. I personally ensured that a 35 mm print got to the Film Institute in Havana. Screenings of *Sicko* were set up in towns all across the country.'[11]

The United States also bans the sale to Cuba of vital medical drugs and devices, such as the inhalant agent Sevoflurane, which has become the pharmaceutical of excellence for applying general anesthesia to children; and the pharmaceutical Dexmetomidine, of particular usefulness to elderly patients, who often must be subjected to extended surgical procedures. Both are produced by the US firm Abbot Laboratories.

Cuban children suffering from lymphoblastic leukemia cannot use Erwinia L-asparaginasa, a medicine commercially known as Elspar, since the US pharmaceuticals company Merck refuses to sell the product to Cuba. Washington has also prohibited the

US-based Pastors for Peace Caravan from donating three Ford ambulances to Cuba.

Cubans are, moreover, upset by the denial of visas requested to attend conferences in the field of anesthesiology and reanimation that take place in the United States. This creates further barriers for Cuba's anesthesiologists to update themselves on state-of-the-art anesthesiology, the care of severely ill patients, and the advances achieved in the treatment of pain.

The foregoing are but a small sample of American warfare against the Cuban medical system presented in a Cuban report to the United Nations General Assembly on October 28, 2009.

Finally, we have the US Cuban Medical Professional Parole (CMPP) immigration program, which encourages Cuban doctors who are serving their government overseas to defect and enter the US immediately as refugees. The *Wall Street Journal* reported in January 2011 that through December 16, 2010, CMPP visas had been issued by US consulates in sixty-five countries to 1,574 Cuban doctors whose education had been paid for by the financially struggling Cuban government.[12] This program, oddly enough, was initiated by the US Department of Homeland Security. Another victory over terrorism? Or socialism? Or are they the same thing?

Wait until the American conservatives hear that Cuba is the only country in Latin America offering abortion on demand, and free.

15

THE COLD WAR
AND ANTI-COMMUNISM

**Flash! The Cold War was not a struggle between the
United States and the Soviet Union** (March 5, 2007)

It was a struggle between the United States and the Third World.
People from all over the Third World were fighting for economic
and political changes against US-supported repressive regimes,
or setting up their own progressive governments. These acts of
self-determination didn't coincide with the needs of the American power elite, and so the United States moved to crush those
governments and movements even though the Soviet Union was
playing virtually no role at all in these scenarios. (It is remarkable
the number of people who make fun of conspiracy theories but
who accepted without question the existence of an international
communist conspiracy.) Washington officials, of course, couldn't
say that they were intervening to block economic or political
change, so they called it 'fighting communism,' fighting a communist conspiracy, fighting for freedom and democracy.

I'm reminded of all this because of a recent article in the
Washington Post about El Salvador. It concerned two men who
had been on opposite sides in the civil war of 1980–92. One was
José Salgado, who had been a government soldier, and is now the
mayor of San Miguel, El Salvador's second-largest city.

Salgado enthusiastically embraced the scorched-earth tactics of his army bosses, the *Post* reports, even massacres of children, the elderly, the sick – entire villages. It was all in the name of beating back communism, Salgado says he remembers being told. But he's now haunted by doubts about what he saw, what he did, and even why he fought. A US-backed war that was defined at the time as a battle against communism is now seen by former government soldiers and former guerrillas as less a conflict about ideology and more a battle over poverty and basic human rights. 'We soldiers were tricked,' says Salgado. 'They told us the threat was communism. But I look back and realize those weren't communists out there that we were fighting – we were just poor country people killing poor country people.' Salgado says he once thought that the guerrillas dreamed of communism, but now that those same men are his colleagues in business and politics he is learning that they wanted what he wanted: prosperity, a chance to move up in the world, freedom from repression. All of which makes what they see around them today even more heartbreaking and frustrating. For all their sacrifices, El Salvador is still among the poorest countries in the Western hemisphere – more than 40 percent of Salvadorans live on less than $2 a day, according to the United Nations. The country is still racked by violence, still scarred by corruption. For some the question remains: was it all worth it? 'We gave our blood, we killed our friends and, in the end, things are still bad,' says Salgado. 'Look at all this poverty, and look how the wealth is concentrated in just a few hands.' The guerrillas Salgado once fought live with the same doubts. Former guerrilla Benito Argueta laments that the future didn't turn out as he'd hoped. Even though some factions of the coalition of guerrilla armies that fought in the civil war were Marxist, he said, ideology had nothing to do with his decision to take up arms and leave the farm where his father earned only a few colones for backbreaking work. Nor did ideology play a role in motivating his friends in the People's Revolutionary Army.

He remembers fighting 'for a piece of land, for the chance that my children might someday get to go to the university.'[1]

The Salvadoran government could never have waged the war as destructively and for as long as it did without a massive influx of military aid and training from Washington, the estimated value of which was $6 billion. In consequence 75,000 Salvadorans died; some twenty American military were killed or wounded in combat; dissidents today still have to fear right-wing death squads; there has been scarcely any significant social change in El Salvador; a small class of the wealthy still own the country; the poor remain poor as ever. But never mind: 'Communism' was defeated and El Salvador remains part of 'the Free World' and a loyal member of the empire, sending troops to Iraq.[2]

This is not merely of historical interest. A civil war still rages in Colombia. Government soldiers and large numbers of right-wing paramilitary forces, with indispensable and endless military support from the United States, battle 'communism,' the FARC guerrillas, year after year, decade after decade. The casualties long ago exceeded those of El Salvador. The irony is monumental, for of those in Colombia labeled 'communist,' a handful of the older ones may have fancied themselves as heirs to Che Guevara ten, twenty or thirty years ago, but for a long time now the primary motivation of these 'left-wing' paramilitary forces has been profits from drugs and kidnappings, obtaining revenge for their comrades' deaths, and staying alive and avoiding capture. Someday the survivors on both sides may well be expressing sentiments and regrets similar to the Salvadorans above, wondering what the hell it was all really about, or at least wondering what the United States' obsessive interest in their country was. (For those who may have forgotten, it should be noted that the Soviet Union has not existed since 1991.)

And someday, as well, survivors on all sides of Washington's 'War on Terror' may wonder who the real terrorists were.

The American myth industry

The Soviet Union signed a pact with the devil, Nazi Germany, in 1939 for no reason other than the commies and the Nazis were just two of a kind who wanted to carve up Poland together.

Without any justification, in 1940 the Soviet Union occupied the three Baltic nations: Lithuania, Latvia, Estonia.

Without any justification the Soviet Union occupied the rest of Eastern Europe after the Second World War.

All this was done, apparently, because the Soviets were an expansionist, brutal empire which liked to subjugate foreign peoples for no particularly good reason – an 'evil empire.' The Soviet Union sabotaged the optimistic plans of the 1945 Yalta Agreement to establish a peaceful, fraternal postwar Europe.

These tales are all set in marble in American media, textbooks, and folklore. However, I'd like to try to correct some of what passes for the official record.

Much Western propaganda mileage has been squeezed out of the Soviet–German treaty of 1939. This is made possible only by entirely ignoring the fact that the Russians were forced into the pact by the repeated refusal of the Western powers, particularly the United States and Great Britain, to sign a mutual defense treaty with Moscow in a stand against Hitler.[3] The Russians had good reasons – their legendary international espionage network being one of them – to believe that Hitler would eventually invade them, which would be just fine with the Western powers, who, at the notorious 1938 Munich conference, were hoping to nudge Adolf eastward. (Thus it was Western 'collusion' with the Nazis, not the oh-so-famous 'appeasement' of them; the latter of course has been invoked over the years on numerous occasions to justify American military action against the dangerous enemy of the month.) The Soviets, consequently, felt obliged to sign the treaty with Hitler to be able to stall for time while they built up their defenses. (Hitler, in the meantime, was focused more on his plans to invade Poland.) Similarly, the Western 'democracies' refused to come to the aid of the socialist-leaning Spanish government under siege by the German, Italian, and Spanish fascists. Hitler derived an important lesson from these happenings. He saw that for the West the real enemy was not fascism; it was communism and socialism. Stalin got the same message.

The Baltic states were part of the Russian empire from 1721 up to the Russian Revolution of 1917, in the midst of World War I. When the war ended in November 1918, and the Germans had been defeated, the victorious Allies (the US, Great Britain, France et al.) permitted/encouraged the German forces to remain in the Baltics for a full year to crush the spread of Bolshevism there; this with ample military assistance from the Allies. In each of the three republics, the Germans installed collaborators in power who declared their independence from the Bolshevik state, which by this time was so devastated by the world war, the revolution, and the civil war (exacerbated and prolonged by Allied intervention) that it had no choice but to accept the fait accompli. The rest of the fledgling Soviet Union had to be saved. To win at least some propaganda points from this unfortunate state of affairs, the Russians announced that they were relinquishing the Baltic republics 'voluntarily' in line with their principles of anti-imperialism and self-determination. But it should not be surprising that the Russians continued to regard the Baltics as a rightful part of their nation or that they waited until they were powerful enough to reclaim the territory.

Within the space of twenty-five years, Western powers invaded Russia three times, during the periods of World War I, 1914–18; the 'intervention' of 1918–20; and World War II, 1939–45, inflicting some 40 million casualties in the two world wars alone. (The Soviet Union lost considerably more people on its own land than it did abroad. There are not too many great powers that can say that.) To carry out these invasions, the West used Eastern Europe as a highway. Should it be any cause for wonder that after World War II the Soviets wanted to close this highway down? In almost any other context, Americans would have no problem in seeing this as an act of self-defense. But in the context of the Cold War such thinking could not find a home in mainstream discourse.

For seventy years the United States used the sins – real and (often) fabricated – of the Soviet Union as a justification for US foreign policy. Thus the horrors carried out by the US in Korea were justified because 'we're fighting communism.' Thus the horrors carried out by the US in Vietnam were justified because 'we're fighting communism.' And similarly the horrors of Cambodia, Laos, Indonesia, Chile, Guatemala, Salvador, Nicaragua, and so on. (Now, of course, 'we're fighting terrorism,' but it's for the same capitalist, imperialist, world-domination reasons.) It's no wonder that many people with a social conscience, who suffered over the horrors of US foreign policy, became anti-anti-communists.[4]

The Yalta Agreement of 1945, in planning for 'the establishment of order in Europe,' affirmed 'the right of all peoples to choose the form of government under which they will live.' We've been told ever since that it was the evil commies who caused this noble agreement to fall apart. But in fact it was the United States and the United Kingdom that cynically violated this affirmation before Stalin did – in Greece, and before the war in Europe even ended! They did so by grossly interfering in the civil war, taking the side of those who had supported the Nazis in the war, thus enabling them to defeat those who had fought against the Nazis. The latter, you see, had among its number some who could be called (choke, gasp) 'communists.'[5]

Anti-communism still holds a death grip on the American psyche. Witness the screams of pain a few years ago – from Bush, Cheney, Rumsfeld, and the media – over Amnesty International's characterization of US torture sites as 'the gulag of our times.' Could anything be more infuriating and humiliating to an inveterate American cold warrior than for the United States to be compared to Stalin's Russia?

The Berlin Wall – another Cold War myth

As the fiftieth anniversary of the erection of the Berlin Wall took place in 2011, all the Cold War clichés about the Free World vs. Communist Tyranny were trotted out and the simple tale of how the wall came to be were repeated: in 1961, the East Berlin communists built a wall to keep their oppressed citizens from escaping to West Berlin and freedom. Why? Because commies don't like people to be free, to learn the 'truth.' What other reason could there have been?

First of all, before the wall went up thousands of East Germans had been commuting to the West for jobs each day and then returning to the East in the evening; many others went back and forth for shopping or other reasons. So they were clearly not being held in the East against their will. Why, then, was the wall built? There were two major reasons.

(1) The West was bedeviling the East with a vigorous campaign of recruiting East German professionals and skilled workers, who had been educated at the expense of the Communist government. This eventually led to a serious labor and production crisis in the East. As one indication of this, the *New York Times* reported in 1963: 'West Berlin suffered economically from the wall by the loss of about 60,000 skilled workmen who had commuted daily from their homes in East Berlin to their places of work in West Berlin.'[6]

In 1999, *USA Today* reported: 'When the Berlin Wall crumbled [1989], East Germans imagined a life of freedom where consumer goods were abundant and hardships would fade. Ten years later, a remarkable 51% say they were happier with communism.'[7] Earlier polls would likely have shown even more than 51 percent expressing such a sentiment, for in the ten years many of those who remembered life in East Germany with some fondness had died; although even ten years later, in 2009, the *Washington Post* could report that 'Westerners say they are fed up with the tendency of their eastern counterparts to wax nostalgic about communist times.'[8]

It was in the post-unification period that a new proverb was born in the east: 'Everything the Communists said about Communism was a lie, but everything they said about capitalism turned out to be the truth.' It should also be noted that the division of Germany into two states in 1949 – setting the stage for forty years of Cold War hostility – was an American decision, not a Soviet one.[9]

(2) During the 1950s, American cold warriors in West Germany instituted a crude campaign of sabotage and subversion against East Germany designed to throw that country's economic and administrative machinery out of gear. The CIA and other US intelligence and military services recruited, equipped, trained, and financed German activist groups and individuals, of West and East, to carry out actions which ran the spectrum from juvenile delinquency to terrorism; anything to make life difficult for the East German people and weaken their support for the government; anything to make the commies look bad.

It was a remarkable undertaking. The United States and its agents used explosives, arson, short-circuiting, and other methods to damage power stations, shipyards, canals, docks, public buildings, gas stations, public transportation, bridges, and so on; they derailed freight trains, seriously injuring workers; burned twelve cars of a freight train and destroyed air pressure hoses of others; used acids to damage vital factory machinery; put sand in the turbine of a factory, bringing it to a standstill; set fire to a tile-producing factory; promoted work slowdowns in factories; killed by poisoning 7,000 cows of a co-operative dairy; added soap to powdered milk destined for East German schools; were in possession, when arrested, of a large quantity of the poison *cantharidin*, with which it was planned to produce poisoned cigarettes to kill leading East Germans; set off stink bombs to disrupt political meetings; attempted to disrupt the World Youth Festival in East Berlin by sending out forged invitations, false promises of free bed and board, false notices of cancellations, and so on; carried out attacks on participants with explosives, firebombs, and tire-puncturing equipment; forged and distributed large quantities of food ration cards to cause confusion, shortages, and resentment; sent out forged tax notices and other government directives and documents to foster disorganization and inefficiency within industry and unions ... all this and much more.[10]

The Woodrow Wilson International Center for Scholars, of Washington, DC, conservative cold warriors, in one of their Cold War International History Project Working Papers (no. 58, p. 9) states: 'The open border in Berlin exposed the GDR [East Germany] to massive espionage and subversion and, as the two documents in the appendices show, its closure gave the Communist state greater security.'

Throughout the 1950s, the East Germans and the Soviet Union repeatedly lodged complaints with the Soviets' erstwhile allies in the West and with the United Nations about specific sabotage and espionage activities and called for the closure of the offices in West Germany they claimed were responsible, and for which they provided names and addresses. Their complaints fell on deaf ears. Inevitably, the East Germans began to tighten up entry into the country from the West, leading eventually to the infamous Wall. However, even after the wall was built there was regular, albeit limited, legal emigration from east to west. In 1984, for example, East Germany allowed 40,000 people to leave. In 1985,

East German newspapers claimed that more than 20,000 former citizens who had settled in the West wanted to return home after becoming disillusioned with the capitalist system. The West German government said that 14,300 East Germans had gone back over the previous ten years.[11]

The American media as the Berlin Wall

In December 1975, while East Timor, which lies at the eastern end of the Indonesian archipelago, was undergoing a process of decolonization from Portugal, a struggle for power took place. A movement of the left, Fretilin, prevailed and then declared East Timor's independence from Portugal. Nine days later, Indonesia invaded East Timor. The invasion was launched the day after US President Gerald Ford and Secretary of State Henry Kissinger had left Indonesia after giving President Suharto permission to use American arms, which, under US law, could not be used for aggression. But Indonesia was Washington's most valuable ally in Southeast Asia and, in any event, the United States was not inclined to look kindly on any government of the left.

Indonesia soon achieved complete control over East Timor, with the help of the American arms and other military aid, as well as diplomatic support at the UN. Amnesty International estimated that by 1989 Indonesian troops had killed 200,000 people out of a population of between 600,000 and 700,000, a death rate which is probably one of the highest in the entire history of wars.[12]

Is it not remarkable that in the numerous articles in the American daily press following President Ford's death on December 26, 2006 there was not a single mention of his role in the East Timor massacre? A search of the extensive Lexis–Nexis and other media databases finds mention of this only in a few letters to the editor from readers; not a word even in the reports of any of the news agencies, like the Associated Press, which generally shy away from controversy less than the newspapers they serve; nor a single mention in the mainstream broadcast news programs.

Imagine if following the death of Augusto Pinochet two weeks earlier the media had made no mention of his overthrow of the Allende government in Chile, or the mass murder and torture that followed. Ironically, articles about Ford also failed to mention his remark a year after Pinochet's coup. President Ford declared that what the United States had done in Chile was 'in the best interest of the people in Chile and certainly in our own best interest.'[13]

During the Cold War, the American government and media never missed an opportunity to point out the news events embarrassing to the Soviet Union which were not reported in the communist media.

Lincoln Gordon: Harvard boy wonder and his crime against humanity

Lincoln Gordon died in December 2009 at the age of 96. He had graduated *summa cum laude* from Harvard at the age of 19, received a doctorate from Oxford as a Rhodes Scholar, published his first book at 22, with dozens more to follow on government, economics, and foreign policy in Europe and Latin America. He joined the Harvard faculty at 23. Dr Gordon was an executive on the War Production Board during World War II, a top administrator of Marshall Plan programs in postwar Europe, ambassador to Brazil and held other high positions at the State Department and the White House, a fellow at the Woodrow Wilson International Center for Scholars, economist at the Brookings Institution, president of Johns Hopkins University. President Lyndon B. Johnson praised Gordon's diplomatic service as 'a rare combination of experience, idealism, and practical judgment.'

You get the picture? Boy wonder, intellectual shining light, distinguished leader of men, outstanding American patriot.

Abraham Lincoln Gordon was also Washington's on-site, and very active, director in Brazil of the military coup in 1964 which overthrew the moderately leftist government of João Goulart and condemned the people of Brazil to more than twenty years of an unspeakably brutal dictatorship. Human-rights campaigners have long maintained that Brazil's military regime originated the idea of the *desaparecidos*, 'the disappeared,' and exported torture methods across Latin America. In 2007, the Brazilian government published a 500-page book, *The Right to Memory and the Truth*, which outlines the systematic torture, rape, and disappearance of nearly 500 left-wing activists, and includes photos of corpses and torture victims.

In a cable to Washington after the coup, Gordon stated – in a remark that might have had difficulty getting past the lips of even John Foster Dulles – that without the coup there could have been a 'total loss to the West of all South American Republics.' (It was actually the beginning of a series of fascistic anti-communist coups that trapped the southern half of South America in a decades-long nightmare, culminating in 'Operation Condor', in which the various dictatorships, aided by the CIA, cooperated in hunting down and killing leftists.)

Gordon later testified at a congressional hearing. While denying completely any connection to the coup in Brazil, he stated that the coup was 'the single most decisive victory of freedom in the mid-twentieth century.'

Consider the transcript of a phone conversation between President Johnson and Thomas Mann, assistant secretary of state for inter-American affairs, of April 3, 1964, two days after the coup:

MANN: I hope you're as happy about Brazil as I am.

LBJ: I am.

MANN: I think that's the most important thing that's happened in the hemisphere in three years.

LBJ: I hope they give us some credit instead of hell.[14]

So the next time you're faced with a boy wonder from Harvard, try to keep your adulation in check no matter what office the man attains, even – oh, just choosing a position at random – the presidency of the United States. Keep your eyes focused not so much on these 'liberal,' 'best and brightest' who come and go, but on US foreign policy, which remains the same decade after decade. There are dozens of Brazils and Lincoln Gordons in America's past, in its present, in its future. They're the diplomatic equivalent of the guys who ran Enron, AIG, and Goldman Sachs.

Of course, not all of our foreign policy officials are like that. Some are worse. The same people who read Dante and went to Yale and were educated in civic virtue recruited Nazis, manipulated the outcome of democratic elections, gave LSD to unwitting subjects, opened the mail of thousands of American citizens, overthrew governments, supported dictatorships, plotted assassinations, and engineered the Bay of Pigs disaster. 'In the name of what?' asked one critic. 'Not civic virtue, but empire.'[15]

Remember the words of convicted spy Alger Hiss: prison was 'a good corrective to three years at Harvard.'

Anti-communism 101: hijacking history

We like to think of death as the time for truth. No matter how much the deceased may have lived a lie, when he goes to meet his presumed maker the real, sordid facts of his life will out. Or at least they should; the obituary being the final chance to set the record straight. But obituaries of those who played an important role in American foreign policy seldom perform this function; the sanitized version surrounding foreign policy and the deceased individual's role therein usually find life in his obituary and thence into State of Texas-approved American history textbooks.

I commented above on the death of Lincoln Gordon and the egregious absence in his obituaries of his crime against humanity in Brazil. Not long afterwards came the death of Phillips Talbot, who was appointed by President Kennedy to be assistant secretary of state for Near Eastern and South Asian affairs, and later became ambassador to Greece. In 1967 the Greek military and intelligence service, both closely tied to the CIA, overthrew another progressive government, that of George Papandreou and his son, cabinet minister Andreas Papandreou. For the next seven years the Greek people suffered utterly grievous suppression and torture. Talbot's obituary states:

> Dr. Talbot was asleep in his bed while tanks rumbled through the streets of Athens and was completely surprised when Armed Forces radio announced at 6:10 a.m. that the military had taken control of the country. Dr. Talbot was adamant that the United States was impartial throughout the transition. 'You may be assured that there has been no American involvement in or, in fact, prior knowledge of the climactic events that those residing in this country have lived through in the past couple of years,' Dr. Talbot told the *New York Times* in 1969 shortly before he returned home.[16]

Andreas Papandreou was arrested at the time of the coup and held in prison for eight months. Shortly after his release, he and his wife Margaret visited Ambassador Talbot in Athens. Papandreou later related the following:

> I asked Talbot whether America could have intervened the night of the coup, to prevent the death of democracy in Greece. He denied that they could have done anything about it. Then Margaret asked a critical question: What if the coup had been a Communist or a Leftist coup? Talbot answered without hesitation. Then, of course, they would have intervened, and they would have crushed the coup.[17]

In November 1999, during a visit to Greece, President Bill Clinton was moved to declare:

> When the junta took over in 1967 here the United States allowed its interests in prosecuting the cold war to prevail over its interest – I should say its obligation – to support democracy, which was, after all, the cause for which we fought the cold war. It is important that we acknowledge that.[18]

Clinton's surprising admission prompted the retired Phillips Talbot to write to the *New York Times*:

> With all due respect to President Clinton, he is wrong to imply that the United States supported the Greek coup in 1967. The coup was the product of Greek political rivalries and was contrary to American interests in every respect. ... Some Greeks have asserted that the United States could have restored a civilian government. In fact, we had neither the right nor the means to overturn the junta, bad as it was.[19]

Or, as Bart Simpson would put it: 'I didn't do it, no one saw me do it, you can't prove anything!'

After reading Talbot's letter in the *New York Times* in 1999 I wrote to him at his New York address reminding him of what Andreas Papandreou had reported on this very subject. I received no reply.

The cases of Brazil and Greece were, of course, just two of many leftist governments overthrown, as well as revolutionary movements suppressed, by the United States during the Cold War on the grounds that America had a moral right and obligation to defeat the evil of Soviet communism that was – we were told – instigating these forces. It was largely a myth. Bolshevism and Western liberalism were united in their opposition to most popular revolution. Russia was a country with a revolutionary past, not a revolutionary present. Even in Cuba, the Soviets were always a little embarrassed by the Castro–Guevara radical fervor. Stalin would have had such men imprisoned.

A cold warrior's nightmare

Jack Kubisch died on May 7, 2007 in North Carolina. You probably have never heard of him. He was a State Department foreign service officer who served in Mexico, France, and Brazil, and as ambassador to Greece. At the time of the September 11, 1973 military coup in Chile which overthrew the democratically elected socialist government of Salvador Allende, he was assistant secretary of state for inter-American affairs.

In the wake of the coup, Kubisch was hard-pressed to counter charges that the United States had been involved. He insisted:

> It was not in our interest to have the military take over in Chile. It would have been better had Allende served his entire term, taking the nation and the Chilean people into complete and total ruin. Only then would the full discrediting of socialism have taken place. Only then would people have gotten the message that socialism doesn't work. What has happened has confused this lesson.[20]

Read that again. It's as concise and as clear a description of the ideological underpinnings of United States foreign policy as you're ever going to find publicly admitted to by a high-ranking American official. Though based on a falsehood made up for the occasion – that Allende's polices were leading Chile to ruin, which was not the case at all – Kubisch's words articulate a basic goal of US foreign policy: to prevent the rise of any society that might serve as a successful example of an alternative to the capitalist model. Many underdeveloped countries were punished terribly during the Cold War by Washington for having such an aspiration; Cuba still is; better that such societies suffer 'complete and total ruin' than achieve such a goal.

Washington knows no heresy in the Third World but genuine independence. In the case of Salvador Allende, independence came clothed in an especially provocative costume – a Marxist constitutionally elected who continued to honor the constitution.

This would not do. It shook the very foundation stones upon which the anti-communist tower was built: the doctrine, painstakingly cultivated for decades, that 'communists' can take power only through force and deception, that they can retain that power only through terrorizing and brainwashing the population. For Washington ideologues there could be only one thing worse than a Marxist in power – an *elected* Marxist in power.

Dr Strangelove
(July 4, 2008)

There have been numerous books published on the 1962 Cuban Missile Crisis. I have not read one of them. There's another one just out: *One Minute to Midnight*, by *Washington Post* writer Michael Dobbs. I will not be reading it. The reason authors keep writing these books and publishers keep publishing them is obvious: how close the world came to a nuclear war between the United States and the Soviet Union! Arthur Schlesinger, Jr, historian and adviser to President Kennedy, termed it 'the most dangerous moment in human history.'[21] But I've never believed that. Such a fear is based on the belief that either or both of the countries was ready and willing to unleash their nuclear weapons against the other. However, this was never in the cards because of MAD – mutually assured destruction. By 1962, the nuclear arsenals of the United States and the Soviet Union had grown so large and sophisticated that neither superpower could entirely destroy the other's retaliatory force by launching a missile first, even with a surprise attack. Retaliation was certain, or certain enough. Starting a nuclear war was committing suicide. If the Japanese had had nuclear bombs, Hiroshima and Nagasaki would not have been destroyed.

Russian leader Nikita Khrushchev was only looking for equality. The United States had missiles and bomber bases already in place in Turkey and other missiles in Western Europe pointed toward the Soviet Union. Khrushchev later wrote:

> The Americans had surrounded our country with military bases and threatened us with nuclear weapons, and now they would learn just what it feels like to have enemy missiles pointing at you; we'd be doing nothing more than giving them a little of their own medicine. ... After all, the United States had no moral or legal quarrel with us. We hadn't given the Cubans anything more than the Americans were giving to their allies. We had the same rights and opportunities as the Americans. Our conduct in the international arena was governed by the same rules and limits as the Americans.[22]

Virtually every president from Truman on has been exhorted by one Dr Strangelove or another, military or civilian, to use the Bomb when things were going badly, such as in Korea or Vietnam or Cuba, or to use it against the Soviets directly, unprovoked, to once and for all get rid of those commie bastards who were causing so much trouble in so many countries. And not one president gave in to this pressure. They would have been MAD to do so. Which is why all the scary talk of recent years about Saddam Hussein and Iran and all their alleged and potential weapons of mass destruction was just that – scary talk. Hussein was not, and the Iranians are not, MAD. The only modern-day leaders I would not make this assumption about are Osama bin Laden and Dick Cheney. The latter is a genuine Dr Strangelove.

The Cold War was a marvelous era for Armageddon humor. Here is US General Thomas Power speaking in December 1960 about things like nuclear war and a first strike by the United States: 'The whole idea is to *kill* the bastards! At the end of the war, if there are two Americans and one Russian, we win!' The response from one of those present was: 'Well, you'd better make sure that they're a man and a woman.'[23]

Saving Japan from pacifism

> Aspiring sincerely to an international peace based on justice and
> order, the Japanese people forever renounce war as a sovereign
> right of the nation and the threat or use of force as means of
> settling international disputes ... In order to accomplish the aim of
> the preceding paragraph, land, sea, and air forces, as well as other
> war potential, will never be maintained. The right of belligerency
> of the state will not be recognized. (Article 9 of the Japanese
> Constitution, 1947, cherished by a majority of the Japanese people)

In the triumphalism of the end of the Second World War, the
American occupation of Japan, in the person of General Douglas
MacArthur, played a major role in the creation of the 1947 constitution. But after the communists came to power in China in
1949, the United States opted for a strong Japan safely ensconced
in the anti-communist camp. It was all downhill after that... step
by step... MacArthur himself ordered the creation of a 'national
police reserve,' which became the embryo of the future Japanese
military... Visiting Tokyo in 1956, US Secretary of State John
Foster Dulles told Japanese officials: 'In the past, Japan had
demonstrated her superiority over the Russians and over China. It
was time for Japan to think again of being and acting like a Great
Power'[24]...Various US–Japanese security and defense cooperation
treaties were signed, which, for example, called on Japan to inte-
grate its military technology with that of the US and NATO... the
US supplying new sophisticated military aircraft and destroyers...
All manner of Japanese logistical assistance was given to the US in
its frequent military operations in Asia... Repeated US pressure
on Japan to increase its military budget and the size of its armed
forces... More than a hundred US military bases were established
in Japan, protected by Japanese armed forces... US–Japanese
joint military exercises and joint research on a missile defense
system... In 2001 the US ambassador to Japan said: 'I think the
reality of circumstances in the world is going to suggest to the

Japanese that they reinterpret or redefine Article 9'[25]... Under pressure from Washington, Japan sent several naval vessels to the Indian Ocean to refuel US and British warships as part of the Afghanistan campaign in 2002, then sent non-combat forces to Iraq to assist the American war... In 2004 US Secretary of State Colin Powell observed: 'If Japan is going to play a full role on the world stage and become a full active participating member of the Security Council, and have the kind of obligations that it would pick up as a member of the Security Council, Article Nine would have to be examined in that light.'[26]

One outcome or symptom of all this can perhaps be seen in the case of Kimiko Nezu, a 54-year-old Japanese teacher, who was punished by being transferred from school to school, by suspensions, salary cuts, and threats of dismissal because of her refusal to stand during the playing of the national anthem, a World War II song chosen in 1999. She opposed the song because it was the same one sung as the Imperial Army set forth from Japan calling for an 'eternal reign' of the emperor. At graduation ceremonies in 2004, 198 teachers refused to stand for the song. After a series of fines and disciplinary actions, Nezu and nine other teachers were the only protesters the following year. Nezu was then allowed to teach only when another teacher was present.[27]

The Germans, too, had to be taught how to kill
(March 2007)

While weaning Japan away from its post-World War II pacifist constitution and foreign policy and setting it back on the righteous path to again being a military power, acting in coordination with US foreign policy needs, the United States of course had the same goal in mind for its other major World War II foe. But recent circumstances indicate that Washington may be losing patience with the rate of Germany's submission to the empire's embrace. Germany declined to send troops to Iraq and sent only non-combat forces to Afghanistan, not quite good enough for the Pentagon war lovers and their NATO allies. Germany's leading news magazine, *Der Spiegel*, reported the following:

> At a meeting in Washington, Bush administration officials, speaking in the context of Afghanistan, berated Karsten Voigt, German government representative for German–American relations: 'You concentrate on rebuilding and peacekeeping, but the unpleasant things you leave to us. ... The Germans have to learn to kill.'

A German officer at NATO headquarters was told by a British officer: 'Every weekend we send home two metal coffins, while you Germans distribute crayons and woollen blankets.' A NATO colleague from Canada remarked that it was about time that 'the Germans left their sleeping quarters and learned how to kill the Taliban.' Bruce George, British MP and head of the House of Commons Defence Committee, observed: 'some drink tea and beer and others risk their lives.' And in Quebec, a Canadian official told a German official: 'We have the dead, you drink beer.'[28]

Yet, in many other contexts since the end of the war the Germans have been unable to disassociate themselves from the image of Nazi murderers and monsters.

Will there come the day when the Taliban and Iraqi insurgents will be mocked by 'the Free World' for living in peace?

Man shall never fly
(January 12, 2007)

The Cold War is still with us. Because the ideological conflict that was the basis for it has not gone away. Because it can't go away. As long as capitalism exists, as long as it puts profit before people, as it must, as long as it puts profit before the environment, as it must, those on the receiving end of its sharp pointed stick must look for a better way.

Thus it is that when Venezuelan President Hugo Chávez announced plans to nationalize telephone and electric utility companies to accelerate his 'socialist revolution,' the spokesperson for Capitalism Central, White House press secretary Tony Snow, was quick to the attack: 'Nationalization has a long and inglorious history of failure around the world,' Snow declared. 'We support the Venezuelan people and think this is an unhappy day for them.'[29]

Snow presumably buys into the belief that capitalism defeated socialism in the Cold War. A victory for a superior idea. The boys of Capital chortle into their martinis about the death of socialism. The word has been banned from polite conversation. And they hope that no one will notice that every socialist experiment of any significance in the past century has been corrupted, subverted, perverted, or destabilized... or crushed, overthrown, bombed, or invaded... or otherwise had life made impossible for it, by the United States. Not one socialist government or movement – from the Russian Revolution to Cuba, the Sandinistas in Nicaragua and the FMLN in Salvador, from Communist China to Grenada, Chile and Vietnam – not one was permitted to rise or fall solely on its own merits; not one was left secure enough to drop its guard against the all-powerful enemy abroad and freely and fully relax control at home. Even many plain old social democracies – such as in Guatemala, Iran, British Guiana, Serbia, and Haiti – which were not in love with capitalism and were looking for another path, even those too were made to bite the dust by Uncle Sam.

It's as if the Wright brothers' first experiments with flying machines all failed because the automobile interests sabotaged each test flight. And the good and God-fearing folk of America looked upon this, took notice of the consequences, nodded their collective heads wisely, and intoned solemnly: Man shall never fly.

Tony Snow would have us believe that the government is no match for the private sector in efficiently getting large and important things done. But is that really true? Let's clear our minds for a moment, push our upbringing to one side, and re-member that the American government has landed men on the moon, created great dams, marvelous national parks, an interstate highway system for a huge land, the peace corps, built up an incredible military machine (ignoring for the moment what it's used for), social security, Medicare, insurance for bank deposits, protection of pension funds against corporate misuse, the Envi-ronmental Protection Agency, the National Institutes of Health, the Smithsonian, the G.I. Bill, and much, much more. In short, the government has been quite good at doing what it wanted to do, or what labor and other movements have made it do, like es-tablishing worker health and safety standards and requiring food manufacturers to list detailed information about ingredients.

When George W. Bush took office one of his chief goals was to examine whether jobs done by federal employees could be performed more efficiently by private contractors. Bush called it his top management priority. By the end of 2005, around 50,000 government jobs had been studied. And federal workers had won the job competitions more than 80 percent of the time.[30]

The American people have to be reminded of what they've instinctively learned but tend to forget when faced with statements like that of Tony Snow: that they don't want *more* government, or *less* government; they don't want *big* government, or *small* government; they simply want government *on their side*.

And by the way, Tony, the great majority of the population in the last years of the Soviet Union had a much better quality of life, including a longer life, under their 'failed nationalized' economy, than they have had under unbridled capitalism.

> When plunder becomes a way of life for a group of men living in society, they create for themselves, in the course of time, a legal system that authorizes it and a moral code that glorifies it.
> (Frédéric Bastiat, *The Law*, 1850)

This is your mind on anti-communism
(April 22, 2006)

Earlier this month, in Miami–Dade county, Florida (where else?) it was reported that the parent of a schoolchild asked the school board to ban a book called *Vamos a Cuba* ('Let's go to Cuba'), a travel book that has smiling kids on the cover and inside depicts happy scenes from a festival held in Cuba. 'As a former political prisoner from Cuba, I find the material to be untruthful,' Juan Amador, wrote to the school board. 'It portrays a life in Cuba that does not exist. I believe it aims to create an illusion and distort reality.' Mr. Amador is presumably claiming that no one in Cuba is ever happy or even smiles.[31]

Italian Premier Silvio Berlusconi declared during his election campaign that communists in Mao's China boiled babies to make fertilizer.[32] He defended his remark by citing *The Black Book of Communism*, a 'history' of communism published in 1997, a book that is to the study of communism what 'The Protocols of the Elders of Zion' is to Judaism, or what the collected statements of George W. Bush are to understanding why we are fighting in Iraq. Berlusconi's remark may actually be regarded as progress in the wonderful world of anti-communism, for following the Russian Revolution of 1917 it was widely and long proclaimed in the Western world that the Bolsheviks killed and ate babies (as the early pagans believed the Christians guilty of devouring their children; the same was believed of Jews in the Middle Ages).

The Victims of Communism Memorial

This is a memorial in Washington, DC installed in 2007 near the US Capitol with an associated Global Museum on Communism on the Internet. Both are monuments to radical one-sidedness. It may be difficult for young people today to believe, but the lies fed to the American people and the world about the Cold War, the Soviet Union, and communism (or 'communism') were even more routine and flagrant than the lies of recent years concerning Iraq, Afghanistan, and terrorism (or 'terrorism'). The most extreme and basic Cold War lie being the existence of something called the 'International Communist Conspiracy,' seeking to take over the world and subvert everything decent and holy.

The ideological hijacking of history is never a pretty sight. Who, it must be asked, will build the Victims of Anti-Communism Memorial and Museum? Who will document and remember the abominable death, destruction, torture, violation of human rights, and killing of hope under the banner of fighting 'communism' that we know under various names: Vietnam, Laos, Chile, Korea, Guatemala, El Salvador, Cambodia, Indonesia, Iran, Brazil, Greece, Argentina, Nicaragua, Haiti, Afghanistan, Iraq, and numerous others.

Why does NATO still exist?

NATO has been taking ambitious steps for years: bombing Yugoslavia in 1999; patrolling the Balkans like a governor general; providing security for the 2004 Olympics in Greece; taking formal charge of the war in Afghanistan; training Iraqi security forces; putting itself into the war on terror; waging a vicious seven-month war against Libya in 2011; seeking to do the same in Syria in 2012 with or without UN Security Council sanction; expanding its membership, which now stands at twenty-six nations plus twenty others brought into the NATO fold under the reassuring name of Partnership for Peace...

Time out. Where does NATO get all this authority? What body of citizens has ever voted for them to do any of this? Why, indeed, does NATO even exist?

We were told during the Cold War that NATO was needed to protect Western Europe from a Soviet invasion. As some may have noticed, the Soviet Union no longer exists. (It has been suggested, plausibly, that NATO was created originally to suppress the left in Italy or France if the Communist Party came to power through an election.)

We have also been told that NATO was there to counter the Warsaw Pact. The Warsaw Pact folded its tent in 1991, calling upon NATO to do the same.

If NATO hadn't begun to intervene outside of Europe it would have highlighted its uselessness and lack of mission. 'Out of area or out of business' it was said.

If NATO had never existed, what argument could be given today in favor of creating such an institution? Other than being a very useful handmaiden of US foreign policy and providing American arms manufacturers with billions of dollars of guaranteed sales to the ever-increasing membership.

The Rosenbergs as heroes

John Gerassi, professor of political science at Queens College in New York City, wrote a letter to the *New York Times*:

To the Editor,

In his 'A Spy Confesses' (Week in Review, September 21, 2008), Sam Roberts claims that folks 'fiercely loyal to the far left believed that the Rosenbergs were not guilty...' I am and have always been, since my stint as a correspondent and editor in Latin America for *Time* and *Newsweek*, a 'far leftist,' and I have never claimed the Rosenbergs were not guilty. Nor have any of my 'far leftist' friends. What we always said, and what I repeat to my students every semester, is that 'if they were guilty, they are this planet's great heroes.' My explanation is quite simple: The US had a first-strike policy, the USSR did not (until Gorbachev). In 1952, the US military, and various intelligence services, calculated that a first strike on all Soviet silos would wipe out all but 6 percent of Russian atomic missiles (and, we now know, create enough radiation to kill us all). But those 6 percent would automatically be fired at US cities. The military then calculated what would happen if one made a direct hit on Denver (why they chose Denver and not New York or Washington was never explained). Their finding: 200,000 would die immediately, two million within a month. They concluded that it was not worth it. In other words, I tell my students, you were born and I am alive because the USSR had a deterrent against our 'preventive' attack, not the other way around. And if it is true that the Rosenbergs helped the Soviets get that deterrent, they end up among the planet's saviors.

John Gerassi

It will not come as a great surprise to learn that the *New York Times* did not allow such thoughts to appear in its exalted pages.

'16

THE 1960S

Carl Oglesby and Students for a Democratic Society

The president of Students for a Democratic Society (SDS), 1965–66, died on September 13, 2011, aged 76. I remember Oglesby best for his speech during the March on Washington, on November 27, 1965, a speech passionately received by the tens of thousands crowding the National Mall:

> The original commitment in Vietnam was made by President Truman, a mainstream liberal. It was seconded by President Eisenhower, a moderate liberal. It was intensified by the late President Kennedy, a flaming liberal. Think of the men who now engineer that war – those who study the maps, give the commands, push the buttons, and tally the dead: Bundy, McNamara, Rusk, Lodge, Goldberg, the President [Johnson] himself. They are not moral monsters. They are all honorable men. They are all liberals.

He insisted that America's founding fathers would have been on his side. 'Our dead revolutionaries would soon wonder why their country was fighting against what appeared to be a revolution.' He challenged those who called him anti-American: 'I say, don't blame me for that! Blame those who mouthed my liberal values and broke my American heart.'

> We are dealing now with a colossus that does not want to be changed. It will not change itself. It will not cooperate with those

who want to change it. Those allies of ours in the government
– are they really our allies? If they are, then they don't need
advice, they need constituencies; they don't need study groups,
they need a movement. And if they are not [our allies], then all the
more reason for building that movement with the most relentless
conviction.

It saddens me to think that virtually nothing has changed for
the better in US foreign policy since Carl Oglesby spoke on the
Mall that day. America's wars are ongoing, perpetual, eternal.
And the current warmonger in the White House is regarded by
many as a liberal, for whatever that's worth.

'We took space back quickly, expensively, with total panic and
close to maximum brutality,' war correspondent Michael Herr
recalled about the US military in Vietnam. 'Our machine was
devastating. And versatile. It could do everything but stop.'

The March on the Pentagon, 1967

October 21, 1967, the March on the Pentagon, surely one of
the most extraordinary and imposing acts of protest and civil
disobedience in history – the government hunkered down in
its trenches in the face of an audacious assault upon its seat of
power by its own citizens; a demonstration much bigger than
the Bonus Marchers of 1932 (those Depression-stricken World
War I veterans demanding payment on their government bonus
certificates *now*, not in some pie-in-the-sky future – the people
peaceably assembled to petition the government for a redress of
grievances, violently and humiliatingly squashed by federal troops
under the command of a general named MacArthur, and his aide
named Eisenhower, and their officer named Patton.)

After a stirring concert at the Reflecting Pool by Phil Ochs, surrounded by 150,000 of his closest friends, most of the protestors
marched over the Memorial Bridge to the war factory. Never to be

forgotten: the roof of the Pentagon when the colossus first came
into view and we marched closer and closer – soldiers standing
guard, spaced across the roof from one side to the other, weapons
at the ready, motionless, looking down upon us from on high with
all the majesty of stone warriors or gods atop a classical Greek
temple. For the first time that day I wondered – not without
excitement – what I was letting myself in for.

This was wholly unlike my first protest at the Pentagon. This
was not a group of Quaker pacifists sworn to non-violence, who
could bring out the least macho side of even professional military men, and who would be received cordially in the Pentagon
cafeteria. Today, we were as welcome and as safe as narcs at a
biker rally. Our numbers included many that the boys at the
Pentagon must have been itching to get their hands on, like those
in the Committee to Aid the National Liberation Front, with their
Vietcong flags, and SDS, and other 'anti-imperialist' groups, who
became involved in some of the earliest confrontations that day.

In sharp contrast to the likes of these were the illuminati like
Norman Mailer, Marcus Raskin, Noam Chomsky, Robert Lowell,
Dwight McDonald – men in dark suits, white shirts and ties as if
to ward off evil spirits with the cross of respectability.

In the vast parking lot to which we were confined, open hostility was kept in check at first, but it was clear that the peace was
only an inch deep. Repeated draft-card burnings took place – a
veritable performance, with flaming cards held high and flaunted
square in the irises of the soldiers, whose faces were masked in
studied indifference. Although this augured conflict of unpredict-
able dimensions, I found it exhilarating to see all those young
people acting in such a principled and fearless way. I was sorry
that I was too old to have a card to burn.

Scattered pockets of mild confrontation broke out, soon un-
folding into more widespread and serious clashes. At one spot a
Vietnam teach-in for the troops was broken up by Military Police

(MP) with clubs. Later, 82nd Airborne Division paratroopers, veterans of Vietnam, entered the scene, bayonets fixed, face to face at last with these people they had been hearing about so much, the privileged little sons of bitches whose incessant crying about international law and morality and God-knows-what-else gave aid and comfort to the enemy, the cowardly little snot-nosed draft-dodgers who wallowed in sex and dope while the GIs wallowed in mud and death (and dope as well).

The paratroopers proceeded to kick ass – after 'Nam this was a church picnic – and many bruised and battered demonstrators were carried away to waiting prison busses, helping to swell the day's total arrestees to near 700. The protestors, whose only defense was to lock arms, appealed to the soldiers to back off, to join them, to just act human, shouting through a bull horn: 'The soldiers are not our enemy, the decision-makers are.' Though this was a sincere declaration, its failure to sway their attackers gave way to angry, impotent curses of 'bastards' and 'motherfuckers.'

I had no big argument with the idea that the soldiers' bosses were the real enemy, but I had real difficulty with the expressions of 'love' for the GIs that some silly hippie types allowed to pass their lips. The soldiers, after all, had made decisions, just as others of their generation had opted for draft evasion or Canada. These soldiers, in particular, were fresh from the killing fields. The idea of 'individual responsibility' is not just a conservative buzzword.

Several eyewitnesses told the *Washington Free Press* that in other areas of the 'battlefield' they saw as many as three soldiers drop their weapons and helmets and join the crowd, and that at least one of them was seized and dragged into the Pentagon by MPs soon afterward. Later attempts to obtain information about these soldiers from the Pentagon were met with denials.

17

IDEOLOGY AND SOCIETY

What a mad raving dinosaur am I!

Leaders of both the Republican and Democratic Parties believe, or pretend to believe, that the American people have resolutely moved to the center, abandoning the 'extremes' of left and right. But is that really so? I maintain that most Americans are clearly liberal, and many even further left. I think that this would be revealed if the public was asked questions along the following lines.

Would you like to have a government-run healthcare system which covered all residents for all ailments at no charge at all?

Would you like to have a government-financed education system where all schooling, including medical school and law school, would be free?

Do you think that when corporations are faced with a choice between optimizing their revenue and doing what's best for the environment, public health, or public safety that they should almost always choose in favor of optimizing their revenue, as they do now?

Do you think that abortion is a question best left up to a woman and her doctor?

Do you think that the United States should officially be a totally secular nation or one officially based on religious beliefs?

Do you think that large corporations and their political action committees exercise too much political power?

Do you think that corporate executive salaries are highly excessive?

Do you think that the tax cuts for the super-rich instituted by the Bush administration should be cancelled and their taxes thus increased?

Do you think that the minimum wage should be increased to what is called a 'living wage,' which would be at least $10 per hour?

Do you think that the government should take all measures necessary to guarantee that corporations have retirement plans for all workers and that the retirement funds are safeguarded?

Do you think that the invasion and occupation of Iraq was a mistake?

Do you think that the invasion and occupation of Afghanistan was a mistake?

Do you think that United States support of Israel is excessive?

Do you approve of the treatment of people captured by the United States as part of its so-called War on Terror – the virtually complete loss of legal and human rights, and subjection to torture?

For those readers who think that I'm presuming too much about Americans' disenchantment with their economic system, I suggest they have a look at my essay 'The United States invades, bombs, and kills for it, but do Americans really believe in free enterprise?'[1]

And for those readers who wonder where all the money would come from to pay for the education, medical care, and so forth, that's the easy part – The Defense Department would have to do what peace groups often have to do: hold bake sales.

To those who like to tell themselves and others that they don't have any particular ideology, I say this: if you have thoughts about why the world is the way it is, why society is the way it is, why people are the way they are, what a better way would look like, and if your thoughts are fairly well organized, then that's your ideology, even if it's not wholly conscious as such.

Humans mourning humans

On April 16, 2007, on the campus of Virginia Polytechnic Institute, a lone student gunman killed thirty-two people. Because of the university's location and the fact that several of the victims came from the Virginia suburbs of Washington, DC, where I live, the *Washington Post* gave book-length coverage to the event. I found myself choking up, at times with tears, repeatedly, each day as I read the stories of the stolen young lives.

Two days after the massacre, the Supreme Court issued a ruling making certain abortions illegal. This led to statements from celebrating anti-abortion activists about how the life of 'unborn children' would be saved, and how the fetus is fully a human being deserving of as much care and respect and legal protection as any other human being. But does anyone know cases of parents grieving over an aborted fetus the way the media showed parents and friends grieving over the slain Virginia Tech students? Of course not. If for no other reason than the fact that parents *choose* to have an abortion.

Does anyone know of a case of the parents of an aborted fetus mourning the fetus for many years after the abortion, perhaps the rest of the parents' lives? Tearfully remembering the fetus's first words, or high school graduation or wedding or the camping trip they all took together? Or the fetus's smile or the way it laughed? Of course not. And why is that? Is it not because the fetus is not a human being in a sufficiently meaningful physical, social, intellectual, and emotional sense? But the anti-abortion activists – often for reasons of sexual prudery, anti-feminism, religion (the Supreme Court ruling derived from the five Catholic members of the court), or other personal or political hang-ups – throw a halo around the fetus, treat the needs and desires of the parents as nothing, and damn all those who differ with them as child murderers. Unfortunately, with many of these activists, their perfect love for human beings doesn't extend to the human beings of Iraq or Afghanistan or the many other victims of their government's foreign policy.

Abortion and war

About half the states in the US require that a woman seeking an abortion be told certain things before she can obtain the medical procedure. In South Dakota, for example, until relatively recently staff were required to tell women: 'The abortion will terminate the life of a whole, separate, unique, living human being'... the pregnant woman has 'an existing relationship with that unborn human being,' a relationship protected by the U.S. Constitution and the laws of South Dakota... and a 'known medical risk' of abortion is an 'increased risk of suicide ideation and suicide' among the women having the procedure. A federal judge has now eliminated the second and third required assertions, calling them 'untruthful and misleading.'[2]

    I personally would question even the first assertion about a fetus or an embryo being a human being, but that's not the point I wish to make here. I'd like to suggest that before a young American man or woman can enlist in the armed forces s/he must be told the following by the staff of the military recruitment office:

> The United States is at war [this statement is always factually correct]. You will likely be sent to a battlefield where you will be expected to do your best to terminate the lives of whole,

separate, unique, living human beings you know nothing about and who have never done you or your country any harm. You may in the process lose an arm or a leg. Or your life. If you come home alive and with all your body parts intact there's a good chance you will be suffering from post-traumatic stress disorder. Do not expect the government to provide you particularly good care for that, or any care at all. In any case, you may wind up physically abusing your spouse and children and/or others, killing various individuals, abusing drugs and/or alcohol, and having an increased risk of suicide ideation and suicide. No matter how bad a condition you may be in, the government may send you back to the battlefield for another tour of duty. They call this 'stop-loss.' And don't ever ask any of your officers what we're fighting for. Even the generals don't know. In fact, the generals *especially* don't know. They would never have reached their high position if they had been able to go beyond the propaganda we're all fed, the same propaganda that has influenced you to come to this office.

Since for so many young people in recent years one of the determining factors in their enlistment has been the economy, this additional thought should be pointed out to them:

You are enlisting to fight, and perhaps kill, and perhaps die, for a country that can't even provide you with affordable education, a decent job, or perhaps any job at all.

These are the words of Carolyn Chute, novelist, of Maine:

I fear for us all, but I especially fear for those already poor. How much lower can they go without being cannon fodder or electric chair fodder or street litter or prison stuffing or just plain lonely suicide?

Why don't church leaders forbid Catholics from joining the military with the same fervor they tell their parishioners to stay away from abortion clinics?

All consciences are equal,
but some consciences are more equal than others
(September 6, 2008)

The Bush administration has proposed stronger job protections for doctors and other healthcare workers who refuse to participate in abortions because of religious or moral objections. Both supporters and critics say that the new regulations are broad enough to allow pharmacists, doctors, nurses and others to refuse to provide birth control pills, Plan B emergency contraception, and other forms of contraception, while explicitly allowing employees to withhold information about such services and refuse to refer patients elsewhere. 'People should not be forced to say or do things they believe are morally wrong,' health and human services secretary Mike Leavitt said. 'Health-care workers should not be forced to provide services that violate their own conscience.'[3]

It's difficult to argue against such a philosophy. It's also difficult to be consistent about it. Do Leavitt and others in the Bush administration extend this concept to those in the military? If a soldier in Iraq or Afghanistan is deeply repulsed by his/her involvement in carrying out the daily horror of the American occupation and asks to be discharged from the military as a conscientious objector, will the Pentagon honor his request because 'people should not be forced to do things they believe are morally wrong'? The fact that the soldier voluntarily enlisted has no bearing on the question. A person's conscience develops from life experiences and continual reflection. Who's to say at what precise point a person's conscience must rebel against committing war crimes for the objection to be considered legally or morally valid? Signing a contract is no reason to be forced to kill people. Moreover, the pharmacist's employees also voluntarily took their positions.

Can a healthcare worker strongly opposed to America's brutal wars refuse to care for a wounded soldier who has been directly involved in the brutality? Can a civilian doctor, pharmacist, or psychologist in the US refuse to treat a soldier on the grounds that if they help to restore his health he'll be sent back to the war front to continue his killing?

Can peace activists be allowed to withhold the portion of their income taxes that supports the military? They've been trying to do this for decades without any government support.

The forbidden 'P' word

> Back now at 8:11 with one of our favorite families, the Duggars. Parents Jim Bob and Michelle became the proud parents of their nineteenth child back in December. This morning we have an exclusive first look at their daughter, Josie Brooklyn. She was born three and a half months premature, but we are happy to report both mom and baby are doing well. (Meredith Vieira, *The Today Show*, NBC, January 28, 2010)

Wow, ain't that just real neat! Their nineteenth child! Wow, and mom and baby are doing so well!

Wow, the Duggars and their children were featured on a television reality show called '19 Kids & Counting.' Wow, just a newborn and already on a reality show! Pass me some more pizza.

Wow, if it was up to me, I would have had mom and/or Jim Bob sterilized after their third child. Wow. Or maybe after their second. Just tie their damn tubes or something!

'D.C. area's population is still blooming: Data shows brisk growth 163,000 gain in 2 years.' This is the *Washington Post* (March 24, 2010) exulting over the fact that the District of Columbia has undergone a sharp increase in population in recent years. Wow, the more the better for the city, right? We all love big crowds and jammed trains and waiting a long time for everything, don't we?

Wow, people, we're suffocating in people, we're drowning in people. So much of importance, so much that we value and take pleasure in, is being choked to death by too many people. But no politician dares touch upon this. Rarely do the mainstream media do so. In fact, rarely do the alternative media do so. Population growth is a driving force behind carbon dioxide emission increases, but it wasn't on the agenda at the international environment conference in Copenhagen last December or at any of the climate talks since then. It appears to be an idea that can not be discussed in polite society.

Imagine if there were 25 million fewer cars on American roads. Imagine the effect on travel time, on air pollution, on accidents, on road rage, on finding a parking space. Imagine what we could build on the huge amount of space now devoted to parking lots.

There is overwhelming evidence that the UN's Millennium Development Goals will not be achieved if population growth is not curbed. These goals include eradicating extreme poverty and hunger, achieving universal primary education, promoting gender equality, combating HIV/AIDS, and ensuring environmental sustainability. A lot of the work of NGOs and other activists all over the world is nullified by population increases.

Many Marxists insist that there's no pressing need to control population if we just change the economic system – eliminate private ownership of the means of production, get rid of the profit motive, curtail all the unnecessary economic 'growth', revise our economic priorities so as to run society on a rational, humane basis. Enough food is already produced in the world, they say, to cover the needs of everyone; it's the distribution of the food that's the problem. There's a lot to what they say, but I think the many serious problems caused by overpopulation – from food and water and transportation to housing, soil erosion, sanitation and much more will continue to plague the world as long as we continue inexorably toward a world of billions more vulnerable beings. All else being equal, imagine the quality of life in the United States with 100 million fewer people. Imagine Chinese society with an additional 400 million people. This is what the Chinese government estimates is what the result would be today if its one-child policy had not been adopted in the 1970s.[4]

So I'm advocating a one- or a two-child per family maximum. This law would not be retroactive.

But I'm not advocating support of US foreign policy, even though it does its share of population control by killing people on a regular basis.

All of you who are activists in any way, I urge you not to be afraid to mention the 'P' word. Be inspired by Britain's Prince Philip, who said: 'If I were reincarnated, I would wish to be returned to Earth as a killer virus to lower human population levels.'[5]

Homosexuality

'Do you think homosexuality is a choice, or is it biological?' was the question posed to presidential candidate Bill Richardson by singer Melissa Etheridge. 'It's a choice,' replied the New Mexico governor at the August 9, 2007 forum for Democratic candidates. Etheridge then said to Richardson, 'Maybe you didn't understand the question,' and she rephrased it. Richardson again said he thought it was a choice.[6]

The next time you hear someone say that homosexuality is a choice, ask them how old they were when they chose to be heterosexual. When they admit that they never made such a conscious choice, the next question to the person should be: 'So only homosexuals choose to be homosexual? Heterosexuals do not choose to be heterosexual? But what comes first, being homosexual so you can make the choice, or making the choice and thus becoming homosexual?'

Marijuana – There's no evidence like no evidence

A 2007 study concluded:

> AIDS patients suffering from debilitating nerve pain got as much
> or more relief by smoking marijuana as they would typically get
> from prescription drugs – and with fewer side effects – according
> to a study conducted under rigorously controlled conditions with
> government-grown pot.[7]

So, yet another study illustrating the absurdity of marijuana use
being illegal. The anti-marijuana forces usually respond to such
studies with one of their fatuous arguments. My favorite one is
that 'marijuana use leads to heroin.' How do they know? Well,
95 percent of all heroin users first used marijuana. That's how
they know. Of course, 100 percent of all heroin users first used
milk. Therefore drinking milk leads to heroin?

How to be (duh) happy

Renowned conservative writer George Will penned a column
celebrating the fact that a survey showed that conservatives
were happier than liberals or moderates. While 34 percent of
all Americans call themselves 'very happy,' only 28 percent of
liberal Democrats do, compared with 47 percent of conservative
Republicans. Will asserted that the explanation for these poll
results lies in the fact that conservatives are more pessimistic and
less angry than liberals. If that seems counterintuitive concerning
pessimism, I could suggest you read his column, except that it
wouldn't be particularly enlightening; the piece is little more
than a vehicle for attacking the welfare state and government
interference in the God-given, wondrous workings of free enterprise. 'Pessimistic conservatives put not their faith in princes
– government – they accept that happiness is a function of fending
for oneself,' writes Will.[8]

I would suggest that one important reason conservative Republicans may be happier is that their social conscience extends no further than themselves and their circle of friends, family, and some groups of other conservative Republicans. George Will gives no hint that the sad state of the world affects, or should affect, conservatives' happiness. In my own case, if my happiness were based solely on the objective conditions of my particular life – work, social relations, health, adventure, material comfort, and so on – I could easily say that I'm very happy. But I'm blessed/cursed with a social conscience that assails my tranquility. Reading the fifty varieties of daily horrors in my morning newspaper – the cruelty of man, the cruelty of nature, the cruelty of chance – I'm frequently frozen in despair and anger.

I wonder how George Will is able to put this all aside and keep on smiling. Does it perhaps have to do with the fact that American foreign policy and American corporations, at home and abroad, directly and indirectly, are responsible for more of the misery than any other human agent? While this makes it even harder for me to take, Mr Will may derive a certain nationalistic pleasure from the way the world works.

Hillary, the closet conservative?

Among the declared candidates for the 2008 presidential elections, who do you think said the following on June 20, 2007?

> The American military has done its job. Look what they accomplished. They got rid of Saddam Hussein. They gave the Iraqis a chance for free and fair elections. They gave the Iraqi government the chance to begin to demonstrate that it understood its responsibilities to make the hard political decisions necessary to give the people of Iraq a better future. So the American military has succeeded. It is the Iraqi government which has failed to make the tough decisions which are important for their own people.[9]

Right, it was the woman who wanted to be president, perhaps still does, because she wants to be president... because she thinks it would be nice to be president... no other reason, no burning cause, no heartfelt desire for basic change in American society or to make a better world... she just thinks it would be nice, even great, to be president of the United States. And keep the American Empire in business, its routine generating of horror and misery being no problem; she wouldn't want to be known as the president who hastened the decline of the empire.

And she spoke the above words at the 'Take Back America' conference; she was speaking to liberals, committed liberal Democrats. She didn't have to cater to them with any flag-waving pro-war rhetoric; they wanted to hear anti-war rhetoric (and she of course gave them a bit of that as well, out of the other side of her mouth), so we can assume that this is how she really feels, if indeed the woman feels anything.

Think of why you were opposed to the Iraq War. Was it not largely because of all the unspeakable suffering brought down upon the heads and souls of the poor people of Iraq by the American military? Hillary Clinton couldn't care less about that. She thinks the American military 'succeeded.' Did she ever label the war 'illegal' or 'immoral'? I used to think that Tony Blair was a member of the right wing or conservative wing of the British Labour Party. I finally realized one day that that was an incorrect description of his ideology. Blair *is* a conservative, a bloody *Tory*. How he wound up in the Labour Party is a matter I haven't studied. Hillary Clinton, however, I've long known is a conservative; going back to at least the 1980s, while the wife of the Arkansas governor, she strongly supported the death-squad torturers known as the Contras, who were the empire's proxy army in Nicaragua.[10]

Roger Morris, in his excellent study of the Clintons, *Partners in Power*, recounts Hillary Clinton aiding Contra fund-raising and her lobbying against people or programs hostile to the Contras or to the Reagan–CIA policies in general. 'As late as 1987–88,' Morris writes, 'amid some of the worst of the Iran–Contra revelations, colleagues heard her still opposing church groups and others devoted to social reform in Nicaragua and El Salvador.'[11]

In 2007 we read in America's venerable conservative magazine, William Buckley's *National Review*, an editorial by Bruce Bartlett, policy adviser to President Ronald Reagan, Treasury official under President George H.W. Bush, a fellow at two of the leading conservative think tanks, the Heritage Foundation and the Cato Institute – you get the picture. Bartlett told his readers that it was almost certain that the Democrats would win the White House in 2008. So what to do? Support the most conservative Democrat. He writes: 'To right-wingers willing to look beneath what probably sounds to them like the same identical views of the Democratic candidates, it is pretty clear that Hillary Clinton is the most conservative.'[12]

We also heard from America's premier magazine for the corporate wealthy, *Fortune*, whose cover at this time featured a picture of Clinton and the headline: 'Business Loves Hillary.'[13]

Yet, despite it all, now as then, Hillary's liberal Democratic Party supporters think of her as one of their own. This kind of ideological dumbness permeates the American media and electoral politics and plays no small part in the voters losing their bearings and their interest.

OUR PRECIOUS ENVIRONMENT

Al Gore: *An Inconvenient Truth*

On March 21, 2007, Al Gore appeared before a House Energy and Commerce Committee hearing on global warming. The star of his documentary film *An Inconvenient Truth* was told by Congressman Joe Barton of Texas: 'You're not just off a little – you're totally wrong.' In the afternoon Gore testified before the Senate Environment and Public Works Committee, during which the former vice president was told by Senator James Inhofe of Oklahoma: 'You've been so extreme in some of your expressions that you're losing some of your own people.'[1]

These members of Congress know the facts of economic life in the United States – fighting global warming is a threat to the principal human generator of it, corporations, who avail themselves of the best Congress members money can buy to keep government regulations as weak as can be.

Does Al Gore know the same facts of American economic life? Of course, but you would have a hard time discerning that from his much-lauded film. It's as cowardly in dealing with the corporations as Gore was in fighting the theft of the 2000 election. In the film's hour and a half, the words 'corporations' or 'profit' are never heard. The closest the film comes to ascribing a link between the rape of the environment and the incessant

corporate drive to optimize profits is a single passing mention
of American automakers' reluctance to increase car gas mileage.
Gore discusses the link between tobacco and lung cancer as an
example of how we have to 'connect the dots' on environmental
issues, with no mention of the tobacco companies or their gross
and deliberate decades-long deception of the American people.
He states at another point that we must choose the environment
over the economy, without any elucidation at all. Otherwise, the
film's message is that it's up to the individual to change his habits,
to campaign for renewable energy, and to write his Congress
member about this or that. In summary, the basic problem, he
tells us, is that we're lacking 'political will.'

It would be most interesting if Al Gore were the president to
see how tough he'd get with the corporations, which every day,
around the clock, are faced with choices: one method of operation
available being the least harmful to the environment, another
method being the least harmful to the bottom line. Of course,
Gore was vice president for eight years and was in a fantastic
and enviable position to pressure the corporations to mend their
ways and Congress to enact tougher regulations, as well as to
educate the public on more than their own bad habits. But what
exactly did he do?

But could Gore be elected without corporate money? And how
much of that money would reach his pocket if he advocated free
government-paid public transportation – rail, bus, ferry, and so
on? That would give birth to a breathtaking – or, rather, breath-
enhancing – reduction in automobile pollution.

The greatest consumer of energy and champion spoiler of the environment is the United States military

Here's Michael Klare, professor of Peace and World Security
Studies at Hampshire College, Massachusetts in 2007:

Sixteen gallons of oil. That's how much the average American soldier in Iraq and Afghanistan consumes on a daily basis – either directly, through the use of Humvees, tanks, trucks, and helicopters, or indirectly, by calling in air strikes. Multiply this figure by 162,000 soldiers in Iraq, 24,000 in Afghanistan, and 30,000 in the surrounding region (including sailors aboard U.S. warships in the Persian Gulf) and you arrive at approximately 3.5 million gallons of oil: the daily petroleum tab for U.S. combat operations in the Middle East war zone. Multiply that daily tab by 365 and you get 1.3 billion gallons: the estimated annual oil expenditure for U.S. combat operations in Southwest Asia. That's greater than the total annual oil usage of Bangladesh, population 150 million – and yet it's a gross underestimate of the Pentagon's wartime consumption.[2]

The United States military, for decades, with its legion of bases and its numerous wars, has also produced and left behind a deadly toxic legacy. From the use of Agent Orange in Vietnam in the 1960s to the open-air burn pits on US bases in Iraq and Afghanistan in the twenty-first century, countless local people have been sickened and killed; and in between those two periods we could read things such as this from a lengthy article on the subject in the *Los Angeles Times* in 1990:

> U.S. military installations have polluted the drinking water of the Pacific island of Guam, poured tons of toxic chemicals into Subic Bay in the Philippines, leaked carcinogens into the water source of a German spa, spewed tons of sulfurous coal smoke into the skies of Central Europe and pumped millions of gallons of raw sewage into the oceans.[3]

The military has caused similar harm to the environment in the United States at a number of its installations.[4]

When I suggest eliminating the military I am usually rebuked for leaving 'a defenseless America open to foreign military invasion'. And I usually reply: 'Tell me who would invade us? Which country?'

'What do you mean which country? It could be *any* country.'

'So then it should be easy to name one.'

'OK, any of the 200 members of the United Nations!'

'No, I'd like you to name a specific country that you think would invade the United States. Name just one.'

'Okay, Paraguay. You happy now?'

'No, you have to tell me *why* Paraguay would invade the United States.'

'How would I know?'

If this charming dialogue continues, I ask the person to tell me how many troops the invading country would have to have to occupy a country of more than 300 million people.

19

THE PROBLEM WITH CAPITALISM

Economics 101 remedial
(July 4, 2008)

The economists who defend the perpetual crises of the capitalist system – the sundry speculative bubbles followed by bursting bubbles followed by a trail of tears – most often turn to 'supply and demand' as the ultimate explanation and justification for the system. This provides an impersonal, neutral-sounding, and respectable, almost scientific, cover for the vagaries of free enterprise. They would have us believe that we shouldn't blame the crises on greed or speculation or manipulation or criminal activity because such flawed human behavior is overridden by 'supply and demand.' It's a law, remember; 'the law of supply and demand' is its full name. You wouldn't want them to break the law, would you?

And where does this 'law' come from? Congress? Our ancestral British Parliament? No, nothing so commonplace, so man-made. No, they would have us believe that it must come from nature. It works virtually like an immutable natural law, does it not? And we violate it or ignore it at our peril.

Thus have we all been raised. But great cracks in the levee have been appearing in recent years, in unlikely places, such as the Senate of the United States, which issued a lengthy report in 2006 (when a gallon of gasoline had already passed the $3 mark) entitled: 'The role of market speculation in rising oil and gas prices.' Here are some excerpts:

> The traditional forces of supply and demand cannot fully account for these increases [in crude oil, gasoline, etc.]. While global demand for oil has been increasing ... global oil supplies have increased by an even greater amount. As a result, global inventories have increased as well. Today, U.S. oil inventories are at an 8-year high, and OECD [mainly European] oil inventories are at a 20-year high. Accordingly, factors other than basic supply and demand must be examined. ...
>
> Over the past few years, large financial institutions, hedge funds, pension funds, and other investment funds have been pouring billions of dollars into the energy commodities markets ... to try to take advantage of price changes or to hedge against them. Because much of this additional investment has come from financial institutions and investment funds that do not use the commodity as part of their business, it is defined as 'speculation' by the Commodity Futures Trading Commission (CFTC). According to the CFTC, a speculator 'does not produce or use the commodity, but risks his or her own capital trading futures in that commodity in hopes of making a profit on price changes.' The large purchases of crude oil futures contracts by speculators have, in effect, created an additional demand for oil, driving up the price of oil to be delivered in the future in the same manner that additional demand for the immediate delivery of a physical barrel of oil drives up the price on the spot market. ... Although it is difficult to quantify the effect of speculation on prices, there is substantial evidence that the large amount of speculation in the current market has significantly increased prices.[1]

The prices arrived at daily on the commodity exchanges (primarily the New York Mercantile Exchange, NYMEX), for the various kinds of oil are used as principal international pricing benchmarks, and play an important role in setting the price of gasoline at the pump.

A good part of the Senate report deals with how the CFTC is no longer able to properly regulate commodity trading to prevent speculation, manipulation, or fraud because much of the trading takes place on commodity exchanges, in the US and abroad, that are not within the CFTC's purview.

> Persons within the United States seeking to trade key U.S. energy commodities – U.S. crude oil, gasoline, and heating oil futures – now can avoid all U.S. market oversight or reporting requirements by routing their trades through the ICE Futures exchange in London instead of the NYMEX in New York. ... To the extent that energy prices are the result of market manipulation or excessive speculation, only a cop on the beat with both oversight and enforcement authority will be effective. ... The trading of energy commodities by large firms on OTC [over-the-counter] electronic exchanges was exempted from CFTC oversight by a provision inserted at the behest of Enron and other large energy traders into the Commodity Futures Modernization Act of 2000.

A tale told many times. While you and I go about our daily lives trying to be good citizens, the Big Boys, the Enron Boys, are busy lobbying the Congress Boys. They call it 'modernization,' or some other eye-rolling euphemism, and we get screwed.

The *Washington Post* recently had this to report on the Enron and Congress Boys:

> Wall Street banks and other large financial institutions have begun putting intense pressure on Congress to hold off on legislation that would curtail their highly profitable trading in oil contracts – an activity increasingly blamed by lawmakers for driving up prices to record levels. ... But the executives were met with skepticism and occasional hostility. 'Spare us your lecture about supply and demand,' one of the Democratic aides said, abruptly cutting off one of the executives. ... A growing number of members of Congress have reacted to public outrage over skyrocketing gasoline prices by introducing at least eight bills that restrict the ability of financial companies to buy futures contracts, [require companies to]

disclose more about those investments or stiffen federal oversight of energy trades.[2]

Some further testimony from the 2006 Senate report:

> There has been no shortage, and inventories of crude oil and products have continued to rise. The increase in prices has not been driven by supply and demand. (Lord Browne, group chief executive of BP, formerly British Petroleum)

> Senator ... I think I have been very clear in saying that I don't think that the fundamentals of supply and demand – at least as we have traditionally looked at it – have supported the price structure that's there. (Lee Raymond, chairman and CEO, ExxonMobil)

> What's been happening since 2004 is very high prices without record-low stocks. The relationship between U.S. [oil] inventory levels and prices has been shredded, has become irrelevant. (Jan Stuart, global oil economist, UBS Securities, which calls itself 'the leading global wealth manager')

In 2008, when a gallon of gasoline had passed the $4 mark, OPEC secretary general Abdalla Salem el-Badri stated: 'There is clearly no shortage of oil in the market.' El-Badri 'blamed high oil prices on investors seeking "better returns" in commodities after a drop in equity prices and the value of the dollar.'[3]

Finally, defenders of the way the system works insist that the oil companies have been experiencing great increases in their costs, due particularly to oil running out, so-called 'peak oil.' It costs much more to find and extricate the remaining oil and the companies have to pass these costs to the consumer. Well, class, if that is so, then the companies should be making about the same net profit as before peak oil – $x more in expenses, $x added to the price, the same amount of profit, albeit a lower percentage of profit to sales, something of interest primarily to Wall Street, not to ordinary human beings. But the oil companies have not done that. Their increases in price and profit defy gravity and are not on the same planet as any increases in costs. Moreover, as economist Robert Weissman of the Multinational Monitor has observed, 'While the price of oil is going up, these companies' drilling expenses are not. Oil can trade at $40 a barrel, $90 a barrel, or $130 a barrel. It still costs ExxonMobil and the rest of Big Oil only about $20 to get a barrel of oil out of the ground.'[4]

The above is not meant to be the last word on the subject of why our gasoline is so expensive. Too much information is hidden, by speculators, oil companies, refiners, and others; too much activity is unregulated; too much is moved by psychology more than economics. The best solution would be to get rid of all the speculative markets – unless they can demonstrate that they serve a useful human purpose – and nationalize the oil companies. (Oh my God, he used the 'N' word!)

A hundred ways to get rich
without doing anything socially useful
(October 1, 2008)

Why do we have this thing called a 'financial crisis'? Why have we had such a crisis periodically ever since the United States was created? What changes occur or what happens each time to bring on the crisis? Do we forget how to make things that people need? Do the factories burn down? Are our tools lost? Do the blueprints disappear? Do we run out of people to work in the factories and offices? Are all the products and services that people need for a happy life so well taken care of that there's hardly any more need for the products and services? In other words: what changes take place in the *real world* to cause the crisis? Nothing, necessarily. The crisis is usually caused by changes in the *make-believe* world of financial capitalism.

All these grown men playing their boys' games. They create an assortment of financial entities, documents, and packages that go by names like hedge funds, derivatives, collateralized debt obligations, index funds, credit default swaps, structured investment vehicles, subprime mortgages, and dozens of other exotic monetary creations. They devise all manner of commercial pieces of paper, of no known real or inherent value, backed up by few if any standards, for which, it must be kept in mind, there had been no public need or strident demand. Then they sell these various pieces of paper to the public and to each other. They slice and dice mortgages into arcane and risky instruments, then bundle them together, and sell the packages to those higher up in the pyramid scheme. And some of those engaged in this Wild West buying and selling become millionaires. Some become billionaires. They get Christmas bonuses greater than what most Americans earn the entire year. Is all this not remarkable?

And much of the buying is not done with the buyer's own money, but with borrowed funds; 'leveraged,' they call it. The pieces of paper sometimes represent commodities, but the actual commodities are not seen, may not even exist; if the seller demanded the buyer's own funds, or the buyer wanted to see the goods, the whole transaction would freeze. They sell 'long,' expecting the price to rise; they sell 'short,' expecting the price to fall; they sell 'naked short,' which means they neither possess nor own what they're selling; a name for each gimmick. They take ever-greater risks buying and selling increasingly esoteric pieces of paper. It's a glorified Las Vegas. Casino capitalism.

These pieces of paper can be so complex and opaque that many of those buying and selling them do not fully understand them; no problem, they just resell the pieces of paper to someone else at a higher price, even when one or both parties know that the paper, while pretending to represent payable debt, is virtually worthless. The government, even when it tries to moderately regulate this Monopoly board, can at times also be confused by the complexities of the pieces of paper, compounded by the less-than-transparent practices that envelop the transactions – a potpourri including speculation, manipulation, fraud. Billionaire financier Warren Buffett has called the pieces of paper 'weapons of mass financial destruction.'

The boys of finance have been playing their games for years, and so at each stage of the process there are insurance policies allowing the players to hedge their bets; they insure, and they re-insure; hopefully covering themselves against the many risks of the game, often knowing that they're trading in questionable debts; the giant corporation AIG, a major player in the insurance game, was taken over by the federal government. And with each transaction, at each level, someone earns a commission or a fee. There are also other firms whose purpose in life is to go around rating various players and their pieces of paper and their creditworthiness and giving seals of approval which are relied upon by investors. The supposedly objective credit-rating agencies told everyone that various firms and their bundles of paper were good investments, but the credit-rating agencies in fact had played a role themselves in putting some of the bundles together. President Roosevelt, confronted in the 1930s with similar players, called them 'banksters.'

It's all built on faith, as fragile as the religious kind, the belief that something is worth something because it comes with a piece of paper with reassuring words and numbers written on it, because it's traded, rated, and insured, because someone will sell it and someone will buy it. The same market psychology, the same herd mentality, that went into constructing this house of cards built on pillars of greed can cause the house to collapse in a heap. But the Monopoly players keep their bonuses, and bow out with multimillion-dollar golden parachutes; while tent cities are springing up all over America.

And the government is in the process of trying to bail out these reckless traders, these parasites, rescuing them and their system from their own nonsense. With our money; without a major restructuring of the Alice in Wonderland rules of the financial games, without instituting the toughest of regulations, oversight, and transparency, and with no guarantee that the spoiled-little-brat Masters of the Universe will act in any way other than in their own narrow self-interest, the rest of us be damned.

Capitalism is the theory that the worst people, acting from their worst motives, will somehow produce the most good.

There is perhaps some consolation. The libertarian and neo-conservative true believers will have a harder time selling their snake oil of privatization of Social Security or any other social program. Government regulation of matters vital to the public's welfare may be taken more seriously. We may hear less of that old bromide that markets are inherently self-correcting. It may even give a boost to the idea of national health insurance.

And the libertarians and neoconservatives are hurting and defensive, albeit not yet admitting to any new-found wisdom. A *Washington Post* interview with some true believers at the Cato Institute, where Ayn Rand's picture prominently hangs, produced these statements: 'Too much regulation got us where we are'... 'The biggest emotion we're feeling right now is frustration that the media narrative is that this is a crisis of the free market, a crisis of capitalism, a crisis of under-regulation. In fact it's a crisis of subsidization and intervention'... 'Capitalism without losses is like religion without hell.'[5]

And just think: Cuba has been tormented without mercy for fifty years because it refuses to live under such a financial system.

Some of the other charms of our capitalist system

The Dow Jones industrial average of blue-chip stocks in New York fell 635 points on Monday August 8, 2011.

On Tuesday it rose by 430 points.

On Wednesday, the market, in its infinite wisdom, decided to fall again, this time by 520 points.

And on Thursday... yes, it rose once again, by 423 points.

The Dow changed directions for eight consecutive trading sessions. The *Washington Post*'s senior economic columnist, Steven Pearlstein, wrote on August 14, 2011 of the four days described above: 'I suppose there are some schnooks who actually believe that those wild swings in stock prices last week represented sober and serious concerns by thoughtful, sophisticated investors about the Treasury debt downgrade or European sovereign debt or a slowdown in global growth. But surely such perceptions don't radically change each afternoon between 2 and 4:30, when the market averages last week were gyrating out of control.'

We go from the dotcom bubble to the stock market bubble to the Enron bubble to the housing bubble to the credit bubble... and with each burst of a bubble many lose jobs, homes, dreams.

'It is difficult to produce a television documentary that is both incisive and probing when every twelve minutes one is interrupted by twelve dancing rabbits singing about toilet paper' (Rod Serling, famed television writer).

Can it be imagined that an American president would openly implore America's young people to fight a foreign war to defend 'capitalism'? The word itself has largely gone out of fashion. The approved references now are to the market economy, free market, free enterprise, or private enterprise. This change in terminology endeavors to obscure the role of wealth in the economic and social system. And avoiding the word 'capitalism' sheds the adverse connotation going back to Karl Marx.

At some unrecorded moment a few years ago, the egg companies of America changed their package labels from small, medium, and large to medium, large, and jumbo. The eggs remained exactly the same size.

'The Federal Trade Commission concluded that there is very little connection between what drug companies charge for a drug and the costs directly associated with it.'[6]

'The makers of aspirin wish you had a headache right now,' says the graffiti.

Slavery is the legal fiction that a person is property, and corporate personhood is the legal fiction that property is a person. 'The private-benefit corporation is an institution granted a legally protected right – some would claim obligation – to pursue a narrow private interest without regard to broader social and environmental consequences. If it were a real person, it would fit the clinical profile of a sociopath,' notes David Korten.

Ralph Nader once charged the Justice Department anti-trust division with going out of business without telling anyone.

Capitalism as practiced in the United States is like chemotherapy: it may kill the cancer cells of consumer shortages, but the side effects are devastating.

Many workers are paid a wage sufficient to allow them to keep on living, even if it's not a living wage. Here's a radical solution to poverty: pay people enough to live on.

'The paradox is that, three centuries after America's colonial beginnings, wealth and income are more unequally distributed in the "New World" than in most of the nations of Europe.'[7] How could the current distribution of property and wealth have emerged from any sort of democratic process?

How many Americans realize that they have a much longer work week, much shorter vacations, much shorter unemployment coverage, much worse maternity leave and other employee benefits, and much worse medical coverage than their West European counterparts?

In expressing elementary truths about the oppression of the poor by the rich in the United States, one runs the risk of being accused of 'advocating class warfare'; because the trick of class war is to not let the victims know the war is being waged.

What do the CEOs do all day that they should earn a thousand times more than schoolteachers, nurses, firefighters, street cleaners, and social workers? Reread some medieval history, about feudal lords and serfs.

The campaigns of the anti-regulationists imply that pure food and drugs will be ours as soon as we abolish the pure food and drug laws.

What takes place in the world of economics is 60 percent power–politics–ideology–speculation, 30 percent psychological, 10 percent immutable laws. (These percentages are immutable.)

The more you care about others, the more you're at a disadvantage competing in the capitalist system.

To say that 1 percent of the population owns 35 percent of the resources and wealth, is deceptive. If you own 35 percent you can control much more than that.

The myth and mystique of 'choice' persuades us to endorse the privatization of almost every sphere of activity.

A study of 17,595 federal government jobs by the Office of Management and Budget in 2004 concluded that civil servants could do their work better and more cheaply than private contractors nearly 90 percent of the time in job competitions.[8]

Communist governments take over companies. Under capitalism, the companies take over the government.

The American oligarchy has less in common with the American people than it does with the oligarchies in Japan and France.

If you lose money gambling, you can't take a tax deduction. But you can if you lose on the glorified slot machine known as the stock market; your loss is thus subsidized by taxpayers.

Do the members of a family relate to each other on the basis of self-interest and greed?

'The idea that egotism is the basis of the general welfare is the principle on which competitive society has been built' (Erich Fromm, German-American social psychologist).

'The twentieth century has been characterized by three developments of great political importance: the growth of democracy; the growth of corporate power; and the growth of corporate propaganda as a means of protecting corporate power against democracy' (Alex Carey, Australian social scientist).

August, 2011: 'Pope Benedict XVI denounced the profit-at-all-cost mentality that he says is behind Europe's economic crisis' as he arrived in hard-hit Spain. 'The economy doesn't function with market self-regulation,' he said, 'but needs an ethical reason to work for mankind. ... Man must be at the center of the economy, and the economy cannot be measured only by maximization of profit but rather according to the common good.'[9]

May, 2010: 'I am a Marxist,' said the Dalai Lama. Marxism has 'moral ethics, whereas capitalism is only how to make profits.'[10]

'The country needs to be born again, she is polluted with the lust of power, the lust of gain' (Margaret Fuller, literary critic, *New York Tribune*, July 4, 1845).

None of the above, of course, will deter the world's only super-power from continuing its jihad to impose capitalist fundamental-ism upon the world.

In the land where happiness is guaranteed in the Declaration of Independence

'Think raising the minimum wage is a good idea?' 'Think again.' That was the message of a full-page advertisement that appeared in major newspapers in January 2007. It was accompanied by statements of approval from the usual eminent suspects: 'The reason I object to the minimum wage is I think it destroys jobs, and I think the evidence on that, in my judgment, is overwhelm-ing' (Alan Greenspan, former Federal Reserve chairman); 'The high rate of unemployment among teenagers, and especially black teenagers, is both a scandal and a serious source of social unrest. Yet it is largely a result of minimum wage laws' (Milton Friedman, Nobel prizewinning economist).

Well, if raising the minimum wage can produce such negative consequences, then surely it is clear what we as an enlightened and humane people must do. We must *lower* the minimum wage. And thus enjoy less unemployment, less social unrest. Indeed, if we lower the minimum wage to zero, particularly for poor blacks... think of it! No unemployment at all! Hardly any social unrest! In fact – dare I say it? – what if we did away with wages altogether?

> The modern conservative is engaged in one of man's oldest exer-cises in moral philosophy: that is, the search for a superior moral justification for selfishness. (John Kenneth Galbraith)

Eat the rich, share your recipes

With Bill Gates's announcement that he'll be phasing out his day-to-day participation in Microsoft, the media have carried a lot of adulatory stories about the *wunderkind*, who became the world's youngest self-made billionaire at age 31. I do not mean to detract from Gates's accomplishments when I point out that for him to have become a billionaire just six years after introducing the MS-DOS 1.0 operating system, Microsoft had to be charging a lot more – an awful lot more – for its software than it had to based on the company's costs.

There are those, enamored by the philosophy, practice, and folklore of free enterprise and rugged individualism, who will declare: 'More power to the guy! He deserves every penny of it!' There are others, enamored by the vision of a more equitable society, who question how the current distribution of property and wealth can reasonably be said to derive from any sort of democratic process. This is the twenty-first century; American society should not be suffocating on 2 percent with breathtaking wealth and 75 percent with a daily struggle for a decent life. In fact, along such lines we're regressing.

This is almost heresy to many Americans, who are unwilling to tamper with political and economic arrangements, though they have no qualms about meddling with other people's sex lives, women's bodies, and other moral issues. Greed and selfishness are natural, they insist, and have to be catered to.

But if the system should cater to selfishness because it's natural, why not cater to aggression, which many of the same people claim is also natural?

Some questions to ask our quaint little Tea Party friends

The Tea Party folks never tire of calling for 'smaller government.' How sweet. Most other Republicans repeat the same mantra ad nauseam as well, as do many liberals (not to be confused with progressives). So, for all these individuals I have some questions:

- When there's a plane crash the government sends investigators to the crash site to try to determine the cause of the accident;

this is information that can be used to make air travel safer. But it's really *big government*, forcing the airlines to fully cooperate, provide all relevant information – secrecy is not permitted – and make changes or face severe penalties. Do you think the government should stop doing this?

- Following the 2010 BP oil spill in the Gulf of Mexico, was the government right to bully and threaten the company for an explanation and solution for the catastrophe, or should it have been 'hands off' for the sake of small government?

- Following a major earthquake there's usually a cry from many quarters: stores should not be raising prices for basic necessities like water, generators, batteries, tree-removal services, diapers, and so on. More grievances soon arise because landlords raise rents on vacant apartments after many dwellings in the city have been rendered uninhabitable. 'How dare they do that?' people wail. Following the 1994 earthquake in Los Angeles the California Assembly proceeded to make it a crime for merchants to increase prices for vital goods and services by more than 10 percent after a natural disaster.[11] Following the destruction caused by Hurricane Isabel in September 2003, the governor and attorney general of Virginia called on the legislature to pass the state's first anti-price-gouging law after receiving around a hundred complaints from residents. North Carolina had enacted an anti-gouging law just shortly before.[12] Does such blatant big-government interference in our God-given supply-and-demand system bother you? Do you think that our legislators should simply allow 'the magic of the marketplace' to do its magic?

- Do you think that the government should continue waging war against what they call 'terrorists' abroad, since there's no bigger or more expensive big-government action than this?

- Do you think the government should continue with its highly intrusive electronic strip searches and body feel-ups at airports or should we allow the risk of bombs being brought on board airplanes?

- If your bank fails – and hundreds have done so in recent years in the United States – are you willing to accept the loss of your life's savings? Or are you thankful that big, big government steps in, takes over the bank, and protects every penny of your savings?

- Do you think that big government – federal, state, or local – should stop haranguing the citizenry about the environment: recycling, air pollution, water pollution, soil runoff, and so on, or that people should simply be allowed to do what is most convenient for them, their families, and their businesses?

- Do you think that American manufacturers should have the right to run their factories like the sweatshops in a Bangkok alley fifty years ago or that big government should throw its weight around to assure modern working conditions, with worker health-and-safety standards?

- When a prescription drug starts to kill or harm more and more people, who should decide when to pull it off the market: big government or the drug's manufacturer?

- Are you glad that food packages list the details of ingredients and nutrition? Who do you think is responsible for this?

- A huge number of Americans would be facing serious hunger if not for their food stamps; more than 45 million receive them. Where do you think food stamps come from?

- And where do you think unemployment insurance, housing subsidies, and Medicare come from? (There were of course, Lord help us, the Tea Party signs: 'Keep your government hands off my Medicare,'[13] while simultaneously ridiculing Obama's push for 'socialized medicine.')

- Would some of you rather see widespread hunger, poverty, homelessness, and illness in America than have people dependent upon the Big Government Monster?

The climax of civilization, American style

Main Street is the climax of civilization.
That this Ford car might stand in front of
the Bon Ton store, Hannibal invaded Rome
and Erasmus wrote in Oxford cloisters.

(Sinclair Lewis, 'Main Street,' 1920)

Piles of advertising circulars clutter the lobby of my apartment building; they're hardly touched, remaining there until the cleaning person decides to toss them in the trash. For this, trees are cut down; dioxin, a by-product of paper-making, exceedingly toxic, is directly expelled into the water from paper mills; incalculable amounts of energy and other resources are used to print all the pages. Imagine all the people and vehicles needed to deliver the circulars. Multiply my building by millions.

'If it takes a $200 billion advertising industry to maintain what economists quaintly call "demand", then perhaps that demand isn't as urgent as conventional theory posits. Perhaps it's not even demand in any sane meaning of the word.'[14]

Advertising is the climax of civilization.
That this circular for Walmart might sit in
the lobbies of apartment buildings, this
television program interrupted to bring you proof that
Coke is superior to Pepsi, and this billboard ruining
the view, George W. Bush invaded Iraq and Paul Wolfowitz
studied at the University of Chicago.

You can't make this stuff up

One of the most quoted aphorisms of the Western world: 'The law, in its majestic equality, forbids the rich as well as the poor to sleep under bridges, to beg in the streets, and to steal bread' (Anatole France, 1844–1924).

On April 14, 2006 a federal appeals court ruled that the Los Angeles Police Department cannot arrest people for sitting, lying, or sleeping on public sidewalks on Skid Row, saying such enforcement amounts to cruel and unusual punishment because there are not enough shelter beds for the city's huge homeless population. Judge Pamela A. Rymer issued a strong dissent against the majority opinion. The Los Angeles code 'does not punish people simply because they are homeless,' wrote Rymer. 'It targets conduct – sitting, lying or sleeping on city sidewalks – that can be committed by those with homes as well as those without.'[15]

'There is no alternative!'
'Really? There had better be or we're all doomed!'
Some thoughts about socialism

'History is littered with post-crisis regulations. If there are undue restrictions on the operations of businesses, they may view it to be their job to get around them, and you sow the seeds of the next crisis.' So said Liz Ann Sonders, chief investment analyst, Charles Schwab & Co., a leading US provider of investment services.[16]

And so it goes. Corporations, whether financial or not, strive to maximize profit as inevitably as water seeks its own level. We've been trying to 'regulate' them since the nineteenth century. Or is it the eighteenth? Nothing helps for long. You close one loophole and the slime oozes out of another hole. Wall Street has not only an army of lawyers and accountants, but a horde of mathematicians with advanced degrees searching for the perfect equations to separate people from their money. After all the stimulus money has come and gone, after all the speeches by our leaders condemning greed and swearing to reform, after the last congressional hearing deploring corporate executives to their faces, the boys of Wall Street, shrugging off a few bruises, will resume churning out their assortment of exotic financial instruments. Speculation, bonuses, and Scotch will flow again, and the boys will be all the wiser, perhaps shaken a bit that they're so reviled, but knowing better now what to flaunt and what to disguise.

This is another reminder that communism or socialism have almost always been given just one chance to work, if that much, while capitalism has been given numerous chances to do so following its perennial fiascos. Ralph Nader has observed: 'Capitalism will never fail because socialism will always be there to bail it out.'

In the West, one of the most unfortunate results of the Cold War was that seventy years of anti-communist education and media stamped in people's minds a lasting association between socialism and what the Soviet Union called communism. Socialism meant a dictatorship, it meant Stalinist repression, a suffocating 'command economy,' no freedom of enterprise, no freedom to change jobs, few avenues for personal expression, and other similar truths, half-truths, and untruths. This is a set of beliefs clung to even among many Americans opposed to US foreign policy. No matter how bad the economy is, Americans think, the only alternative available is something called 'communism,' and they know how awful that is.

Adding to the purposeful confusion, the conservatives in Britain, for thirty years following the end of World War II, filled the minds of the public with the idea that the Labour Party was socialist, and when recession hit (as it does regularly in capitalist countries) the public was then told, and believed, that 'socialism had failed.'

Yet, ever since the dissolution of the Soviet Union in 1991, polls taken in Russia have shown a nostalgia for the old system. In 2009, for example, *Russia Now*, a Moscow publication that appears as a supplement in the *Washington Post*, asked Russians: 'What socio-economic system do you favor?' The results were: 'State planning and distribution' – 58 percent; 'Based on private property and market relations' – 28 percent; 'Hard to say' – 14 percent.[17]

In 1994, Mark Brzezinski (son of Zbigniew) was a Fulbright scholar teaching in Warsaw. He has written:

> I asked my students to define democracy. Expecting a discussion on individual liberties and authentically elected institutions, I was surprised to hear my students respond that to them, democracy means a government obligation to maintain a certain standard of living and to provide health care, education and housing for all. In other words, socialism.[18]

Many Americans cannot go along with the notion of a planned, centralized society. To some extent it's the terminology that bothers them because they were raised to equate a planned society with the worst excesses of Stalinism. OK, let's forget the scary labels; let's describe it as people sitting down to discuss a particular serious societal problem, what the available options there are to solve the problem, and what institutions and forces in the society have the best access, experience, and assets to deliver those options. So, the idea is to prepare these institutions and forces to deal with the problem in a highly organized, rational manner without having to worry about which corporation's profits might be adversely affected, without having to rely on 'the magic of the marketplace.' Now it happens that all this is usually called 'planning,' and if the organization and planning stem from a government body it can be called 'centralized planning.' There's no reason to assume that this has to result in some kind of very authoritarian regime. All of us over a certain age – individually and collectively – have learned a lot about such things from the past. We know the warning signs; that's why the Bush and Obama administrations' assaults on civil liberties and human rights have been so strongly condemned.

The overwhelming majority of people in the United States work for a salary. They don't need to be motivated by the quest for profit. It's not in our genes. Virtually everybody, if given the choice, would prefer to work at jobs where the main motivations are to produce goods and services that improve the quality of life of the society, to help others, and to provide themselves with meaningful and satisfying work. It's not natural to be primarily motivated by trying to win or steal 'customers' from other people, no holds barred, survival of the fittest or the most ruthless.

A major war can be the supreme test of a nation, a time when it's put under the greatest stress. In World War II, the US government commandeered the auto manufacturers to make tanks and jeeps instead of private cars. When a pressing need for an atom bomb was seen, Washington did not ask for bids from the private sector; it created the Manhattan Project to do it itself, with no concern for balance sheets or profit-and-loss statements. Women and blacks were given skilled factory jobs they had been traditionally denied. Hollywood was enlisted to make propaganda films. Indeed, much of the nation's activities, including farming, manufacturing, mining, communications, labor, education, and cultural undertakings were in some fashion brought under new and significant government control, with the war effort coming before private profit. In peacetime, we can think of socialism as putting people before profit, with all the basics guaranteed – healthcare, all education, decent housing, food, jobs. Those who swear by free enterprise argue that the 'socialism' of World War II was instituted only because of the exigencies of the war. That's true, but it doesn't alter the key point that it had been immediately recognized by the government that the wasteful and inefficient capitalist system, always in need of proper financial care and feeding, was no way to run a country trying to win a war.

It's also no way to run a society of human beings with human needs. Most Americans agree with this but are not consciously aware that they hold such a belief. In 1987, nearly half of 1,004 Americans surveyed by the Hearst press believed that Karl Marx's aphorism 'From each according to his ability, to each according to his need' was to be found in the US Constitution.[19]

I cannot describe in detail what every nut and bolt of my socialist society would look like. That might appear rather pretentious on my part; most of it would evolve through trial and error anyway; the important thing is that the foundation – the crucial factors in making the important decisions – would rest on people's welfare and the common good coming before profit. Humankind's desperate need to halt environmental degradation regularly runs smack into the profit motive, as does the American healthcare system. It's more than a matter of ideology; it's a matter of the quality of life, sustainability, and survival.

20

THE MEDIA

National Pentagon Radio

In 2008, WAMU, the Washington, DC National Public Radio (NPR) station, asked its listeners to write and tell it what they used the station as a source for. Some of those who replied were invited in for a recorded interview, and a tape of part of the interview was played on the air. I sent them the following email:

> June 13, 2008
>
> Dear People,
>
> I use WAMU to listen to *All Things Considered*. I use *All Things Considered* to get the Pentagon point of view on US foreign policy. It's great hearing retired generals explain why the US has just bombed or invaded another country. I'm not bothered by any naive anti-war protesters. I get the official truth right from the horse's mouth. Is this a great country, or what? I hope you're lining up some more great retired generals to tell me why we had to bomb Iran and kill thousands more people. Just make sure you don't make me listen to anyone on the left.
>
> Sincerely, William Blum, who should be on Diane Rehm, but never will be asked.
> [This was followed by some information about my books.]

I had no expectation of any kind of positive reply. I figured that if my letter didn't do it, then surely the titles of my books would reveal that I'm not actually a lover of the American military or their wars. But I don't really want to believe the worst about the mainstream media. That's too discouraging. So it was a pleasant surprise when someone at the station invited me to come in for an interview. It lasted more than half an hour and went very well. I expressed many of my misgivings about US foreign policy and NPR's coverage of it in no uncertain terms, even pointing out that anti-war activists referred to NPR as National Pentagon Radio. The interviewer said he was very pleased. He expected this was going to be an interesting piece for the station to broadcast. But, as it turned out, that was the end of the matter. I never heard from the station again, and my interview was never broadcast.

About two months later I sent an email to the interviewer asking if the interview would be aired. I could verify that he received it, but I got no reply. I think the interviewer had been sincere, which is why I'm not mentioning his name. Someone above him must have listened to the tape, remembered where 'public' radio's real loyalty lay (with its primary funder, Congress), and vetoed the whole thing. My (lack of) faith in American mass media has not been challenged. And those who work in the mass media will continue to believe in what they practice, something they call 'objectivity.'

The audience contributes its share to the syndrome. Consumers of news, if fed American-exceptionalism junk food long enough, come to feel at home with it, equate it with objectivity, and equate objectivity with getting a full and balanced picture, or the 'truth'; it appears neutral and unbiased, like the old comfortable living-room sofa they're sitting on as they watch NBC or CNN. They view the 'alternative media,' with a style rather different from what they're accustomed to, as not being 'objective' enough, therefore suspect.

The president of NPR, incidentally, is a gentleman named Kevin Klose. Previously he helped coordinate all US-funded international broadcasting: Radio Free Europe/Radio Liberty (Central Europe and the Soviet Union), Voice of America, Radio Free Asia, Radio/TV Martí (Cuba), Worldnet Television (Africa and elsewhere); all created specifically to disseminate world news to a target audience through the prism of US foreign policy beliefs and goals. He also served as president of Radio Free Europe/Radio Liberty. Would it be unfair to say that Americans then became his newest target audience? All unconscious of course; that's what makes the mass media so effective; they really believe in their own objectivity; while I will continue to believe that objectivity is no substitute for honesty.

Diane Rehm has a large and loyal listenership on National Public Radio, and I think she does a pretty good job with her very wide-ranging interviews, but the woman has a deep-seated flaw: she doesn't understand ideology very well – right from left, conservative from liberal, liberal from radical leftist, and so on. Time and time again she gathers a group to discuss some very controversial issue, and there is not among their number a single person of genuine leftist credentials, or even close to it; and, from a number of remarks I've heard her make, my guess is that this is not because she has a conservative bias, but rather that she has an inadequate comprehension of what distinguishes left from right; although whoever helps her choosing guests may well be conscious of what they're doing.

The program of February 27, 2007 (with someone sitting in for Rehm) is a case in point. The topic was Iran – all the controversial issues surrounding that country were on the table. The discussants were: (i) someone from the Council on Foreign Relations (CFR), the oldest, most traditional private institution in support of US imperialism; (ii) someone from the American Enterprise Institute, which makes CFR look positively progressive; (iii) someone from the Brookings Institution, which is about on a par with CFR ideologically. The Brookings representative was Kenneth Pollack, former CIA analyst and National Security Council staffer, who will always be remembered (or at least should be) for his 2002 book *The Threatening Storm: The Case for Invading Iraq*. Can we look forward to his next book, *The Case for Global Warming?*

In a society which pays so much lip service to dissent, free speech, and town-hall 'balanced' discussions, the lineup of Diane Rehm's guests is depressingly typical in the mainstream world. Whether it's the 9/11 Commission, the Iraq Study Group, the Congressional JFK assassination committee, or any of dozens of other congressional investigating committees over the years, the questioning, challenging, progressive point of view is almost always represented by an empty chair.

'In America you can say anything you want – as long as it doesn't have any effect' – Paul Goodman

Progressive activists and writers bemoan the fact that the news they generate and the opinions they express are consistently ignored by the mainstream media, and thus kept from the masses of the American people. This disregard of the progressive point of view is tantamount to a definition of the mainstream media. It doesn't have to be a conspiracy; it's a matter of who owns the mainstream media and the type of journalists they hire – men and women who would like to keep their jobs; so it's more insidious than a conspiracy, it's what's built into the system, it's how the system works. The disregard of the progressive world is of course not total; at times some of that world makes too good copy to ignore, and, on rare occasions, progressive ideas, when they threaten to become very popular, have to be countered.

So it was with Howard Zinn's *A People's History of the United States*, a history of the US written primarily from the point of view of those below – workers, farmers, soldiers, the poor, and so on, instead of from the point of view of traditional history books – government officials, corporate executives, law enforcement officials, the rich, and so on. Here's Barry Gewen, an editor at the *New York Times Book Review*, June 5, 2005, writing of Zinn's book and others like it:

> There was a unifying vision, but it was simplistic. Since the victims and losers were good, it followed that the winners were bad. From the point of view of downtrodden blacks, America was racist; from the point of view of oppressed workers, it was exploitative; from the point of view of conquered Hispanics and Indians, it was imperialistic. There was much to condemn in American history, little or nothing to praise.... Whereas the Europeans who arrived in the New World were genocidal predators, the Indians who were already there believed in sharing and hospitality (never mind the profound cultural differences that existed among them), and raped Africa was a continent overflowing with kindness and communalism (never mind the profound cultural differences that existed there).

One has to wonder whether Mr Gewen thought that all the victims of the Holocaust were saintly and without profound cultural differences.

Prominent American historian Arthur Schlesinger, Jr once said of Zinn: 'I know he regards me as a dangerous reactionary. And I don't take him very seriously. He's a polemicist, not a historian.'

In the obituaries that followed Zinn's death, this particular defamation was picked up around the world, from the *New York Times*, *Washington Post*, and the leading American wire services to the *New Zealand Herald* and *Korea Times*.

Regarding reactionaries and polemicists, it is worth noting that Mr Schlesinger as a top adviser to President John F. Kennedy, played a key role in the overthrow of Cheddi Jagan, the democratically elected progressive prime minister of British Guiana (now Guyana). In 1990, at a conference in New York City, Schlesinger publicly apologized to Jagan, saying: 'I felt badly about my role thirty years ago. I think a great injustice was done to Cheddi Jagan.'[1] This is to Schlesinger's credit, although the fact that Jagan was present at the conference may have awakened his conscience after thirty years. Like virtually all the American historians of the period who were granted attention and respect by the mainstream media, Schlesinger was a cold warrior. Those like Zinn, who questioned the basic suppositions of the Cold War abroad and capitalism at home, were regarded as polemicists.

America's presstitutes

Imagine that the vicious police attack of October 25, 2011 on the Occupy Oakland encampment had taken place in Iran or Cuba or Venezuela or in any other ODE (officially designated enemy) ... Page One Righteous Indignation with Shocking Photos! But here's the *Washington Post* the next day, with a three-inch story on page three with a headline: 'Protesters wearing out their welcome nationwide'; no mention of the Iraqi veteran left unconscious from a police projectile smashing into his head. As to photos, just one: an Oakland police officer petting a cat that was left behind by the protesters.

And here's television comedian Jay Leno the same night as the police attack in Oakland: 'They say Moammar Gaddafi may have been one of the richest men in the world ... 200 billion dollars. With all of the billions he had, he spent very little on education or health care for his country. So I guess he was a Republican.'[2]

The object of Leno's humor was of course the Republicans, but it served the cause of further demonizing Gaddafi and thus adding to the 'justification' for America's murderous attack on Libya. If I had been one of Leno's guests sitting there, I would have turned to the audience and said: 'Listen people, under Gaddafi healthcare and education were completely free. Wouldn't you like to have that here?' I think that enough people in the audience would have applauded or shouted to force Leno to back off a bit from his indoctrinated, made-in-America remark.

And just for the record, the $200 billion is not money found in Gaddafi's personal bank accounts anywhere in the world, but money belonging to the Libyan state. But why quibble?

'Goyim [non-Jews] were born only to serve us. Without that, they have no place in the world; only to serve the People of Israel,' said Rabbi Ovadia Yosef in a sermon in Israel on October 16, 2010. Rabbi Yosef is the former Sephardi chief rabbi of Israel and the founder and spiritual leader of the Shas party, at that time one of the three major components of the Israeli government. 'Why are gentiles needed?' he continued. 'They will work, they will plow, they will reap. We will sit like an effendi [master] and eat,' he said to some laughter.

Pretty shocking, right? Apparently not shocking enough for the free and independent American mainstream media. Not one daily newspaper picked it up. Not one radio or television station. Neither did the two leading US news agencies, Associated Press and United Press International, which usually pick up anything at all newsworthy. And the words, of course, did not cross the lips of any American politician or State Department official. Rabbi Yosef's words were reported in English only by the Jewish Telegraph Agency, a US-based news service (October 18), and then picked up by a few relatively obscure news agencies or progressive websites. We can all imagine the news coverage if someone like Iranian president Mahmoud Ahmadinejad said something like 'Jews have no place in the world but to serve Islam.'

On October 8, 2001, the second day of the US bombing of Afghanistan, the transmitters for the Taliban government's Radio Shari were bombed, and shortly after this the US bombed some twenty regional radio sites. US Secretary of Defense Donald

Rumsfeld defended the targeting of these facilities, saying: 'Naturally, they cannot be considered to be free media outlets. They are mouthpieces of the Taliban and those harboring terrorists.'[3]

In 1999, during the US/NATO bombing of the former Yugoslavia, state-owned Radio Television Serbia (RTS) was targeted because it was broadcasting reports *which the United States and NATO did not like* (like how much horror the bombing was causing). The bombs took the lives of many of the station's staff, and both legs of one of the survivors, which had to be amputated to free him from the wreckage.[4] UK prime minister Tony Blair told reporters that the bombing was 'entirely justified,' for the station was 'part of the apparatus of dictatorship and power of Milosevic.'[5] Threatening more such attacks on Serbian media, Pentagon spokesman Kenneth Bacon declared a few hours after the bombing: 'Stay tuned. It is not difficult to track down where TV signals emanate from.'[6]

Accordingly, it should not be surprising if some of the leading members of the United States mainstream media – from the *New York Times* to CNN, from NPR to Fox News – were to fall victim to a bomb, placed by someone who felt that naturally these could not be considered to be free media outlets, but mouthpieces of imperialism and the destructive power of the United States.

'Omission is the most powerful form of lie' – George Orwell

I am asked occasionally why I am so critical of the mainstream media when I quote from them repeatedly in my writings. The answer is simple. The American media's gravest shortcoming is much more their errors of omission than their errors of commission. It's what they leave out, or seriously underemphasize, that distorts the news more than any factual errors or out-and-out lies. So I can make good use of the facts they report, which a large, rich, and well-connected organization can provide more easily than the alternative media.

A Pullet Surprise for the *New York Times* history of the CIA (*Legacy of Ashes* by Tim Weiner)

In 1971 the *New York Times* published its edition of the Pentagon Papers, based on the government documents concerning Vietnam policy which had been borrowed by Daniel Ellsberg. In its preface to the book, the *Times* commented about certain omissions and distortions in the government's view of political and historical realities as reflected in the papers:

> Clandestine warfare against North Vietnam, for example, is not seen ... as violating the Geneva Accords of 1954, which ended the French Indochina War, or as conflicting with the public policy pronouncements of the various administrations. Clandestine warfare, because it is covert, does not exist as far as treaties and public posture are concerned. Further, secret commitments to other nations are not sensed as infringing on the treaty-making powers of the Senate, because they are not publicly acknowledged.[7]

In his 2007 book *Legacy of Ashes: The History of the CIA*, the *New York Times* reporter Tim Weiner also relies heavily on government documents in deciding what events to include and what not to, and the result is often equally questionable. 'This book,' Weiner writes, 'is on the record – no anonymous sources, no blind quotations, no hearsay. It is the first history of the CIA compiled entirely from firsthand reporting and primary documents.'

Thus for Tim Weiner, if US government officials did not put something in writing or if someone did not report their firsthand experience concerning a particular event, the event doesn't exist, or at least is not worth recounting. British journalist Stewart Steven has written: 'If we believe that contemporary history must be told on the basis of documentary evidence before it becomes credible, then we must also accept that everything will either be written with the government's seal of approval or not be written at all.'

As to firsthand reporting, for Weiner it apparently has to be from someone 'reputable.' Former CIA officer Philip Agee wrote a book in 1974, *Inside the Company: CIA Diary*, which provided more detail about CIA covert operations in Latin America than any book ever written. And it was certainly firsthand. But Agee and his revelations are not mentioned at all in Weiner's book. Could it be because Agee, in the process of becoming the Agency's leading dissident, also became a socialist radical and close ally of Cuba?

Former CIA officer John Stockwell also penned a memoir, *In Search of Enemies* (1978), revealing lots of CIA dirty laundry in Africa. He later also became a serious Agency dissident. The Weiner book ignores him as well.

Also ignored is a book written by Joseph Burkholder Smith, another Agency officer, not quite a left-wing dissident like Agee or Stockwell but a heavyweight critic nonetheless. The memoir, titled *Portrait of a Cold Warrior* (1976), reveals numerous instances of CIA illegality and immorality in the Philippines, Indonesia and elsewhere in Asia.

There's also Cambodian leader Prince Sihanouk, who provided his firsthand account in *My War with the CIA* (1974). Sihanouk is also a non-person in the pages of *Legacy of Ashes*.

Even worse, Weiner ignores a veritable mountain of impressive 'circumstantial' and other evidence of CIA misdeeds that do not meet his stated criteria, which any thorough researcher or writer on the Agency should give serious attention to, or certainly at least mention for the record. Among the many CIA transgressions and crimes left out of *Legacy of Ashes*, or very significantly played down, are:

• The extensive CIA role in the 1950s' provocation and sabotage activities in East Berlin/East Germany which contributed considerably to the communists' decision to build the Berlin Wall is not mentioned; although the wall is discussed.

- The US role in instigating and supporting the coup that overthrew Sihanouk in 1970, which led directly to the rising up of the Khmer Rouge, Pol Pot, and the infamous Cambodian 'killing fields.' Weiner, without providing any source, writes: 'The coup shocked the CIA and the rest of the American government' (p. 304). Neither does the book make any mention of the deliberate Washington policy to support Pol Pot in his subsequent war with Vietnam. Pol Pot's name does not appear in the book.

- The criminal actions carried out by Operation Gladio, created by the CIA, NATO, and several European intelligence services beginning in 1949. The operation was responsible for numerous acts of terrorism in Europe, foremost of which was the bombing of the Bologna railway station in 1980, claiming 86 lives. The purpose of the terrorism was to place the blame for these atrocities on the left and thus heighten public concern about a Soviet invasion and keep the left from electoral victory in Italy, France, and elsewhere. In Weiner's book this is all down the Orwellian memory hole.

- A discussion of the alleged 1993 assassination attempt against former president George H.W. Bush in Kuwait presents laughable evidence, yet states: 'But the CIA eventually concluded that Saddam Hussein had tried to kill President Bush' (p. 444). Weiner repeats this, apparently, solely because it appears in a CIA memorandum. That qualifies it as a 'primary document.' But what does this have to do with, y'know, the actual facts?

Moreover, the book scarcely scratches the surface concerning the dozens of foreign elections the CIA has seriously interfered in; the large number of assassination attempts, successful or unsuccessful, against foreign political leaders; the widespread planting of phoney stories in the international media, stories that were at times picked up in the American press as a result; manipulation and corruption of foreign labor movements; extensive book, newspaper, and magazine publishing fronts; CIA drug trafficking; and a virtual world atlas of overthrown governments, or attempts at same.

A Legacy of Ashes is generally a good read, even for someone familiar with the world of the CIA, but it's actually often rather superficial, albeit that it is 700 pages long. Why has so much of importance and interest been omitted from a book which has the subtitle *The History of the CIA*, not, it must be noted, *A History of the CIA*?

Whatever jaundiced eye Weiner focuses on the CIA, he still implicitly accepts the two basic myths of the Cold War: (1) There existed out there something called the 'International Communist Conspiracy,' fueled by implacable Soviet expansionism; (2) United States foreign policy meant well. It may have been frequently bumbling and ineffective, but its intentions were noble, and still are.

The Pentagon tells the media the full and shocking truth for once

Arthur Sylvester, assistant secretary of defense for public affairs, was the man most responsible for 'giving, controlling, and managing the war news from Vietnam.' One day in July 1965 Sylvester told American journalists that they had a patriotic duty to disseminate only information that made the United States look good. When one of the newsmen exclaimed: 'Surely, Arthur, you don't expect the American press to be handmaidens of government,' Sylvester replied: 'That's exactly what I expect,' adding 'Look, if you think any American official is going to tell you the truth, then you're stupid. Did you hear that? – stupid.' And when a correspondent for a New York paper began a question, he was interrupted by Sylvester, who said: 'Aw, come on. What does someone in New York care about the war in Vietnam?'[8]

How I spent the fifteen minutes of fame granted me by Osama bin Laden

On January 19, 2006 an audiotape from Osama bin Laden was released in which he declared: 'If you [Americans] are sincere in your desire for peace and security, we have answered you. And if Bush decides to carry on with his lies and oppression, then it would be useful for you to read the book *Rogue State*, which states in its introduction...' He then goes on to quote the opening of a paragraph I wrote (which actually appears only in the Foreword of the Zed Books edition that was later translated into Arabic), which in full reads:

> If I were the president, I could stop terrorist attacks against the United States in a few days. Permanently. I would first apologize – very publicly and very sincerely – to all the widows and the orphans, the impoverished and the tortured, and all the many millions of other victims of American imperialism. I would then announce that America's global interventions – including the awful bombings – have come to an end. And I would inform Israel that it is no longer the 51st state of the union but – oddly enough – a foreign country. I would then reduce the military budget by at least 90% and use the savings to pay reparations to the victims. There would be more than enough money. One year's military budget of $330 billion is equal to more than $18,000 an hour for every hour since Jesus Christ was born. That's what I'd do on my first three days in the White House. On the fourth day, I'd be assassinated.

Within hours I was swamped by the media and I appeared on many of the leading television news shows, dozens of radio programs, with long profiles in the *Washington Post*, Salon.com, and elsewhere. In the previous ten years the *Post* had declined to print a single one of my letters, most of which had pointed out errors in their foreign news coverage. Now my photo was on page one.

Much of the media wanted me to say that I was repulsed by bin Laden's 'endorsement.' I did not say I was repulsed, because I was not. After the first day or so of interviews I got my reply together and it usually went something like this:

> There are two elements involved here. On the one hand, I totally despise any kind of religious fundamentalism and the societies spawned by such, like the Taliban in Afghanistan. On the other hand, I'm a member of a movement which has the very ambitious goal of slowing down, if not stopping, the American Empire, to keep it from continuing to go round the world doing things like bombings, invasions, overthrowing governments, and torture. To have any success, we need to reach the American people with our message. And to reach the American people we need to have access to the mass media. What has just happened has given me the opportunity to reach millions of people I would otherwise never reach. Why should I not be glad about that? How could I let such an opportunity go to waste?

Celebrity – modern civilization's highest cultural achievement – is a peculiar phenomenon. It really isn't worth anything unless you do something with it.

The callers into the programs I was on, and sometimes the host, in addition to numerous emails, repeated two main arguments against me:

(1) Where else but in the United States could I have the freedom to say what I was saying on national media?

Besides their profound ignorance in not knowing of scores of countries with at least equal freedom of speech (particularly since September 11), what they were saying in effect was that I should be so grateful for my freedom of speech that I should show my gratitude by not exercising that freedom. If they were not saying that, they were not saying anything.

(2) America has always done marvelous things for the world, from the Marshall Plan and defeating Communism and the Taliban to rebuilding destroyed countries and freeing Iraq.

I had dealt with these myths and misconceptions in various writings; like sub-atomic particles, they behave differently when observed. For example, I had pointed out in detail that 'destroyed countries' had usually been destroyed by American bombs; and America typically did not rebuild them. As to the Taliban, the United States had overthrown a secular, women's-rights-supporting government in Afghanistan, which led to the Taliban coming to power; so the US could hardly be honored for ousting the Taliban a decade later, replacing it with an American occupation, an American puppet president, assorted warlords, and women chained.

But try to explain all these fine points in the minute or so one has for an answer on radio or television. However, I think I managed to squeeze in a lot of information and thoughts new to the American psyche.

Some hosts and many callers were clearly pained to hear me say that anti-American terrorists are retaliating against the harm done to their countries by US foreign policy, and are not necessarily just evil, mindless, madmen from another planet. Many of them assumed, with lots of certainty and no good reason at all, that I was a supporter of the Democratic Party and they proceeded to attack Bill Clinton. When I pointed out that I was no fan at all of the Democrats or Clinton, they were usually confused into silence for a few moments before jumping to some other piece of nonsense. They did not know that an entire alternative world exists above and beyond the Republicans and the Democrats.

In the news around this time we had been hearing and reading comments in the American media about how hopelessly backward and violent were those Muslims in Denmark protesting the Danish cartoons which had depicted Muhammad, with protestors carrying signs calling for the beheading of those who insult Islam. It's not quite as bad in America, but a caller to a radio program I was on said I 'should be taken care of,' and one of the hundreds of nasty emails I received began 'Death to you and your family.'

One of my personal favorite moments was on an AM radio program in Pennsylvania, discussing the Israeli–Palestinian conflict:

> HOST (with anguish in her voice): 'What has Israel ever done to the Palestinians?'
>
> ME: 'Have you been in a coma the past twenty years?'

This is a question I could have asked many of those who interrogated me during the previous two weeks. Actually, sixty years would have been more appropriate when it comes to US foreign policy.

21

BARACK OBAMA

**Obama and the empire – the 2008 campaign:
the warning signs were all there** (August 5, 2008)

The *New Yorker* magazine in its July 14, 2008 issue ran a cover cartoon that achieved instant fame. It showed Barack Obama wearing Muslim garb in the Oval Office with a portrait of Osama bin Laden on the wall. Obama is delivering a fist bump to his wife, Michelle, who has an Afro hairdo and an assault rifle slung over her shoulder. An American flag lies burning in the fireplace. The magazine says it's all satire, a parody of the crazy right-wing fears, rumors, and scare tactics about Obama's past and ideology.

The cartoon is making fun of the idea that Barack and Michelle Obama are some kind of mixture of Black Panther, Islamist jihadist, and Marxist revolutionary. But how much more educational for the American public and the world it would be to make fun of the idea that Obama is even some kind of progressive.

I'm more concerned here with foreign policy than domestic issues because it's in this area that the US government can do, and indeed does do, the most harm to the world, to put it mildly. And in this area what do we find? We find Obama threatening, several times, to attack Iran if it doesn't do what the United States wants it to do nuclear-wise; threatening more than once to attack Pakistan if its anti-terrorist policies are not tough enough or if there was a regime change in the nuclear-armed country not to his liking; calling for a large increase in US troops and tougher policies for Afghanistan; wholly and unequivocally embracing Israel as if it were the fifty-first state; totally ignoring Hamas, an elected Palestinian ruling party in the occupied territory; decrying the Berlin Wall in his recent talk in that city, about the safest thing a politician can do, but with no mention of the Israeli Wall while in Israel, nor the numerous American-built walls in Baghdad (designed to keep people in or out) while in Iraq; referring to the Venezuelan government of Hugo Chávez as 'authoritarian' (Would he refer similarly to the Bush government for which the term, or even 'police state,' is more appropriate?); talking with the usual disinformation and hostility about Cuba, albeit with a minimal token reform re visits and remittances. (Would he dare mention the outrageous case of the imprisoned Cuban Five[1] in his frequent references to fighting terrorism?)

While an Illinois state senator in January 2004, Obama declared that it was time 'to end the embargo with Cuba' because it had 'utterly failed in the effort to overthrow Castro.' But speaking as a presidential candidate to a Cuban-American audience in Miami in August 2007, he declared that he would not 'take off the embargo' as president because it is 'an important inducement for change.'[2] He thus went from a good policy for the wrong reason to the wrong policy for the wrong reason. Does Mr Obama care any more than Mr Bush that the United Nations General Assembly has voted – virtually unanimously – sixteen years in a row against the embargo?

In summary, it would be difficult to name a single ODE (officially designated enemy) that Obama has not been critical of, or to name one that he has supported in any way. Can this be mere coincidence?

The fact that Obama says he's willing to 'talk' to some of the 'enemies' more than the Bush administration has done sounds good, but one doesn't have to be too cynical to believe that it will not amount to more than a public-relations gimmick. It's only a change of policy that counts. Why doesn't he simply and clearly state that he would not attack Iran unless Iran first attacked the US or Israel or anyone else?

As to Iraq, if you're sick to the core of your being about the horrors US policy brings down upon the heads of the people of that unhappy land, then you must support withdrawal – immediate, total, all troops, combat and non-combat, all the Blackwater-type killer contractors, not moved to Kuwait or Qatar to be on call. All bases out. No permanent bases. No permanent war. No timetables. No approval by the US military necessary. No reductions in forces. Just *out*. *All*. Just as the people of Iraq want. Nothing less will give them the opportunity to try to put an end to the civil war and violence instigated by the American invasion and occupation and to re-create their failed state.

Has Obama ever said that the war is categorically illegal and immoral? A war crime? Or that anti-American terrorism in the world is the direct result of oppressive US policies? Instead he tells us: 'To ensure prosperity here at home and peace abroad, we all share the belief we have to maintain the strongest military on the planet.'[3] Why of course! All Americans rejoice in the strongest military on the planet and a veritable overflowing of prosperity at home and near heavenly peace abroad. That's what the people of the United States and the people of Iraq and Afghanistan and the rest of the people in this sad world desperately desire and need – *greater American killing power! State of the art!*

And has Obama ever dared to raise the obvious question: why would Iran, even if nuclear-armed, be a threat to the US or Israel? Any more than Iraq was such a threat. Which was zero. Instead, he has said things like 'Iran continues to be a major threat' and repeats the tiresome lie that the Iranian president called for the destruction of Israel.[4]

Obama, one observer has noted, 'opposes the present US policy in Iraq not on the basis of any principled opposition to neo-colonialism or aggressive war, but rather on the grounds that the Iraq war is a mistaken deployment of power that fails to advance the global strategic interests of American imperialism.'[5]

Obama and his supporters have made much of the speech he delivered in the Illinois state legislature in 2002 against the upcoming US invasion of Iraq. But two years later, when he was running for the US Senate, he declared: 'There's not that much difference between my position and George Bush's position at this stage.'[6] Since taking office in January 2005, he has voted to approve almost every war appropriation the Republicans have put forward. He also voted to confirm Condoleezza Rice as secretary of state despite her complicity in the Bush administration's false justifications for going to war in Iraq. In doing so, he lacked the courage of twelve of his Democratic Party Senate colleagues who voted against her confirmation.

If you're one of those who would like to believe that Obama has to present moderate foreign policy views to be elected, but once he's in the White House we can forget that he lied to us repeatedly and the true, progressive man of peace and international law and human rights will emerge, keep in mind that as a US Senate candidate in 2004 he threatened missile strikes against Iran,[7] and winning that election apparently did not put him in touch with his inner peacenik.

When, in 2005, the other Illinois Senator, Dick Durbin, stuck his neck out and compared American torture at Guantánamo to 'Nazis, Soviets in their gulags, or some mad regime – Pol Pot or others – that had no concern for human beings,' and was angrily denounced by the right wing, Obama stood up in the Senate and... defended him? No, he joined the critics, thrice calling Durbin's remark a 'mistake.'[8]

One of Obama's chief foreign policy advisers is Zbigniew Brzezinski, a man instrumental in provoking Soviet intervention in Afghanistan in 1979, which was followed by massive US military supplies to the opposition and widespread war. This gave rise to a generation of Islamic jihadists, the Taliban, Osama bin Laden, al-Qaeda, and more than two decades of anti-American terrorism. Asked later if he had any regrets about this policy, Brzezinski replied: 'Regret what? That secret operation was an excellent idea. It had the effect of drawing the Russians into the Afghan trap and you want me to regret it? The day that the Soviets officially crossed the border, I wrote to President Carter, in substance: we now have the opportunity of giving to the USSR its Vietnam war.'[9]

Another prominent Obama adviser – from a list entirely and depressingly establishment-imperial – is Madeleine Albright, who played key roles in the merciless bombings of Iraq and Yugoslavia in the 1990s.

In a primary campaign talk in March, Obama said that 'he would return the country to the more "traditional" foreign policy efforts of past presidents, such as George H.W. Bush, John F. Kennedy and Ronald Reagan.'[10] 'Traditional' indeed; they were all serial interventionists.

Why have well-known media conservatives like George Will, David Brooks, Joe Scarborough, and others spoken so favorably about Obama's candidacy?[11] Whatever else, they know he's not a threat to their most cherished views and values.

Given all this, can we expect a more enlightened, less bloody, more progressive and humane foreign policy from Mr Barack Obama? Forget the alleged eloquence and charm; forget the warm feel-good stuff; forget the interminable clichés and platitudes about hope, change, unity, and America's indispensable role as world leader; forget all the religiobabble; forget John McCain and George W. Bush ... All that counts is putting an end to the horror – the bombings, the invasions, the killings, the destruction, the overthrows, the occupations, the torture, the American Empire.

Al Gore and John Kerry both took the progressive vote for granted. They themselves had never been particularly progressive. Each harbored a measure of disdain for the left. Both paid a heavy price for the neglect. I and millions like me voted for Ralph Nader, or some other third-party candidate, or stayed home. Obama is doing the same as Gore and Kerry. Progressives should let him know that his positions are not acceptable, keeping up the anti-war pressure on him and the Democratic Party at every opportunity. For whatever good it just might do.

I'm afraid that if Barack Obama becomes president he's going to break a lot of young hearts. And some older ones as well.

What does this man named Barack Obama truly believe in?
(October 1, 2010)

For many years I have not paid a great deal of attention to party politics in the United States. I usually have only a passing knowledge of who's who in Congress. It's policies that interest me much more than politicians. But during the 2008 presidential campaign I kept hearing the name Barack Obama when I turned on the radio, and repeatedly saw his name in headlines in various newspapers. I knew no more than that he was a senator from Illinois and... was he black?

Then one day I turned on my kitchen radio and was informed that Obama was about to begin a talk. I decided to listen, and did so for about fifteen or twenty minutes while I washed the dishes. I listened, and listened, and then it hit me... This man is not *saying* anything! It's all platitude and cliché, with very little of what I would call substance. His talk could have been written by a computer, touching all the appropriate bases and saying just what could be expected to give some hope to the pessimistic and to artfully challenge the skepticism of the cynical; feel-good language for every occasion; conventional wisdom for every issue. His supporters, I would later learn, insisted that he had to talk this way to be elected, but once elected – Aha! The real genuine-progressive, anti-war Barack Obama would appear. 'Change you can believe in!' Hallelujah!... They're still saying things like that.

Last week Obama gave the traditional annual speech at the opening of the United Nations General Assembly.[12] To give you an idea of whether the man now sincerely expresses himself 'outside the box' at all, here's what he had to say about Pakistan: 'Since the rains came and the floodwaters rose in Pakistan, we have pledged our assistance, and we should all support the Pakistani people as they recover and rebuild.' Does he think no one in the world knows that airplanes of the United States of America have flown over Pakistan and dropped bombs on dozens of recent occasions? Did he think he was speaking before sophisticated international diplomats or making a campaign speech before Iowa farmers?

Plus endless verbiage about the endless Israeli–Palestine issue, which could have been lifted out of almost any speech by any American president of the past thirty years. But no mention at all of Gaza. Oh, excuse me – there was one line: 'the young girl in Gaza who wants to have no ceiling on her dreams.' Gosh, choke. One would never know that the United States possesses huge leverage over the state of Israel – billions/trillions of dollars of military and economic aid and gifts. An American president with a minimum of courage could force Israel to make some concessions, and in a struggle between a thousand-pound gorilla (Israel) and an infant (Hamas) it's the gorilla that has to give some ground.

And this: 'We also know from experience that those who defend these [universal] values for their people have been our closest friends and allies, while those who have denied those rights – whether terrorist groups or tyrannical governments – have chosen to be our adversaries.' In fact, however, it would be difficult to name a single brutal dictatorship of the second half of the twentieth century that was not supported by the United States; not only supported, but often put into power and kept in power against the wishes of the population. And in recent years as well Washington has supported very repressive governments, such as Saudi Arabia, Honduras, Indonesia, Egypt, Kosovo, Colombia, and Israel. As to terrorist groups being adversaries of the United States – another item for the future Barack Obama Presidential Liebrary, the United States has supported terrorist groups for decades. These groups have fought alongside the United States in Afghanistan, Bosnia, and Kosovo [added in 2012: and in Libya and Syria.]

> Yes, of course it's nice to have a president who speaks in complete sentences. But that they're coherent doesn't make them honest. (John R. MacArthur, publisher of *Harper's* magazine[13])

Obama's popularity around the world is enhanced to an important extent by the fact that he has successfully concealed or obscured his real ideology (assuming he has one, which is to be doubted). As an example, in an interview with the *New York Times* (March 7, 2009), he was asked: 'Is there a one word name for your philosophy? If you're not a socialist, are you a liberal? Are you progressive? One word?'

'No, I'm not going to engage in that,' replied the president.

Obama, his mother, and the CIA

In his autobiography, *Dreams from My Father*, Barack Obama writes of taking a job at some point after graduating from Columbia University in 1983. He describes his employer as 'a consulting house to multinational corporations' in New York City, and his functions as a 'research assistant' and 'financial writer.'

Oddly, Obama doesn't mention the name of his employer. However, a *New York Times* story of 2007 identifies the company as Business International Corporation.[14] Equally odd is that the *Times* did not remind its readers that the newspaper itself had disclosed in 1977 that Business International had provided cover for four CIA employees in various countries between 1955 and 1960.[15]

The British journal *Lobster* – which, despite its incongruous name, is a venerable international publication on intelligence matters – has reported that Business International was active in the 1980s promoting the candidacy of Washington-favored candidates in Australia and Fiji.[16] In 1987, the CIA overthrew the Fiji government after but one month in office because of its policy of maintaining the island as a nuclear-free zone, meaning that American nuclear-powered or nuclear-weapons-carrying ships could not make port calls.[17] After the Fiji coup, the candidate supported by Business International, who was much more amenable to Washington's nuclear desires, was reinstated to power – R.S.K. Mara was prime minister or president of Fiji from 1970 to 2000, except for the one-month break in 1987.

In his book, Obama not only doesn't mention his employer's name; he fails to say exactly when he worked there, or why he left the job. There may well be no significance to these omissions, but inasmuch as Business International has a long association with the world of intelligence, covert actions, and attempts to penetrate the radical left – including Students for a Democratic Society (SDS)[18] – it's reasonable to wonder if the inscrutable Mr Obama is concealing something about his own association with this world.

Adding to the wonder is the fact that his mother, Ann Dunham, had been associated during the 1970s and 80s – as employee, consultant, grantee, or student – with at least five organizations with *intimate* CIA connections during the Cold War: the Ford Foundation, the Agency for International Development (AID), the Asia Foundation, Development Alternatives, Inc., and the East–West Center of Hawaii.[19] Much of this time she worked as an anthropologist in Indonesia and Hawaii, being in a good position to gather intelligence about local communities.

As examples of the CIA connections of these organizations, consider the disclosure by John Gilligan, director of AID during the Carter administration (1977–81): 'At one time, many AID field offices were infiltrated from top to bottom with CIA people.' 'The idea was to plant operatives in every kind of activity we had overseas, government, volunteer, religious, every kind.'[20] And Development Alternatives, Inc. is the organization for whom Alan Gross was working when arrested in Cuba and charged with being part of the ongoing American operation to destabilize the Cuban government.

Love me, love me, love me, I'm a liberal
(Thank you, Phil Ochs. We miss you)

Angela Davis, star of the 1960s, like most members of the Communist Party, was/is no more radical than the average American liberal. Here she is addressing Occupy Wall Street in January 2012: 'When I said that we need a third party, a radical party, I was projecting toward the future. We cannot allow a Republican to take office... Don't we remember what it was like when Bush was president?'[21]

Yes, Angela, we remember that time well. How can we forget it since Bush, by all important standards, is still in the White House? Waging perpetual war, relentless surveillance of the citizenry, kissing the corporate ass, police brutality?... What's changed? Except for the worse. Where's our single-payer national health insurance? Nothing even close. Where's our affordable university education? Still the most backward in the 'developed' world. Where's our legalized marijuana – I mean really legalized? If you think that's changed, you must be stoned. Where's our abortion on demand? What does your guy Barack think about that? Are the indispensable labor unions being rescued from oblivion? Ha! The ultra-important minimum wage? Inflation adjusted, it's equal to that in the mid-1950s.

Has the American threat to the environment and the world environmental movement ceased? Tell that to a dedicated activist-internationalist. Has the fifty-year-old embargo against Cuba finally ended? It has not, and I can still not go there legally. The police-state War on Terror at home? Scarcely a month goes by without the FBI entrapping some young 'terrorists.' Are any banksters and Wall Street society-screwers (except for the harmless insider traders) being imprisoned? Name one. The really tough regulations of the financial area so badly needed? Keep waiting. How about executives of the BP oil spill company being arrested? Or war criminals, mass murderers, and torturers with names like... Oh, I don't know, let's see... maybe like Cheney or Bush or Rumsfeld or Wolfowitz or Rice? All walking completely free, all celebrated.

'A major decline of progressive America occurred during the Clinton years as many liberals and their organizations accepted the presence of a Democratic president as an adequate substitute for the things liberals once believed in. Liberalism and a social democratic spirit painfully grown over the previous 60 years withered during the Clinton administration' (Sam Smith)[22]

'A change of Presidents is like a change of advertising campaigns for a soft drink; the product itself still tastes the same, but it now has a new "image"' (Richard K. Moore).

Barack 'I'd kill for the peace prize' Obama (March 28, 2011)

Is anyone keeping count? I am. Libya makes six. Six countries that Barack H. Obama has waged war against in his twenty-six months in office. (To anyone who disputes that dropping bombs on a populated land is an act of war, I would ask what they think of the Japanese bombing of Pearl Harbor.)

America's first black president has now waged war in Africa. Is there anyone left who still thinks that Barack Obama is some kind of improvement over George W. Bush?

Probably two types still think so: (1) those to whom color matters a lot; (2) those who are very impressed by the ability to put together grammatically correct sentences.

It certainly can't have much otherwise to do with intellect or intelligence. Obama has said numerous things which if uttered by Bush would have inspired lots of rolled eyeballs, snickers, and chuckling reports in the columns and broadcasts of mainstream media. Like the one the president has repeated on a number of occasions when pressed to investigate Bush and Cheney for war crimes, along the lines of 'I prefer to look forward rather than backwards.' Picture a defendant before a judge asking to be found innocent on such grounds. It simply makes laws, law enforcement, crime, justice, and facts irrelevant. By Obama's stated standard *no one* would ever be found guilty of any crime because the crimes would all be in the past.

There's also the excuse given by Obama not to prosecute those engaged in torture: because they were following orders. Has this 'educated' man never heard of the Nuremberg Trials, where this defense was summarily rejected? Forever, it was assumed.

Just eighteen days before the Gulf oil spill Obama said: 'It turns out, by the way, that oil rigs today generally don't cause spills. They are technologically very advanced.'[23] Picture George W. having said this, and the later reaction.

'All the forces that we're seeing at work in Egypt are forces that naturally should be aligned with us, should be aligned with Israel,' Obama said in early March.[24] Imagine if Bush had implied this – that the Arab protesters in Egypt against a man receiving billions in US aid, as well as the tools to repress and torture them, should 'naturally' be aligned with the United States and – God help us – Israel.

A week later, on March 10, State Department spokesman P.J. Crowley told a forum in Cambridge, Massachusetts that WikiLeaks hero Bradley Manning's treatment by the Defense Department in a Marine prison was 'ridiculous, counterproductive and stupid.' The next day our 'brainy' president was asked about Crowley's comment. Replied the Great Black Hope: 'I have actually asked the Pentagon whether or not the procedures that have been taken in terms of his confinement are appropriate and are meeting our basic standards. They assure me that they are.'

Right, George. I mean Barack. Bush should have asked Donald Rumsfeld whether anyone in US custody was being tortured anywhere in the world. He could then have held a news conference like Obama did to announce the happy news – 'No torture by America!' We would still be chortling at that one.

Obama closed his remarks with: 'I can't go into details about some of their concerns, but some of this has to do with Pvt. Manning's safety as well.'[25] Ah yes, of course, Manning is being tortured for his own good. Someone please remind me: did George ever stoop to using that particular absurdity to excuse prisoner hell at Guantánamo?

Is it that Barack Obama is not bothered by the insult to Bradley Manning's human rights, the daily wearing away of this brave young man's mental stability? The answer to the question is No. The president is not bothered by these things. How do I know? Because Barack Obama is not bothered by anything as long as he can exult in being the president of the United States, eat his hamburgers, and play his basketball. The problem is that the man doesn't really believe strongly in anything, certainly not in controversial areas. He learned a long time ago how to take positions that avoid controversy, how to express opinions without clearly taking sides, how to talk eloquently without actually saying anything, how to leave his listeners' heads filled with stirring clichés, platitudes, and slogans. And it worked. Oh how it worked! What could happen now, having reached the presidency of the United States, to induce him to change his style?

Remember that in his own book, *The Audacity of Hope*, Obama wrote: 'I serve as a blank screen on which people of vastly different political stripes project their own views.' Obama is a product of marketing. He is the prime example of the product 'As seen on TV.'

Sam Smith has written that Obama is the most conservative Democratic president we've ever had. 'In an earlier time, there would have been a name for him: Republican.' Indeed, if John McCain had won the 2008 election, and then done everything that Obama has done in exactly the same way, liberals would be raging about such awful policies.

I believe that Barack Obama is one of the worst things that has ever happened to the American left. The millions of young people who jubilantly supported him in 2008, and numerous older supporters, will need a long recovery period before they're ready to once again offer their idealism and their passion on the altar of political activism.

If you don't like how things have turned out, next time find out exactly what your candidate means when he talks of 'change.'

Team Obama/cult Obama: his 2009 Cairo speech

The praise heaped on President Obama for his speech to the Muslim world by writers on the left, both here and abroad, is disturbing. I'm referring to people who I think should know better, who've taken Politics 101 and can easily see the many hypocrisies in Obama's talk, as well as the distortions, omissions, and contradictions, the true but irrelevant observations, the false-hoods, the optimistic words without any matching action, the insensitivities to victims. Yet, these commentators are impressed, in many cases very impressed. In the world at large, this frame of mind borders on a cult.

In such cases one must look beyond the intellect and examine the emotional appeal. We all know the world is in big trouble The Three Great Problems are: (1) incessant war and violence; (2) financial crises provoking widespread economic suffering; (3) environmental degradation bordering on catastrophe. In all three areas the United States bears more culpability than any other single country. Who better to satisfy humankind's craving for relief than a new American president who makes it a point to convince you that he understands the problems, who admits, to one degree or another, his country's responsibility for them; and who 'eloquently' expresses his desire and determination to change American policies and embolden the rest of the world to follow his inspiring example? Is it any wonder that it's 1964, the Beatles have just arrived in New York, and everyone is a teenage girl?

I could go through the Cairo speech and point out line by line all the political and moral shortcomings, the plain nonsense, and the rest. ('I have unequivocally prohibited the use of torture by the United States.' No mention of it being outsourced to various countries, likely including the very country in which he was speaking. 'No single nation should pick and choose which nation holds nuclear weapons.' But this is precisely what the United States is trying to do concerning Iran and North Korea.)

The problem is that of well-educated people, as well as the not-so-well-educated, being so moved by a career politician saying 'all the right things' to give food for hope to billions starving for it, and swallowing it all as if they had been born yesterday. I'd like to take them back to another charismatic figure, Adolf Hitler, speaking to the German people two years and four months after becoming chancellor, addressing a Germany still reeling with humiliation from its being the defeated nation in the world war, with huge losses of its young men; a country still being punished by the world for its militarism, suffering mass unemployment and other effects of the Great Depression. Here are excerpts from the speech of May 21, 1935. Imagine how it fed the hungry German people...

> I conceive it my duty to be perfectly frank and open in addressing the nation. I frequently hear from Anglo-Saxon tribes expressions of regret that Germany has departed from those principles of democracy, which in those countries are held particularly sacred. This opinion is entirely erroneous. Germany, too, has a democratic constitution.
>
> Our love of peace perhaps is greater than in the case of others, for we have suffered most from war. None of us wants to threaten anybody, but we all are determined to obtain the security and equality of our people.
>
> The world war should be a cry of warning here. Not for a second time can Europe survive such a catastrophe.
>
> Germany has solemnly guaranteed France her present frontiers, resigning herself to the permanent loss of Alsace-Lorraine. She has made a treaty with Poland and we hope it will be renewed and renewed again at every expiry of the set period.
>
> The German Reich, especially the present German government, has no other wish except to live on terms of peace and friendship with all the neighboring states.

Germany has nothing to gain from a European war. What we want is liberty and independence. Because of these intentions of ours we are ready to negotiate non-aggression pacts with our neighbor states.

Germany has neither the wish nor the intention to mix in internal Austrian affairs, or to annex or to unite with Austria.

The German government is ready in principle to conclude non-aggression pacts with its individual neighbor states and to supplement those provisions which aim at isolating belligerents and localizing war areas.

In limiting German air armament to parity with individual other great nations of the West, it makes possible that at any time the upper figure may be limited, which limit Germany will then take as a binding obligation to keep within.

Germany is ready to participate actively in any efforts for drastic limitation of unrestricted arming. She sees the only possible way in a return to the principles of the old Geneva Red Cross convention. She believes, to begin with, only in the possibility of the gradual abolition and outlawing of fighting methods which are contrary to this convention, such as dum-dum bullets and other missiles which are a deadly menace to civilian women and children.

To abolish fighting places, but to leave the question of bombardment open, seems to us wrong and ineffective. But we believe it is possible to ban certain arms as contrary to international law and to outlaw those who use them. But this, too, can only be done gradually. Therefore, gas and incendiary and explosive bombs outside of the battle area can be banned and the ban extended later to all bombing. As long as bombing is free, a limitation of bombing planes is a doubtful proposition. But as soon as bombing is branded as barbarism, the building of bombing planes will automatically cease.

Just as the Red Cross stopped the killing of wounded and prisoners, it should be possible to stop the bombing of civilians. In the adoption of such principles, Germany sees a better means of pacification and security for peoples than in all the assistance pacts and military conventions.

The German government is ready to agree to every limitation leading to abandonment of the heaviest weapons which are especially suitable for aggression. These comprise, first, the heaviest artillery and heaviest tanks.

Germany declares herself ready to agree to the delimitation of caliber of artillery and guns on dreadnoughts, cruisers and torpedo boats. Similarly, the German government is ready to adopt any limitation on naval tonnage, and finally to agree to the limitation of tonnage of submarines or even to their abolition, provided other countries do likewise.

The German government is of the opinion that all attempts effectively to lessen tension between individual states through international agreements or agreements between several states are doomed to failure unless suitable measures are taken to prevent poisoning of public opinion on the part of irresponsible individuals in speech, writing, in the film and the theatre.

The German government is ready any time to agree to an international agreement which will effectively prevent and make impossible all attempts to interfere from the outside in affairs of other states. The term 'interference' should be internationally defined.

If people wish for peace it must be possible for governments to maintain it. We believe the restoration of the German defense force will contribute to this peace because of the simple fact that its existence removes a dangerous vacuum in Europe. We believe if the peoples of the world could agree to destroy all their gas and inflammable and explosive bombs this would be cheaper than using them to destroy one another. In saying this I am not speaking any longer as the representative of a defenseless state which could reap only advantages and no obligations from such action from others.

I cannot better conclude my speech to you, my fellow-figures and trustees of the nation, than by repeating our confession of faith in peace: whoever lights the torch of war in Europe can wish for nothing but chaos. We, however, live in the firm conviction our times will see not the decline but the renaissance of the West. It is our proud hope and our unshakable belief that Germany can make an imperishable contribution to this great work.[26]

How many people in the world, including numerous highly educated Germans, reading or hearing that speech in 1935, doubted that Adolf Hitler was a sincere man of peace and an inspiring, visionary leader for troubled times?

After his June 4 Cairo speech, President Obama was much praised for mentioning the 1953 CIA overthrow of Iranian prime minister Mohammad Mossadegh. But in his talk in Ghana on July 11 he failed to mention the CIA coup that ousted Ghanian president Kwame Nkrumah in 1966, referring to him only as a 'giant' among African leaders. The Mossadegh coup is definitely one of the most well-known CIA covert actions. Obama could not easily get away without mentioning it in a talk in the Middle East looking to mend fences. But the Nkrumah ouster is one of the least known; indeed, not a single print or broadcast news report in the American mainstream media saw fit to mention it at the time of the president's talk. As if it never happened.[27]

And the next time you hear that Africa can't produce good leaders, people who are committed to the welfare of the masses of their people, think of Nkrumah and his fate. And think of Patrice Lumumba, overthrown in the Congo 1960–61 with the help of the United States; of Agostinho Neto of Angola, against whom Washington waged war in the 1970s, making it impossible for him to institute progressive changes; of Samora Machel of Mozambique, against whom the CIA supported a counterrevolution in the 1970s–80s period; and of Nelson Mandela of South Africa (now married to Machel's widow), who spent twenty-eight years in prison thanks to the CIA.[28]

22

PATRIOTISM

Some thoughts on 'patriotism'
(July 4, 2010)

Most important thought: I'm sick and tired of this thing called 'patriotism.'

The Japanese pilots who bombed Pearl Harbor were being patriotic. The German people who supported Hitler and his conquests were being patriotic, fighting for the Fatherland. All the Latin American military dictators who overthrew democratically elected governments and routinely tortured people were being patriotic – saving their beloved country from 'communism.'

General Augusto Pinochet of Chile, mass murderer and torturer: 'I would like to be remembered as a man who served his country.'[1]

P.W. Botha, former president of apartheid South Africa: 'I am not going to repent. I am not going to ask for favours. What I did, I did for my country.'[2]

As Pol Pot, mass murderer of Cambodia, lay on his death bed in 1997, he was interviewed by a journalist, who later wrote: 'Asked whether he wants to apologize for the suffering he caused, he looks genuinely confused, has the interpreter repeat the question, and answers "No". ... "I want you to know that everything I did, I did for my country."'[3]

Tony Blair, former British prime minister, defending his role in the murder of hundreds of thousands of Iraqis: 'I did what I thought was right for our country.'[4]

'In these three decades I have been actuated solely by love and loyalty to my people in all my thoughts, acts, and life': Adolf Hitler, 'Last Will and Testament', written in his bunker in his final hours, April 29, 1945.

Fast forward now to 2036... George W. Bush lies dying, Fox News Channel is in the room recording his last words:

> I know that people think the whole thing... that thing in Iraq... was a bad thing, and they hold it against me... I appreciate their view... I can understand how they feel... But y'know, I did it for America, and the American people, and their freedom... The more you love freedom, the more likely it is you'll be attacked... Saddam was a real threat... I still think he had weapons of mass destruction... and someday we'll find 'em... someday we'll say 'Mission accomplished!'... that will really be a turning point!... So I'm prepared to meet my maker and whatever he has in mind for me... in fact I say *Bring it on!*

At the end of World War II, the United States gave moral lectures to its German prisoners and to the German people on the inadmissibility of pleading that their participation in the war and the Holocaust was in obedience to their legitimate government. To prove to them how legally and morally inadmissable this defense was, the World War II allies hanged the leading examples of such patriotic loyalty.

I was once asked after a talk: 'Do you love America?' I answered: 'No.' After pausing for a few seconds to let that sink in amidst several nervous giggles in the audience, I continued with: 'I don't love *any* country. I'm a citizen of the world. I love certain principles, like human rights, civil liberties, meaningful democracy, an economy which puts people before profits.'

I don't make much of a distinction between patriotism and nationalism. Some people equate patriotism with allegiance to one's country and government or the noble principles they supposedly stand for, while defining nationalism as sentiments of ethno-national superiority. However defined, in practice the psychological and behavioral manifestations of nationalism and patriotism are not easily distinguishable; indeed they feed upon each other.

Howard Zinn called nationalism

> a set of beliefs taught to each generation in which the Motherland or the Fatherland is an object of veneration and becomes a burning cause for which one becomes willing to kill the children of other Motherlands or Fatherlands. ... Patriotism is used to create the illusion of a common interest that everybody in the country has.[5]

Strong feelings of patriotism lie near the surface in the great majority of Americans. They're buried deeper in the more 'liberal' and 'sophisticated', but are almost always reachable, and ignitable.

Alexis de Tocqueville, the mid-nineteenth-century French historian, commented about his long stay in the United States: 'It is impossible to conceive a more troublesome or more garrulous patriotism; it wearies even those who are disposed to respect it.'[6]

George Bush, Sr., pardoning former defense secretary Caspar Weinberger and five others in connection with the Iran–Contra arms-for-hostages scandal, said: 'First, the common denominator of their motivation – whether their actions were right or wrong – was patriotism.'[7]

What a primitive underbelly there is to this rational society. The US is the most patriotic, as well as the most religious, country of the so-called developed world. The entire American patriotism thing may be best understood as the biggest case of mass hysteria in history, whereby the crowd adores its own power as troopers of the world's only superpower, a substitute for the lack of power in the rest of their lives. Patriotism, like religion, meets people's need for something greater to which their individual lives can be anchored.

So this July 4, my dear fellow Americans, some of you will raise your fists and yell: 'U! S! A! ... U! S! A!' And you'll parade with your flags and your images of the Statue of Liberty. But do you know that the sculptor copied his mother's face for the statue, a domineering and intolerant woman who had forbidden another child to marry a Jew?

'Patriotism,' Dr Samuel Johnson famously said, 'is the last refuge of a scoundrel.' American writer Ambrose Bierce begged to differ: it is, he said, the first. For George Bernard Shaw 'Patriotism is the conviction that this country is superior to all other countries because you were born in it.'

George Orwell observed:

> Actions are held to be good or bad, not on their own merits but according to who does them, and there is almost no kind of outrage – torture, the use of hostages, forced labour, mass deportations, imprisonment without trial, forgery, assassination, the bombing of civilians – which does not change its moral colour when it is committed by 'our' side. ... The nationalist not only does not disapprove of atrocities committed by his own side, but he has a remarkable capacity for not even hearing about them.[8]

'Pledges of allegiance are marks of totalitarian states, not democracies,' says David Kertzer, a Brown University anthropologist who specializes in political rituals. 'I can't think of a single democracy except the United States that has a pledge of allegiance.'[9] Or, he might have added, any that insists that its politicians display their patriotism by wearing a flag pin. Hitler criticized German Jews and Communists for their internationalism and lack of national patriotism, demanding that 'true patriots' publicly vow and display their allegiance to the fatherland. In reaction to this, postwar Germany has made a conscious and strong effort to minimize public displays of patriotism.

Oddly enough, the American Pledge of Allegiance was written by Francis Bellamy, a founding member, in 1889, of the Society of Christian Socialists, a group of Protestant ministers who asserted that 'the teachings of Jesus Christ lead directly to some form or forms of socialism.' Tell that to the next Tea Party ignoramus who angrily accuses President Obama of being a 'socialist.'

British writer H.G. Wells had this to say about the destructive effects of nationalism:

> Throughout the nineteenth century, and particularly throughout its latter half, there had been a great working up of this nationalism in the world. ... Nationalism was taught in schools, emphasized by newspapers, preached and mocked and sung into men. It became a monstrous cant which darkened all human affairs. Men were brought to feel that they were as improper without a nationality as without their clothes in a crowded assembly. Oriental peoples, who had never heard of nationality before, took to it as they took to the cigarettes and bowler hats of the West.[10]

And the Russian anarchist Mikhail Bakunin, for his part, understood very well its ideological function:

> The very existence of the state demands that there be some privileged class vitally interested in maintaining that existence. And it is precisely the group interests of that class that are called patriotism.[11]

American exceptionalism

The leaders of imperial powers have traditionally told themselves and their citizens that their country was exceptional and that their subjugation of a particular foreign land should be seen as a 'civilizing mission,' a 'liberation,' 'God's will,' and of course bringing 'freedom and democracy' to the benighted and downtrodden.

It is difficult to kill large numbers of people without a claim to virtue. I wonder if this sense of exceptionalism has been embedded anywhere more deeply than in the United States, where it is drilled into every cell and ganglion of American consciousness from kindergarten on.

If we measure the degree of indoctrination (I'll resist the temptation to use the word 'brainwashing') of a population as the gap between what the people believe about their government's behavior in the world and what the government's actual behavior has been, the American people are clearly the most indoctrinated people on the planet. The role of the American media is of course indispensable to this process – try naming a single American daily newspaper or television network that was *unequivocally* against the US attacks on Libya, Iraq, Afghanistan, Yugoslavia, Panama, Grenada, and Vietnam. Or even against any two of them. How about one?

Overloaded with a sense of America's moral superiority, each year the State Department judges the world, issuing reports evaluating the behavior of all other nations, often accompanied by sanctions of one kind or another. There are different reports rating how each lesser nation has performed in the previous year in the areas of religious freedom, human rights, the war on drugs, trafficking in persons, and counterterrorism. The State Department also maintains a list of international 'terrorist' groups. The criteria used in these reports are mainly political, wherever applicable; Cuba, for example, is always listed as a supporter of terrorism whereas anti-Castro exile groups in the United States, which have committed hundreds of terrorist acts, are not listed as terrorist groups.

> The causes of the malady are not entirely clear but its recurrence is one of the uniformities of history: power tends to confuse itself with virtue and a great nation is peculiarly susceptible to the idea that its power is a sign of God's favor, conferring upon it a special

responsibility for other nations – to make them richer and happier and wiser, to remake them, that is, in its own shining image. (Former US senator William Fulbright, *The Arrogance of Power*, 1966)

We Americans are the peculiar, chosen people – the Israel of our time; we bear the ark of the liberties of the world. … God has predestined, mankind expects, great things from our race; and great things we feel in our souls. (Herman Melville, *White-Jacket*, 1850)

God appointed America to save the world in any way that suits America. God appointed Israel to be the nexus of America's Middle Eastern policy and anyone who wants to mess with that idea is (a) anti-Semitic, (b) anti-American, (c) with the enemy, and (d) a terrorist. (John le Carré, *The Times*, London, January 15, 2003)

Neoconservatism … traded upon the historic American myths of innocence, exceptionalism, triumphalism and Manifest Destiny. It offered a vision of what the United States should do with its unrivaled global power. In its most rhetorically-seductive messianic versions, it conflated the expansion of American power with the dream of universal democracy. In all of this, it proclaimed that the maximal use of American power was good for both America and the world. (Columbia University professor Gary Dorrien, *The Christian Century* magazine, January 22, 2007)

To most of its citizens, America is exceptional, and it's only natural that it should take exception to certain international standards. (Michael Ignatieff, *Legal Affairs*, May–June, 2002)

Our country is a force for good without precedent. (Lieutenant (Colonel Ralph Peters, US Army War College, 1997)

The US military is a force for global good that … has no equal. (Thomas Barnett, US Naval War College, *Guardian*, London, December 27, 2005)

John Bolton, future US ambassador to the United Nations, wrote in 2000 that, because of its unique status, the United States could not be 'legally bound' or constrained in any way

by its international treaty obligations. The US needed to 'be un-
ashamed, unapologetic, uncompromising American constitutional
hegemonists,' so that their 'senior decision makers' could be free
to use force unilaterally.

Condoleezza Rice, future US Secretary of State, writing in
2000, was equally contemptuous of international law. She claimed
that in the pursuit of its national security the United States no
longer needed to be guided by 'notions of international law and
norms' or 'institutions like the United Nations' because it was 'on
the right side of history' (*Z magazine*, Boston MA, July/August
2004).

> The president [George W. Bush] said he didn't want other coun-
> tries dictating terms or conditions for the war on terrorism. 'At
> some point, we may be the only ones left. That's okay with me. We
> are America.' (*Washington Post*, January 31, 2002)

> Reinhold Niebuhr got it right a half-century ago: what persists
> – and promises no end of grief – is our conviction that Providence
> has summoned America to tutor all of humankind on its pilgrim-
> age to perfection. (Andrew Bacevich, professor of international
> relations, Boston University)

In commenting on Woodrow Wilson's moral lecturing of his European colleagues at the Versailles peace table following the First
World War, Winston Churchill remarked that he found it hard to
believe that the European emigrants, who brought to America the
virtues of the lands from which they sprang, had left behind all
their vices (*The World Crisis*, Vol. V: *The Aftermath*, 1929)

> Behold a republic, gradually but surely becoming the supreme
> moral factor to the world's progress and the accepted arbiter of the
> world's disputes. (William Jennings Bryan, US secretary of state
> under Woodrow Wilson, *In His Image*, 1922)

> U.S. allies must accept that some U.S. unilateralism is inevitable,
> even desirable. This mainly involves accepting the reality of

America's supreme might – and truthfully, appreciating how historically lucky they are to be protected by such a relatively benign power. (Michael Hirsch, *Newsweek* editor, *Foreign Affairs*, November, 2002)

[The United States is] a country that exists by the grace of a divine providence. (Colin Powell, Republican National Convention, August 13, 1996)

The US media always has an underlying acceptance of the mythology of American exceptionalism, that the US, in everything it does, is the last best hope of humanity. (Rahul Mahajan, author of *The New Crusade: America's War on Terrorism* and *Full Spectrum Dominance*)

The fundamental problem is that the Americans do not respect anybody except themselves. They say, 'We are the God of the world,' and they don't consult us. (Col. Mir Jan, spokesman for the Afghan Defense Ministry, *Washington Post*, August 3, 2002)

If we have to use force, it is because we are America! We are the indispensable nation. We stand tall. We see further into the future. (Madeleine Albright, US secretary of state, 1998)

Sports and the Flag

2005: A television ad for Anheuser–Busch shown during the Super Bowl. An airport, a contingent of US soldiers in uniform is passing through, presumably on the way to or just returning from Iraq; the people in the terminal look up one by one, and slowly realize who's walking by – It's (choke) … Can it (gasp) be? … Yes! HEROES! Real honest-to-God heroes! The faces of the onlookers are filled with deep gratitude and pride. The soldiers begin to realize what's happening as the waves of adulation sweep over them; their faces, bursting with gratitude and matching pride, say 'Thanks.' The screen says 'Thanks.' Not a dry eye in the whole damn terminal. In the Soviet Union they might have been a group of Stakhanovite hero workers on the way to the factory.

2008: The United States Tennis Open women's final in New York. A woman comes out to sing 'America the Beautiful.' Pretty common, of course, at sporting events in beautiful America. If it's not that, it's another well-known hymn to athleticism like 'God Bless America' or 'The Star Spangled Banner.' But this time, as she finishes singing, dozens of marines in full uniform march out and unfurl an American flag a mile long. The crowd eats it up. Two days later, at the men's final, it's the same thing plus four jet planes roar past above the stadium.

I wish I had been there. So I could have yelled out: 'What the fuck does this have to do with tennis?' Hardly anyone would have heard me above the din of the patriotic orgy, but if anyone did I would not be surprised if they reported me to the nearest authorities (and in present-day America one is never too far from authorities), and I'd be asked to accompany the authorities to the security office (and in present-day America one is never too far from a security office).

Norman Mailer wrote in 2003, a few weeks before the US invasion of Iraq:

> My guess is that, like it or not, or want it or not, we are going to go to war because that is the only solution Bush and his people can see. The dire prospect that opens, therefore, is that America is going to become a mega-banana republic where the army will have more and more importance in our lives. ... And before it is all over, democracy, noble and delicate as it is, may give way. ... Indeed, democracy is the special condition ... we will be called upon to defend in the coming years. That will be enormously difficult because the combination of the corporation, the military and the complete investiture of the flag with mass spectator sports has set up a pre-fascistic atmosphere in America already.[12]

23

DISSENT AND RESISTANCE
IN AMERICA

The crime of making Americans aware of their own history
(October 4, 2011)

Is history getting too close for comfort for the fragile little American heart and mind? Their schools and their favorite media have done an excellent job of keeping them ignorant of what their favorite country has done to the rest of the world, but lately some discomforting points of view have managed to find their way into this well-defended American consciousness.

First, Congressman Ron Paul during a presidential debate last month expressed the belief that those who carried out the September 11 attack were retaliating for the many abuses perpetrated against Arab countries by the United States over the years. The audience booed him, loudly.

Then, popular-song icon Tony Bennett, in a radio interview, said the United States caused the 9/11 attacks because of its actions in the Persian Gulf, adding that President George W. Bush had told him in 2005 that the Iraq War was a mistake. Bennett of course came under some nasty fire; so much so that he felt obliged to post a statement on Facebook saying that his experience in World War II had taught him that 'war is the lowest form of human behavior.' He said there's no excuse for terrorism, and he added, 'I'm sorry if my statements suggested anything other than an expression of love for my country' (NBC September 21). Fox News, discussing Bennett, carefully chose its comments charmingly as usual, using words like 'insane,' 'twisted mind,' and 'absurdities' (September 24).

Then came the Islamic cleric, Anwar al-Awlaki, an American citizen, who for some time had been blaming US foreign policy in the Middle East as the cause of anti-American hatred and terrorist acts. So the United States killed him. Ron Paul and Tony Bennett can count themselves lucky.

What, then, is the basis of all this? What has the United States actually been doing in the Middle East in the recent past?

- the shooting down of two Libyan planes in 1981
- the bombing of Lebanon in 1983 and 1984
- the bombing of Libya in 1986
- the bombing and sinking of an Iranian ship in 1987
- the shooting down of an Iranian passenger plane in 1988
- the shooting down of two more Libyan planes in 1989
- the massive bombing of the Iraqi people in 1991
- the continuing bombings and draconian sanctions against Iraq from 1991 to 2003
- the bombing of Afghanistan and Sudan in 1998
- the habitual support of Israel despite the routine devastation and torture it inflicts upon the Palestinian people
- the habitual condemnation of Palestinian resistance to this
- the abduction of 'suspected terrorists' from Muslim countries, such as Malaysia, Pakistan, Lebanon and Albania, who were then taken to places like Egypt and Saudi Arabia, where they were tortured
- the large military and hi-tech presence in Islam's holiest land, Saudi Arabia, and elsewhere in the Persian Gulf region
- the support of numerous undemocratic, authoritarian Middle

East governments from the Shah of Iran to Mubarak of Egypt
to the Saudi royal family

- the invasion, bombing, and occupation of Afghanistan, 2001
  to the present, and Iraq, 2003 to the present
- the bombings and continuous firing of missiles to assassinate
  individuals in Somalia, Yemen, Pakistan, and Libya during
  the period of 2006–2011
- the overthrow of the Libyan government of Muammar Gaddafi
  in 2011.

It can't be repeated or emphasized enough. The biggest lie
of the 'war on terror', although weakening, is that the targets of
America's attacks have an irrational hatred of the United States
and its way of life, based on religious and cultural misunder-
standings and envy. The large body of evidence to the contrary
includes a 2004 report from the Defense Science Board, 'a Federal
advisory committee established to provide independent advice to
the Secretary of Defense.' The report states:

> Muslims do not hate our freedom, but rather they hate our
> policies. The overwhelming majority voice their objections to
> what they see as one-sided support in favor of Israel and against
> Palestinian rights, and the long-standing, even increasing, support
> for what Muslims collectively see as tyrannies, most notably Egypt,
> Saudi Arabia, Jordan, Pakistan and the Gulf states. Thus, when
> American public diplomacy talks about bringing democracy to Is-
> lamic societies, this is seen as no more than self-serving hypocrisy.

The report concludes: 'No public relations campaign can save
America from flawed policies.'[1]

In the words of Sam Smith, editor of *The Progressive Review*,
'Homeland security is a rightwing concept fostered following 9–11
as the answer to the effects of 50 years of bad foreign policies in
the middle east. The amount of homeland security we actually
need is inversely related to how good our foreign policy is.'

The difference between a congressman
and a normal human being

A report in the *Washington Post* (January 30, 2007), headlined 'Soldier's Death Strengthens Senators' Antiwar Resolve', informs us that Senators Christopher Dodd (D–Conn.) and John Kerry (D–Mass.) have been rather upset upon learning of the death in Iraq of an army captain whom they had met on a visit to the country in December, 2006 and who made a strong impression upon them. Dodd has been 'radicalized,' the story says, and Kerry has been 'energized' in his opposition to the war.

Why, it must be asked, does it take the death of someone they met by chance to fire up their anti-war sentiments? Many millions of Americans, and many millions more around the world, have protested the war vehemently and passionately without having met any of the war's casualties. What do these protestors have inside of them that so many members of Congress seem to lack?

'This was the kind of person you don't forget,' said Dodd. 'You mention the number dead, 3,000, the 22,000 wounded, and you almost see the eyes glaze over. But you talk about an individual like this, who was doing his job, a hell of a job, but was also willing to talk about what was wrong, it's a way to really bring it to life, to connect.'

Dear reader, is it the same for you? Do your eyes glaze over when you read or hear about the dead and wounded of Iraq?

Neither senator has apparently been 'energized' enough to call for the immediate withdrawal of American forces from Iraq. That would be too 'radical.'

This gap – emotional and intellectual – between members of Congress and normal human beings has been with us for ages of course. The anti-Vietnam War movement burst out of the starting gate back in August 1964, with hundreds of people demonstrating in New York. Many of these early dissenters took apart and critically examined the administration's statements about the war's origin, its current situation, and its rosy picture of the future. They found continuous omission, contradiction, and duplicity, became quickly and wholly cynical, and called for immediate and unconditional withdrawal. This was a state of intellect and principle it took members of Congress – and then only a minority – until the 1970s to reach. The same can be said of the mass media. And even then – even today – our political and media elite viewed Vietnam only as a 'mistake'; that is, it was 'the wrong way' to fight communism, not that the United States should not be traveling all over the globe to spew violence against anything labeled 'communism' in the first place. Essentially, the only thing these best and brightest have learned from Vietnam is that we should not have fought in Vietnam.

The revolution was televised

In his seminal song, 'The Revolution Will Not Be Televised', Gil Scott-Heron told people in the 1970s (which, I maintain, were not unlike the fabled 1960s) that a revolution was coming, that they would no longer be able to live their normal daily life, that they should no longer *want* to live their normal daily life, that they would have to learn to be more serious about this thing they were always prattling about, this thing they called 'revolution.'

Fast Forward to 2009 … Gil Scott-Heron, now a ripe old 60, was interviewed by the *Washington Post* (August 26):

> WP: In the early 1970s, you came out with 'The Revolution Will Not Be Televised,' about the erosion of democracy in America. You all but predicted that there would be a revolution in which a brainwashed nation would come to its senses. What do you think now? Did we have a revolution?
>
> GS-H: Yes, the election of President Obama was the revolution.

Oh? So *that's* it? That's what we took clubs over our heads for... tear gas, jail cells, and permanent police and FBI files... published a million issues of the underground press? To get a president who doesn't have a revolutionary bone in his body? Not a muscle or nerve or tissue or organ that seriously questions cherished establishment beliefs concerning terrorism, permanent war, Israel, torture, marijuana, healthcare, and the primacy of profit over the environment and all else? Karl Marx is surely turning over in his London grave. If the modern counterrevolutionary United States had existed at the time of the American Revolution, it would have crushed that revolution. And a colonial (white) Barack Obama would have worked diligently to achieve some sort of bipartisan compromise with the King of England, telling him we need to look forward, not backward.

Democracy American Style. You gotta problem wit dat?

Here's White House spokeswoman Dana Perino at a March 20, 2008 press briefing:

REPORTER: The American people are being asked to die and pay for this, and you're saying that they have no say in this war?

PERINO: I didn't say that ... this President was elected –

REPORTER: Well, what it amounts to is you saying we have no input at all.

PERINO: You had input. The American people have input every four years, and that's the way our system is set up.[2]

In 1941, Edward Dowling, editor and priest, commented: 'The two greatest obstacles to democracy in the United States are, first, the widespread delusion among the poor that we have a democracy, and second, the chronic terror among the rich, lest we get it.'

There have as often been the same 'causes' for wars that did not happen as for wars that did

Henry Allingham died in Britain on July 18, 2009 at age 113, believed to have been the world's oldest man. A veteran of World War I, he spent his final years reminding the British people about their service members killed during the war, which came to about a million: 'I want everyone to know,' he said during an interview in November. 'They died for us.'[3]

The whole million? Each one died for Britain? In the most useless imperialist war of the twentieth century? No, let me correct that – the most useless imperialist war *of all time*. The British Empire, the French Empire, the Russian Empire, and the wannabe American Empire joined in battle against the Austro-Hungarian Empire and the Ottoman Empire as youthful bodies and spirits sank endlessly into the wretched mud of Belgium and Germany, the pools of blood of Russia and France. The wondrous nobility of it all is enough to make you swallow hard, fight back the tears, light a few candles, and throw up. Imagine, by the middle of this century Vietnam veterans in their nineties and hundreds will be speaking of how each of their 58,000 war buddies died for America. By 2075 we'll be hearing the same stirring message from ancient vets of Iraq and Afghanistan. How many will remember that there were mammoth protest movements against their glorious, holy crusades?

The time hundreds of thousands of American soldiers refused to fight

It's a very long shot to get large numbers of soldiers to angrily protest a military action. But consider the period following the end of World War II. Late 1945 and early 1946 saw what is likely the greatest troop revolt that has ever occurred in a victorious army. Hundreds of thousands, if not millions, of American soldiers protested all over the world because they were not being sent home even though the war was over. The GIs didn't realize it at first, but many soon came to understand that the reason they were being transferred from Europe and elsewhere to various places in the Pacific area, instead of being sent home, was that the United States was concerned about uprisings against colonialism, which, in the minds of Washington foreign-policy officials, was equated with communism and other nasty un-American things. The uprisings were occurring in British colonies, in Dutch colonies, in French colonies, as well as in the American colony of the Philippines.

In the Philippines there were repeated mass demonstrations by GIs who were not eager to be used against the left-wing Huk guerrillas. The *New York Times* reported in January 1946 about one of these demonstrations: "'The Philippines are capable of handling their own internal problems,' was the slogan voiced by several speakers. Many extended the same point of view to China."[4]

American marines were sent to China to support the Nationalist government of Chang Kai-shek against the Communists of Mao Tse-tung and Chou En-lai. They were sent to the Netherlands Indies (Indonesia) to be of service to the Dutch in their suppression of native nationalists. And American troop ships were used to transport the French military to France's former colony in Vietnam. (Did anyone say 'imperialism'?) These and other actions of Washington led to numerous large GI protests in Japan, Guam, Saipan, Korea, India, Germany, England, France, and Andrews Field, Maryland, all concerned with the major slowdown in demobilization and the uses for which the soldiers were being employed. There were hunger strikes and mass mailings to Congress from the soldiers and their huge body of support in the States. In January 1946, Senator Edwin Johnson of Colorado declared 'It is distressing and humiliating to all Americans to read in every newspaper in the land accounts of near mutiny in the Army.'[5]

On January 13, 1946, five hundred American servicemen in Paris adopted a set of demands called 'The Enlisted Man's Magna Charta,' calling for radical reforms of the master–slave relationship between officers and enlisted men; also demanding the removal of Secretary of War Robert Patterson. In the Philippines, soldier sentiment against the reduced demobilization crystalized in a meeting of GIs that voted unanimously to ask Secretary Patterson and certain senators: 'What is the Army's position in the Philippines, especially in relation to the reestablishment of the Eighty-sixth Infantry Division on a combat basis?'[6]

By the summer of 1946 there had been a huge demobilization of the armed forces, although there's no way of knowing with any exactness how much of that was due to the GIs' protests.[7]

If this is how American soldiers could be inspired and organized in the wake of 'The Good War,' imagine what can be done today in the midst of America's 'God-awful Wars.'

24

RELIGION

Christopher Hitchens, Saddam Hussein, and religion
(June 8, 2007)

Christopher Hitchens published his book *God Is Not Great* in the spring of 2007. It's a compilation of the many terrible things done in the name of God (or god) by various religions over the centuries, far in excess, the book posits, of the terrible things done by the secular world. The holy horrors continue today, of course, perhaps worse than ever. If the leaders and would-be leaders of Lebanon, Pakistan, the United States, Israel, Palestine, Afghanistan, Somalia, and some other countries were secular humanists our poor old world would not appear to be another planet's hell. Organized religion has a lot to answer for.

I have no particular quarrel with the Hitchens book's general theme. But when I first read a review of it I wondered how the author dealt with Saddam Hussein and his secular government in Iraq. Here was a guy who was genuinely a baddie, but not a religious fanatic at all. The problem for Hitchens was that being an ardent supporter of the US war against Iraq he had to dispel the notion that the United States had overthrown a secular government. Hitchens, however, came up with a simple but elegant solution: he made Saddam and his regime 'religious'! Saddam, he writes, 'had decked out his whole rule ... as one of piety and jihad' [against whom he doesn't say, and I can't either]. 'Those who regarded his regime as a "secular" one are deluding themselves.'[1]

Islamic sharia law is now imposed in many parts of Iraq, with numerous horror stories of its enforcement against young men and women for their co-mingling, their clothing, their music, dancing, and so on. The number of family honor killings based on religion has jumped. Mosques and the buildings of other religions, including Christian Assyrians, have suffered many serious attacks. These things were rare to non-existent under Saddam Hussein, when Shias and Sunnis regularly intermarried and Muslims did not need to escape from Iraq by the thousands in fear of other Muslims; neither did Jews or Christians. (In his last year or so in power, Saddam Hussein spoke in religious terms more often than earlier, but this appeared to be little more than paying lip service to the anger stirred up in Iraq, as elsewhere in the Middle East, by Washington's War on Terror.)

This, then, is what Hitchens's 'Oh what a lovely war!' has given birth to. The irony for a person like him might be unbearable if he were not rescued by denial.

It will not have passed unnoticed that Saddam Hussein's Iraq is not the only secular government overthrown by the United States which led to a very religious successor. In Afghanistan in the 1980s and early 1990s, the US masterminded the overthrow of the 'communist' government, which led to rule by Islamic fundamentalists, from which the Taliban emerged.

Imperialist fundamentalists also have a lot to answer for.

You can love your mom, eat lotsa apple pie, and wave the American flag, but if you don't believe in God you are a hell-bound subversive

A 2006 study by the University of Minnesota's Department of Sociology identified atheists as 'America's most distrusted minority.' University researchers found that Americans rate atheists below Muslims, recent immigrants, homosexuals and other minority groups in 'sharing their vision of American society.' Atheists are also the minority group most Americans are least willing to allow their children to marry. The researchers conclude that atheists offer 'a glaring exception to the rule of increasing social tolerance over the last 30 years.'

Many of the study's respondents associated atheism with an array of moral indiscretions ranging from criminal behavior to rampant materialism and cultural elitism. The study's lead researcher believes a fear of moral decline and resulting social disorder is behind the findings. 'Americans believe they share more than rules and procedures with their fellow citizens, they share an understanding of right and wrong. Our findings seem to rest on a view of atheists as self-interested individuals who are not concerned with the common good.'[2]

Hmmm. I've been a political activist for more than forty years. I've marched and fought and published weekly newspapers along-side countless atheists and agnostics who have risked jail and police brutality, and who have forsaken a much higher standard of living for no purpose other than the common good. Rampant materialism? Hardly. 'Secular humanism,' many atheists call it. And we don't read about mobs of atheists stoning, massacring, or otherwise harming or humiliating human beings who do not share their non-beliefs. Never. That's what the believers do. All over the world.

The public attitude depicted by this survey may derive in part from the Cold War upbringing of so many Americans – the idea and the image of the 'Godless atheistic communist.' But I think even more significant than that is the deep-seated feeling of insecurity, even threat, that atheists can bring out in the religious, putting into question, consciously or unconsciously, their core beliefs and way of life.

You must wonder at times, as I do, how this world became so unbearably cruel, corrupt, unjust, and stupid. Can it have descended to this remarkable level by chance, or was it planned? It's enough to make one believe in God. Or the Devil.

American Muslims and other conservatives

In March of 2006 I agreed to speak on a panel at the American-Arab Anti-Discrimination Committee convention, to be held in June in Washington, DC. The panel was called 'America, Empire, Democracy and the Middle East.' Then someone at the ADC apparently realized that I was the person whose book had been recommended by Osama bin Laden in January, and they tried to cancel my appearance with phoney excuses. I objected, calling them cowards; they relented, then changed their mind again, telling me finally 'all of the seats on the journalism panel, for the ADC convention, are filled.' Two months after our agreement, they had discovered that all the panel seats were filled.

American Muslims are very conservative. 72 percent of them voted for Bush in 2000, before they got a taste of his police state. University officials are also conservative, or can easily be bullied by campus conservative organizations which are part of a well-financed national campaign (think David Horowitz's Campus Watch) to attack the left on campus, be they faculty, students, or outside speakers. In the six years following the bin Laden recommendation I had virtually no university speaking engagements, compared with five to ten per year earlier; on several occasions students tried to arrange something for me but were not successful at convincing school officials.

Speakout, a California agency which places progressive speakers on campuses, informed me that the Horowitz-type groups have succeeded in cutting sharply into their business.

Blasphemers and heros

In January of 2011 Salman Taseer was murdered in Pakistan. He was the governor of Punjab province and a member of the secular Pakistan People's Party. The man who killed him, Mumtaz Qadri, was lauded by some as a hero, showering rose petals on him. Photos taken at the scene show him smiling.

Taseer had dared to speak out against Pakistan's stringent anti-blasphemy law, calling for leniency for a Christian mother sentenced to death under the blasphemy ban. A national group of 500 religious scholars praised the assassin and issued a warning to those who mourned Taseer. 'One who supports a blasphemer is also a blasphemer,' the group said in a statement, which warned journalists, politicians, and intellectuals to 'learn' from the killing. 'What Qadri did has made every Muslim proud.'[3]

Nice, really nice, very civilized. It's no wonder that decent, God-fearing Americans believe that this kind of thinking and behavior justify Washington's multiple wars; that this is what the United States is fighting against – Islamic fanatics, homicidal maniacs, who kill their own countrymen over some esoteric piece of religious dogma, who want to kill Americans partly over some other imagined holy sin, because we're 'infidels' or 'blasphemers.' How can we reason with such people? Where is the common humanity the naive pacifists and anti-war activists would like us to honor?

But war can be seen as America's religion – most recently Pakistan, Iraq, Afghanistan, Somalia, Yemen, Libya, and many more in the past, all non-believers in Washington's Church of Our Lady of Eternal Invasion, Sacred Bombing, and Immaculate Torture, all condemned to death for blasphemy, as each day the United States unleashes blessed robotic death machines called Predators flying over their lands to send 'Hellfire' (*sic*) missiles screaming into wedding parties, funerals, homes; thousands of them killed by now, as long as the US can claim each time – whether correctly or not – that among their number was a prominent blasphemer, call him Taliban, or al-Qaeda, or 'insurgent,' or 'militant.' How can we reason with such people, the ones in the CIA who operate these drone bombers? What is the difference between them and Mumtaz Qadri? Qadri was smiling in satisfaction after carrying out his holy mission. The CIA man sits comfortably in a room in Nevada and plays his holy video game, then goes out to a satisfying dinner while his victims lay dying. Mumtaz Qadri believes passionately in something called Paradise. The CIA man believes passionately in something called American Exceptionalism.

Extending the comparison: in 2008 a young American named Sharif Mobley moved to Yemen to study Arabic and religion. American officials maintain that his purpose was actually to join a terror group. They 'see Mobley as one of a growing cadre of native-born Americans who are drawn to violent jihad.'[4] Can one not say as well that the many young native-born Americans who voluntarily join the military to fight in one of America's many foreign wars 'are drawn to violent jihad'?

And are they not lauded by many as a hero, showered with rose petals as they smile?

25

LAUGHING DESPITE THE EMPIRE

Happy New Year. Here's what to look forward to in the coming year

JANUARY 22: Congress passes a law requiring that all persons arrested in anti-war demonstrations be sterilized. House Speaker John Boehner declares it is 'God's will.' House Minority Leader Nancy Pelosi says that she has some reservation because there's no provision for a right of appeal.

FEBRUARY 15: Ron Paul assassinated by a man named Oswald Harvey.

FEBRUARY 18: Oswald Harvey, while in solitary confinement and guarded round the clock by 1,200 policemen and the entire 3rd Army Brigade, is killed by man named Ruby Jackson.

FEBRUARY 26: Ruby Jackson suddenly dies in prison of a rare Asian disease heretofore unknown in the Western hemisphere

MARCH 6: US president Hopey Changey announces new draconian sanctions against Iran, Syria, North Korea, Pakistan, Nicaragua, Venezuela, and Cuba, declaring that they all possess weapons of mass destruction, are an imminent threat to the United States, have close ties to al-Qaeda and the Taliban, are aiding Islamic terrorists in Somalia, were involved in 9/11, played a role in the assassination of John F. Kennedy and the attack on Pearl Harbor, do not believe in God or American Exceptionalism, and are all 'really bad guys.'

APRIL 1: Bolivian military forces overthrow President Evo Morales. The US State Department decries the loss of democracy.

APRIL 2: The US recognizes the new Bolivian military junta, sells it 100 jet fighters and 200 tanks.

APRIL 3: Revolution breaks out in Bolivia endangering the military junta; 40,000 American marines are sent to La Paz to quell the uprising.

APRIL 8: Dick Cheney announces from his hospital bed that the United States has finally discovered caches of weapons of mass destruction in Iraq – 'So all those doubters can now just go "F" themselves.' The former vice president, however, refuses to provide any details of the find because, he says, to do so might reveal intelligence sources or methods.

APRIL 10: ExxonMobil, ChevronTexaco, General Electric, General Motors, AT&T, Ford, and IBM merge to form 'Free Enterprise, Inc.'

APRIL 16: Free Enterprise, Inc. seeks to purchase Guatemala and Haiti. Citigroup refuses to sell.

APRIL 18: Free Enterprise, Inc. purchases Citigroup.

MAY 5: The Democratic Party changes its name to the Republican Lite Party, and announces the opening of a joint bank account with the Republicans so that corporate lobbyists need make out only one check. In celebration of the change the new party calls for eliminating the sales tax on yachts.

MAY 11: China claims to have shot down an American spy plane over the center of China. The State Department categorically denies the story.

MAY 12: The State Department admits that an American plane may have 'inadvertently' strayed 2,000 miles into China, but denies that it was a spy plane.

MAY 13: The State Department admits that the plane may have been a spy plane but denies that it was piloted by a US government employee.

MAY 14: The State Department admits that the pilot was a civilian employee of a Defense Department contractor but denies that China exists.

JUNE 11: Homeland Security announces plan to collect the DNA at birth of every child born in the United States.

JULY 1: The air in Los Angeles reaches so bad a pollution level that the rich begin to hire undocumented workers to breathe for them.

AUGUST 6: The Justice Department announces that six people have been arrested in New York in connection with a plan to bomb the United Nations, the Empire State Building, the Times Square subway station, Madison Square Garden, and Lincoln Center.

AUGUST 7: Charges are dropped against four of 'The New York Six' when it is determined that they are FBI agents.

AUGUST 16: At a major demonstration in Washington, the Tea Party demands an end to all government expenditures. They also warn Congress not to touch Social Security or Medicare.

AUGUST 26: Texas executes a 16-year-old girl for having an abortion and a 12-year-old boy for possession of marijuana.

SEPTEMBER 3: The Labor Department announces that Labor Day will become a celebration of America's gratitude to its corporations, a day dedicated to the memory of J.P. Morgan and Pinkerton strikebreakers killed in the line of duty.

SEPTEMBER 12: The draft is reinstated for males and females, aged 16 to 45. Those who are missing a limb or are blind can apply for non-combat roles.

SEPTEMBER 14: Riots breaks out in twenty-four American cities in protest at the new draft. 200,000 American troops are brought home from Afghanistan, Iraq, and twenty-five other countries to put down the riots.

SEPTEMBER 28: The Tea Party calls for giving embryos the vote.

OCTOBER 19: Cops the world over form a new association, Policemen's International Governing Society. PIGS announces that its first goal will be to mount a campaign against the notion that a person is innocent until proven guilty, in those countries where the quaint notion still dwells.

NOVEMBER 8: The turnout for the US presidential election is 9.6 percent. The voting ballots are all imprinted: 'From one person, one vote, to one dollar, one vote.' The winner is 'None of the above.'

NOVEMBER 11: The US prison population reaches 2.5 million. It is determined that at least 70 percent of the prisoners would not have been incarcerated a century ago, for the acts they committed were then not criminal violations.

DECEMBER 3: The Supreme Court rules that police may search anyone if they have reasonable grounds for believing that the person has pockets.

DECEMBER 16: The Occupy Movement sets up a tent on the White House lawn. An hour later a missile fired from a drone leaves but a thin wisp of smoke.

People who like this sort of thing will find this the sort of thing they like

To my dear readers in the United States and around the world, in the spirit of the season, I wish each of you your choice of the following:

Merry Christmas
Happy Chanukah
Joyous Eid

Festive Kwanza

Happy New Year

Gleeful Occupy

Erotic Pagan Rite

Internet Virtual Holiday

Heartwarming Satanic Sacrifice

Devout Atheist Season's Greetings

Possessed Laying-on-of-Hands Ceremony

Really Neat Reincarnation with Auras and Crystals

And may your name never appear on a Homeland Security 'No-fly list'.

May you not vex a marginally literate high-school graduate with a badge, a gun, and a can of pepper spray.

May your abuses at the hands of authority be only cruel, degrading and inhuman, nothing that Mr Obama or Mr Cheney would call torture.

May you or your country never experience a NATO or US humanitarian intervention, liberation, or involuntary suicide.

May neither your labor movement nor your elections be supported by the National Endowment for Democracy.

May the depleted uranium, cluster bombs, white phosphorous, and napalm which fall upon your land be as precisely guided and harmless as the State Department says they are.

May you receive for Christmas a copy of *An Arsonist's Guide to the Homes of Pentagon Officials*.

May you not fall sick in the United States without health insurance, nor desire to go to an American university while being less than wealthy.

May you rediscover what the poor in eighteenth-century France discovered, that rich people's heads can be mechanically separated from their shoulders if they refuse to listen to reason.

May you be given the choice of euthanasia instead of having to watch Republican primary debates.

26

BUT WHAT CAN WE DO?

Some thoughts that Occupy my mind
(December 2, 2011)

When the Vietnam War became history, and the protest signs and the bullhorns were put away, so too was the serious side of most protestors' alienation and hostility toward the government. They returned, with minimal resistance, to the restless pursuit of success, and the belief that the choice facing the world was either 'capitalist democracy' or 'communist dictatorship.' The war had been an aberration was the implicit verdict, a blemish on an otherwise humane American record. The fear felt by the powers-that-be that society's fabric was unraveling and that the Republic was hanging by a thread turned out to be little more than media hype; it had been great copy.

I mention this to explain why I've been reluctant to jump with both feet on the Occupy bandwagon. I first thought that if nothing else the approaching winter would do them in; if not, it would be the demands of their lives – they have to make some money at some point, attend classes somewhere, lovers and friends and family they have to cater to somewhere; lately I've been thinking it's the police that will do them in, writing *finis* to their marvelous movement adventure – if you hold the system up to a mirror the system can go crazy.

But now I don't know. Those young people, and the old ones as well, keep surprising me, with their dedication and energy, their camaraderie and courage, their optimism and innovation, their non-violence and their keen awareness of the danger of being co-opted, their focusing on the economic institutions more than on the politicians or political parties. There is also their splendid signs and slogans, walking from New York to Washington, and not falling apart following the despicable police destruction of the Occupy Wall Street encampment. They've given a million young people other ideas about how to spend the rest of their lives, and commandeered a remarkable amount of media space. The *Washington Post* on several occasions has devoted full-page or near-full-page sympathetic coverage. Occupy is being taken increasingly seriously by virtually all media.

Yet the 1960s and 1970s were also a marvelous movement adventure – for me as much as for anyone – but nothing actually changed in US foreign policy as a result of our endless protests, many of which were also very innovative. American imperialism has continued to add to its brutal record right up to this very moment. We can't even claim Vietnam as a victory for our protests. The anti-Vietnam protest movement lasted nine years, 1964–73, before the United States left the country. It's difficult to ascribe cause and effect to that.

It has greatly helped Occupy's growth and survival that they have seldom mentioned foreign policy. That's much more sensitive ground than corporate abuse. Foreign policy gets into flag-waving, 'our brave boys' risking their lives, American exceptionalism, nationalism, patriotism, loyalty, treason, terrorism, 'anti-American,' 'conspiracy theorist' … all those emotional icons that mainstream America uses to separate a Good American from one who *ain't really one of us.*

Foreign policy cannot be ignored permanently, of course, if for no other reason than that the nation's wealth that's wasted on war could be used to pay for anything Occupy calls for... or anything *anyone* calls for.

The education which Occupy has caused to be thrust upon the citizenry – about corporate abuse and criminality, political corruption, inequality, poverty, and so on, virtually all unprosecuted – would be highly significant if America were a democracy. But, as it is, more and more people can learn more and more about these matters, and get more and more angry, but have nowhere to turn to, to effectuate meaningful change. Money must be removed from the political process. Completely. It is my favorite Latin expression: *sine qua non* – 'without which, nothing.'

If not now, when? If not here, where? If not you, who?
(October 1, 2007)

I used to give thought to what historical time and place I would like to have lived in. Europe in the 1930s was usually my first choice. As the war clouds darkened, I'd be surrounded by intrigue, spies omnipresent, matters of life and death pressing down, the opportunity to be courageous and principled. I pictured myself helping desperate people escape to America. It was real Hollywood stuff; think *Casablanca*. And when the Spanish Republic fell to Franco and his fascist forces, aided by the German and Italian fascists (while the United States and Britain stood aside, when not actually aiding the fascists), everything in my imaginary scenario would have heightened – the fate of Europe hung in the balance. Then the Nazis marched into Austria, then Czechoslovakia, then Poland... one could have devoted one's life to working against all this, trying to hold back the fascist tide. What could be more thrilling, more noble?

Miracle of miracles, miracle of time machines, I'm actually living in this imagined period, watching as the Bush fascists march into Afghanistan, bombing it into a 'failed state'; then they march into Iraq – death, destruction, and utterly ruined lives for 24 million human beings; threatening more of the same endless night of hell for the people of Iran; overthrowing Jean-Bertrand Aristide in Haiti; bombing helpless refugees in Somalia; relentless attempts to destabilize and punish Cuba, Venezuela, Bolivia, Nicaragua, Gaza, and other non-believers in the empire's God-given mission. Sadly, my most common reaction to this real-life scenario, daily in fact, is less heroic and more feeling scared or depressed; not for myself personally but for our one and only world. The news every day, which I consume in large portions, slashes away at my *joie de vivre*; it's not just the horror stories of American military power run amok abroad and the injustices of the ever-expanding police state at home, but all the lies and stupidity which drive me up the wall, making me constantly changing stations, turning the television or radio off, turning the newspaper page.

Nonetheless, I must tell you, comrades, that at the same time our contemporary period also brings out in me a measure of what I imagined for my 1930s' life. Our present world is in just as great peril, even more so when one considers the impending environmental catastrophe. The Bush [and now Obama] fascist tide must be stopped.

Usually when I'm asked 'But what can we do?', my reply is something along the lines of what I said earlier about educating yourself and as many others as you can until your numbers reach a critical mass; see it as the planting of seeds, to provide the raw sprouts that can grow into direct action. I'm afraid that this advice, whatever historical correctness it may embody, is not terribly inspiring. However, I've assembled four wise men to add their thoughts, hopefully raising the inspiration level a little. Let's call them the 'patron saints of lost causes.'

I.F. Stone:

> The only kinds of fights worth fighting are those you are going to
> lose because somebody has to fight them and lose and lose and lose
> until someday, somebody who believes as you do wins. In order for
> somebody to win an important, major fight 100 years hence, a lot
> of other people have got to be willing – for the sheer fun and joy of
> it – to go right ahead and fight, knowing you're going to lose. You
> mustn't feel like a martyr. You've got to enjoy it.

Howard Zinn:

> People think there must be some magical tactic, beyond the tradi-
> tional ones – protests, demonstrations, vigils, civil disobedience
> – but there is no magical panacea, only persistence.

Noam Chomsky:

> There are no magic answers, no miraculous methods to overcome
> the problems we face, just the familiar ones: honest search for
> understanding, education, organization, action that raises the
> cost of state violence for its perpetrators or that lays the basis for
> institutional change – and the kind of commitment that will persist
> despite the temptations of disillusionment, despite many failures
> and only limited successes, inspired by the hope of a brighter
> future.

Sam Smith:

> Those who think history has left us helpless should recall the
> abolitionist of 1830, the feminist of 1870, the labor organizer of
> 1890, and the gay or lesbian writer of 1910. They, like us, did not
> get to choose their time in history but they, like us, did get to
> choose what they did with it. Knowing what we know now about
> how these things turned out, but also knowing how long it took,
> would we have been abolitionists in 1830, or feminists in 1870, and
> so on?

NOTES

INTRODUCTION

1. http://killinghope.org/essays6/othrow.htm.
2. See chapter 18 of William Blum, *Rogue State: A Guide to the World's Only Superpower* (Common Courage Press, Monroe ME, 2005).
3. http://killinghope.org/bblum6/assass.htm Depending on how you count it, the total attempts can run into the hundreds; targeting Fidel Castro alone totals 634 according to Cuban intelligence; see Fabian Escalante, *Executive Action: 634 Ways to Kill Fidel Castro* (Ocean Press, Melbourne, 2006).
4. http://killinghope.org/superogue/bomb.htm.
5. http://killinghope.org/bblum6/suppress.html.
6. Afghanistan, Albania, Algeria, Angola, Australia, Bolivia, Bosnia, Brazil, British Guiana (now Guyana), Bulgaria, Cambodia, Chad, Chile, China, Colombia, Congo (also as Zaire), Costa Rica, Cuba, Dominican Republic, East Timor, Ecuador, Egypt, El Salvador, Fiji, France, Germany (plus East Germany), Ghana, Greece, Grenada, Guatemala, Haiti, Honduras, India, Indonesia, Iran, Iraq, Italy, Jamaica, Japan, Kuwait, Laos, Lebanon, Libya, Mongolia, Morocco, Nepal, Nicaragua, North Korea, Pakistan, Palestine, Panama, Peru, Philippines, Portugal, Russia, Seychelles, Slovakia, Somalia, South Africa, South Korea, Soviet Union, Sudan, Suriname, Syria, Thailand, Uruguay, Venezuela, Vietnam (plus North Vietnam), Yemen (plus South Yemen).
7. *Washington Post*, March 5, 2003, p. 19, column by Al Kamen.
8. *Washington Post*, December 27, 2001, p. C1.
9. White House, Office of the Press Secretary, June 1, 2002.
10. Steve Vogel, *The Pentagon: A History* (Random House, New York, 2008).
11. *The Black Commentator* (weekly progressive Internet magazine), www.blackcommentator.com, June 8, 2006.
12. *Aviation Week and Space Technology*, August 5, 1996, p. 51.
13. Speaking to the National Space Club, Washington, DC, September 15, 1997.
14. Excerpts are in the same sequence as found in the August 1997 brochure beginning on page 1.

15. March 2004, www.stratcom.mil/fact_sheets/fact_sm.html. In 2002, the US Space Command was merged with the US Strategic Command.
16. From article in *Dissident Voice* (online magazine), February 10, 2003.
17. Natalia Narochnitskaya, vice chairman of the international affairs committee in the state Duma, the lower house of Russia's parliament, *Washington Post*, April 3, 2006, p. 14.
18. *Village Voice* (New York), November 27, 2001, p. 46; *Scotland on Sunday*, November 25, 2001.
19. Elting E. Morison, ed., *The Letters of Theodore Roosevelt*, vol. 2 (Harvard University Press, Cambridge MA, 1951), pp. 1176-7.
20. *Z magazine*, Noam Chomsky's ZSpace Page, www.zmag.org/znet, July 21, 2005.
21. Associated Press, CNN.com, December 25, 2007.

CHAPTER 1

1. *New York Times*, December 22, 1989, p. 17.
2. Ibid., p. 16.
3. *Los Angeles Times*, December 1, 1990.
4. *Washington Post*, January 1, 2007.
5. National Prayer Breakfast, Washington, DC, February 7, 2008.
6. Testimony before the House Committee on Oversight and Government Reform, October 2, 2007.
7. *Washington Post*, May 28, 2003.
8. Washington Post, July 20, 2004, statement attributed to President Bush in the Lancaster (PA) *New Era* newspaper from a private meeting with Amish families on July 9. The White House later said Bush said no such thing. (Yes, we know how the Amish lie.)
9. *Los Angeles Times*, June 7, 1991.
10. CBS, *60 Minutes*, May 12, 1996.
11. Associated Press, December 22, 2006.
12. Associated Press, April 6, 2011; some obvious errors in the original have been corrected.
13. *New York Times*, November 6, 2003.
14. *New York Times*, April 16, 2002.
15. *Los Angeles Times*, February 24, 1994.
16. Guatemala: Stephen Schlesinger and Stephen Kinzer, *Bitter Fruit: The Untold Story of the American Coup in Guatemala* (Dooubleday, New York, 1982), p. 183. Jagan: Arthur Schlesinger, *A Thousand Days* (Houghton Mifflin, Boston MA, 1965), pp. 774-9. Bishop: Associated Press, 'Leftist Government Officials Visit United States,' May 29, 1983.
17. *The Pentagon Papers* (*New York Times* edition, 1971), pp. 4, 5, 8, 26; William Blum, *Killing Hope: US Military and CIA Interventions since World War II* (Zed Books, London, 2003), p. 123.
18. www.alys.be/pauwels/2publi_the_myth.htm. Available in English, Spanish, French, German, Italian, and Dutch editions.
19. See my essay on the use of the atomic bomb: http://killinghope.org/essays6/abomb.htm.

20. US Agency for International Development, 'Direct Economic Benefits of U.S. Assistance Programs,' 1999.
21. For discussion of various aspects of the Marshall Plan, see for example Joyce and Gabriel Kolko, *The Limits of Power: The World and US Foreign Policy 1945–1954* (Harper & Row, New York, 1972), chs 13, 16, 17; Sallie Pisani, *The CIA and the Marshall Plan* (University Press of Kansas, Lawrence, 1991) *passim*; Frances Stonor Saunders, *The Cultural Cold War: The CIA and the World of Arts and Letters* (New Press, New York, 2000) *passim*.
22. *New York Times*, August 10, 2003.
23. Frances Fitzgerald, *America Revised* (Vintage, New York, 1980), pp. 129, 139.
24. www.foreignpolicy.com/articles/2010/09/07/jared_cohen; *Washington Post*, June 24, 2011.
25. Reuters, August 3, 2009.
26. See my discussion of this question at killinghope.org/essays6/myth.htm.
27. States News Service, July 22, 2005.
28. *Washington Post*, September 29, 2005.
29. *Los Angeles Times*, September 29, 2005.
30. *Washington Post*, October 7, 2005.
31. *Washington Post*, September 30, 2005.
32. *Washington Post*, June 11, 2005.
33. *Boston Globe*, October 12, 2001.
34. White House press briefing, January 7, 2010.
35. *Washington Post*, February 15, 2009.
36. For the full list of US bombings since World War II, see http://killinghope.org/superogue/bomb.htm.
37. *Washington Post*, February 22, 2008.
38. Associated Press, February 21, 2008.
39. *Observer*, October 17 and November 28, 1999.
40. *New York Times*, June 25, 1999.
41. *Observer*, October 17 and November 28, 1999.
42. Associated Press, 'France Confirms It Denied U.S. Jets Air Space, Says Embassy Damaged,' April 15, 1986.
43. Interfax news agency (Moscow), April 2, 2003.
44. CBS News, April 9, 2003.
45. *Los Angeles Times*, May 5, 2004.
46. *Washington Post*, April 17, 2007.
47. Veterans of Foreign Wars convention, August 17, 2009.
48. *Washington Post*, May 26, 2005.
49. Associated Press, May 14, 2002.
50. *New York Times*, September 20, 1999.

CHAPTER 2

1. *Seattle Times*, March 31, 2007.
2. *Washington Post*, March 30, 2007.
3. *Financial Times*, October 4, 2004.
4. *Wall Street Journal*, January 26, 2005.

5. Testimony before the House Subcommittee on Western Hemisphere Affairs, US Congress, April 16, 1985.
6. ABC News, April 3, 2007.
7. *Sunday Telegraph*, February 25, 2007.
8. *Washington Post*, March 18, 2007.
9. Richard Ackland, 'Innocence Ignored at Guantanamo,' *Sydney Morning Herald*, February 24, 2006.
10. *New York Times*, January 17, 2003.
11. Vorin Whan, ed., *A Soldier Speaks: Public Papers and Speeches of General of the Army Douglas MacArthur* (Praeger, New York, 1965).
12. *The Daily News*, February 10, 2006.
13. *Washington Post*, April 14, 2005; United Press International, April 18, 2005.
14. *Time*, July 7, 2006, article by Joshua Marshall; Associated Press, July 14, 2006.
15. Sears case: Knight Ridder Newspapers, June 23, 2006; *Independent*, June 25, 2006; *St. Petersburg Times* (Florida), June 24, 2006; *New York Times*, August 13, 2006.
16. Associated Press, July 14, 2006.
17. Toledo: Associated Press, April 18, 2006; Sears: *South Florida Sun Sentinel*, July 26, 2006.
18. Associated Press, July 8, 2006.
19. *Christian Science Monitor*, October 29, 2010.
20. *Washington Post*, April 14, 2006.
21. Deutsche Presse-Agentur, April 13, 2006.
22. *Miami Herald*, March 26, 1983.
23. www.unodc.org/unodc/terrorism_convention_civil_aviation.html.

CHAPTER 3

1. *Washington Post*, December 18, 2011.
2. *New York Times*, May 19, 2006.
3. BBC, March 4, 2010; *Washington Post*, December 3, 2005.
4. Associated Press, November 11, 2006.
5. United Press International, July 25, 2007.
6. *New York Times*, November 30, 2003.
7. *Washington Post*, September 7, 2007.
8. Mary Eberstadt, ed., *Why I Turned Right: Leading Baby Boom Conservatives Chronicle Their Political Journeys* (Simon & Schuster, New York, 2007), p. 73.
9. National Public Radio (NPR), *Day to Day*, June 6, 2006.
10. Associated Press, December 4, 2006.
11. William Blum, *Rogue State: A Guide to the World's Only Superpower* (Common Courage Press, Monroe ME, 2005), p. 304.
12. CBS, *Evening News*, August 20, 2002.
13. ABC Nightline, December 4, 2002.
14. *60 Minutes II*, February 26, 2003.
15. *Washington Post*, March 1, 2003.

16. Associated Press, July 28, 2010.
17. *60 Minutes*, January 27, 2008. See also Fairness and Accuracy in Reporting, Action Alert, February 1, 2008.
18. *New York Times,* August 21, 2004.
19. www.crudedesigns.org.
20. Interview with Institute for Public Accuracy, Washington, DC, November 22, 2005.
21. Interview by Andy Clark, Amsterdam Forum, December 18, 2005; audio and text at www.informationclearinghouse.info/article11330.htm.
22. *Washington Post*, September 6, 2007.
23. For a good discussion of this, see the Inter Press Service report of November 14, 2007 by Ali al-Fadhily.
24. Associated Press, November 6, 2007.
25. *New York Times*, November 26, 2007.
26. *Washington Post*, December 5, 2007.
27. Joseph Farah, editor of the conservative *WorldNetDaily* (worldnetdaily.com/news/article.asp?article_id=56769), August 6, 2007.
28. Mona Charen, *National Review Online*, July 20, 2007.
29. Search Google News: <bloodbath iraq vietnam> for more examples.
30. *Newsweek*, April 3, 2006.
31. *Washington Post*, April 15, 2006.
32. Associated Press, March 27, 2006.
33. *Philadelphia Inquirer*, March 26, 2006.
34. Dahlia Lithic, Slate.com, March 28, 2006.
35. *Washington Post*, January 2, 2006.
36. Ibid.
37. William Blum, *Freeing the World to Death: Essays on the American Empire* (Common Courage Press, Monroe ME, 2004), pp. 134–8.
38. *Washington Post*, January 3, 2006.
39. Associated Press, September 8, 2002.
40. *New York Times*, November 6, 2003.
41. *Washington Post*, October 22, 2005.
42. *New York Times*, April 10, 1988, sect. 4, p. 3, re Iran; *Washington Post*, August 4 and September 4, 1988.
43. *New York Times*, January 31, 2003.
44. Barry Lando, 'Saddam Hussein, a Biased Trial,' *Le Monde*, October 17, 2005.
45. *New York Times*, October 3, 2005.
46. Reuters news agency, October 17, 2005.
47. *Washington Post*, September 20, 21; Al Jazeera, September 19, 2005.

CHAPTER 4

1. Talk given by the president at Veterans of Foreign Wars convention, August 17, 2009.
2. Talk at the Paul H. Nitze School for Advanced International Studies, Washington, DC, September 20, 2007.
3. See, for example, 'Oil Barons Court Taliban in Texas,' *Telegraph*, December

17, 1997. For further discussion of the TAPI pipeline and related issues, see the article by international petroleum engineer John Foster: www.ensec.org/index.php?option=com_content&view=article&id=233: afghanistan_the_tapi_pipeline_and_energy_geopolitics&cati.

4. *The Times Online*, May 31, 2010.
5. Associated Press, May 31. 2010.
6. Vermont television station WCAX, July 4, 2009, WCAX.com.
7. *Los Angeles Times*, July 6, 2007.
8. Article by Kim Barker, *Chicago Tribune*, July 8, 2007.
9. *Los Angeles Times*, July 6, 2007.
10. *Washington Post*, April 22, 1999.
11. William Blum, *Rogue State: A Guide to the World's Only Superpower* (Common Courage Press, Monroe ME, 2005), pp. 103–4.
12. US Department of the Army, *Afghanistan, A Country Study* (1986), pp. 121, 128, 130, 223, 232.

CHAPTER 5

1. AlterNet, www.alternet.org/, May 5, 2006.
2. Associated Press, December 12, 2006.
3. washingtonpost.com/wp_dyn/content/article/2007/09/24/AR2007092401042.html.
4. nkusa.org/activities/Speeches/2006Iran-ACohen.cfm (Cohen's talk); Alex Spillius, *Telegraph*, December 13, 2006; Associated Press, December 12, 2006.
5. *Globe and Mail* (Toronto), December 13, 2006.
6. Associated Press, December 12, 2006.
7. counterpunch.org/tilley08282006.html.
8. Associated Press, December 16, 2006.
9. *Washington Post*, March 5, 1987.
10. whitehouse.gov/the_press_office/2012/03/04/remarks_president_aipac_policy_conference_0.
11. Haaretz.com (Israel), October 25, 2007; print edition October 26.
12. *Washington Post*, March 5, 2009.
13. CBS, 'Face the Nation,' January 8, 2012; see video at http://ufohunterorguk.com/2012/01/12/us_defense_secretary_leon_panetta_admits_iran_not_making_nuclear_weapons.
14. *Guardian*, January 31, 2012.
15. Fairness and Accuracy in Reporting, www.fair.org/index.php.
16. Reuters, January 12, 2012.
17. killinghope.org/bblum6/assass.htm.
18. Video of Pletka making these remarks at http://politicalcorrection.org/fpmatters/201112020008.
19. www.brookings.edu/~/media/Files/rc/reports/2010/08_arab_opinion_poll_telhami/08_arab_opinion_poll_telhami.pdf.
20. *Washington Post*, December 7, 2007, p. 8.
21. *New York Times*, December 3, 2007.
22. *Washington Post*, December 9, 2007.

23. *Washington Post*, December 4, 2007.
24. *Washington Post*, December 5, 2007.
25. 'How They Stole the Bomb from Us,' December 8, 2007, http://zope.
gush_shalom.org/index_en.html.
26. *New York Times*, February 3, 1992, p. 8.
27. *Guardian*, October 10, 1983.
28. Haaretz.com, October 1, 2007.
29. Haaretz.com, October 25, 2007; print edition October 26.
30. *Newsweek*, October 20, 2007.
31. *Washington Post*, May 6, 2004.
32. *Washington Post*, July 22, 2007, p. B7, op-ed by Dobbins.
33. *Washington Post*, June 18, 2006.

CHAPTER 6

1. *Washington Post*, May 5, 2006, p. B1.
2. *New York Times*, June 30, 2004.
3. *Washington Post*, April 12, 2006, p. C3.
4. Associated Press, November 16, 2005.
5. Talk by Bush at Freedom House, Washington, DC, March 29, 2006.
6. *Los Angeles Times*, May 31, 1991.
7. Associated Press, January 2, 2006.
8. Copley News Service, October 10, 2005.
9. *Washington Post*, June 16, 2007, letter from Andrew Apostolou.
10. killinghope.org/bblum6/bulgaria.htm.
11. For further discussion of this, see William Blum, *Freeing the World to Death* (Common Courage Press, Monroe ME, 2004), pp. 166–71.

CHAPTER 8

1. From a March 5, 2007 press release by Archives of General Psychiatry.
2. *Guardian*, February 17, 2006.
3. Testimony before the International Commission of Inquiry On Crimes Against Humanity Committed by the Bush Administration, New York, session of January 21, 2006.
4. Associated Press, August 1, 2007.
5. Press conference, February 25, 2009, transcript by Federal News Service.
6. Agence France Presse (AFP), January 20, 2009.
7. *New York Times*, December 29, 1998.
8. Associated Press, November 17, 2008.
9. See William Blum, *Rogue State: A Guide to the World's Only Superpower* (Common Courage Press, Monroe ME, 2005), ch. 10, 'Supporting Pol Pot.'
10. See William Blum, *Killing Hope: US Military and CIA Interventions since World War II* (Zed Books, London, 2003), ch. 20, 'Cambodia, 1955–1973.'
11. www.realclearpolitics.com/articles/2009/02/jones_munich_conference.html.
12. Reuters news agency, January 30, 2009.
13. The War Crimes Act (18 U.S.C. 2441).
14. *Haaretz*, January 30, 2009.

15. Blum, *Rogue State*, pp. 71–6.
16. *Los Angeles Times*, February 1, 2009.
17. *New York Times*, February 6, 2009.
18. Fars News Agency (Iran), November 21, 2006.
19. Senate Committee on Veterans' Affairs, 'Is Military Research Hazardous to Veterans' Health? Lessons Spanning Half a Century,' December 8, 1994, p. 5.
20. Ibid., *passim*.
21. *Washington Post*, October 2 and 23, 1996, and July 31, 1997 for the estimated numbers of affected soldiers.
22. *Journal of the American Medical Association*, September 1, 1999, p. 822.
23. *Washington Post*, December 20, 2006, p. 19.
24. Associated Press, January 15, 2006.
25. *Los Angeles Times*, January 29, 2006.
26. *Washington Post*, November 15, 2005.
27. *Washington Post*, November 18, 1996.
28. Reuters, June 10, 2002.
29. Ellen Messer and Marc J. Cohen, 'US Approaches to Food and Nutrition Rights, 1976–2008.'

CHAPTER 9

1. *Sunday Telegraph* (Australia), December 19, 2010.
2. Salon.com, December 15, 2010, www.salon.com/news/wikileaks/index.html?story=/opinion/greenwald/2010/12/14/manning; *Washington Post*, December 16, 2010.
3. *Guardian*, December 17, 2010.
4. *New York Times*, December 19, 2010.
5. *Washington Post*, December 20, 2010.
6. National Public Radio, *Diane Rehm Show*, December 9, 2010.
7. *Guardian*, December 21, 2010.
8. www.informationclearinghouse.info/article27119.htm.
9. Associated Press, February 3, 2012.

CHAPTER 10

1. *Washington Post*, October 17, 2004, p. C10.
2. Jonathan Vankin, *Conspiracies, Cover-ups and Crimes: Political Manipulation and Mind Control in America* (Paragon House, St Paul MN, 1991), p. 120.

CHAPTER 11

1. www.un.org/icty/legaldoc-e/basic/statut/statute-feb08-e.pdf.
2. This and most of the other material concerning the complaints to the Tribunal mentioned here were transmitted to this writer by Mandel and other complainants. See also Michael Mandel, *How America Gets Away With Murder* (Pluto Press, London, 2004).
3. Press release from Chief Prosecutor Louise Arbour, The Hague, May 13, 1999.
4. http://un.org/icty/cases_e/factsheets/achieve_e.htm.

5. *Observer*, December 26, 1999; *Washington Times*, December 30 and 31, 1999; *New York Times*, December 30, 1999.
6. There are numerous articles in the world press of the past twenty years about the KLA's inordinate thuggery; Google <KLA> and one or more of the key words, such as 'drugs,' 'prostitution,' 'ethnic cleansing,' 'transplants,' etc.
7. http://wikipedia.org, under 'Camp Bondsteel.'
8. Del Ponte's book and the turmoil it has produced have been almost entirely ignored in the US media, but if one Googles her name and the book, one will find many reports from Europe.

CHAPTER 12

1. Viagra: Reuters, April 29, 2011.
2. See, for example, www.mathaba.net/news/?x=627196?rss. For further discussion of why Libyans may have been motivated to support Gaddafi, have a look at this video: www.youtube.com/watch?v=17HopG7Yxw8&feature=related.
3. *Guardian*, September 3, 2011.
4. *Washington Post*, 'Islamists Rise to Fore in New Libya,' September 15, 2011.
5. *USA Today*, October 24, 2011.
6. www.thehumanitarianwar.com.
7. Rashid Khalidi, professor of Arab studies, Columbia University, *Washington Post*, November 11, 2007.
8. For a counter-view of the Libyan 'massacre' stories, see www.abovetopsecret.com/forum/thread691464/pg1.
9. You can find the figures at the NATO site: www.aco.nato.int/page424201235.aspx.
10. For a history of this hostility, including the continual lies and scare campaigns, see the Libya chapter in my *Killing Hope: US Military and CIA Interventions Since World War II* (Zed Books, London, 2003).

CHAPTER 13

1. Paul Sigmund, *The Overthrow of Allende and the Politics of Chile, 1964–1976* (University of Pittsburgh Press, Pittsburgh, PA, 1977), p. 297.
2. 'Covert Action in Chile, 1963–1973, a Staff Report of the Select Committee to Study Governmental Operations with Respect to Intelligence Activities (US Senate),' December 18, 1975, p. 4.
3. Sigmund, *The Overthrow of Allende and the Politics of Chile*, p. 34.
4. A report of Venezuelanalysis.com, an English-language news service published by Americans in Caracas, November 27, 2007, article by Michael Fox.
5. For further information, see John Perkins, *Confessions of an Economic Hit Man* (Berrett-Koehler, San Francisco, 2004), *passim*.
6. *Newsweek* magazine, June 18, 1973, p. 22.
7. See Michael Parenti, *The Anti-Communist Impulse* (Random House, New York, 1969) for these and similar examples.
8. Associated Press, February 4, 2006.
9. For further detail, see Bart Jones, op-ed, *Los Angeles Times*, May 30, 2007;

also www.venezuelanalysis.com; www.misionmiranda.com/rctv.htm.

10. Edward Schumacher-Matos, *Washington Post*, February 14, 2009.

11. *New York Times*, February 13, 2009.

12. *Washington Post*, February 12, 2009.

13. *Washington Post*, February 8, 2009.

14. Holly Sklar, *Washington's War on Nicaragua* (South End Press, Boston MA, 1988), p. 243.

15. *New York Times*, October 7, 1990, p. 10.

16. For the full report of October 28, 2006, see Nicaragua Network of Washington, DC: nicanet.org; chuck@afgy.org.

17. Nicaragua Network, October 29, 2001, www.nicanet.org/pubs/hotline1029_2001.html; *New York Times*, November 4, 2001, p. 3.

18. *Miami Herald*, October 29, 2001.

19. *Independent*, September 6, 2006; contact Nicaragua Network, nicanet.org; Kathy@afgy.org, for list of US interventions into the Nicaraguan democratic process. *Independent*, September 6, 2006; '2006 Nicaraguan Elections and the US Government Role. Report of the Nicaragua Network delegation to investigate US intervention in the Nicaraguan elections of November 2006,' www.nicanet.org/pdf/Delegation%20Report.pdf.

CHAPTER 14

1. Department of State, *Foreign Relations of the United States, 1958–1960*, Vol. VI: *Cuba* (1991), p. 885.

2. White House press release, October 10, 2003.

3. Press release from the Cuban Mission to the United Nations, October 17, 2007, re this and preceding three paragraphs.

4. For a detailed discussion of Cuba's alleged political prisoners, see www.huffingtonpost.com/salim-lamrani/cuba-and-the-number-of-po_b_689845.html.

5. *Washington Post*, May 13, 2006, p. 10.

6. Reuters, March 17, 2006.

7. NPR, *Day to Day*, August 1, 2006.

8. Prensa Latina (Cuban news agency), March 12, 2011.

9. *The Militant* (US Socialist Workers Party weekly newspaper), April 4, 2011.

10. Bloomberg news agency, September 19, 2007.

11. Huffington Post, December 18, 2010.

12. Presented in a *Wall Street Journal* video: http://online.wsj.com/video/cuban_doctors_come_in_from_the_cold/069ECoEA_840F_4B3C_B8C6_2372B52D107A.html.

CHAPTER 15

1. *Washington Post*, January 29, 2007.

2. For further details of the civil war period, see William Blum, *Killing Hope: US Military and CIA Interventions Since World War II* (Zed Books, London, 2003), ch. 54.

3. See the British Cabinet papers for 1939, summarized in the *Washington Post*,

January 2, 1970 (reprinted from the *Manchester Guardian*); also D.F. Fleming, *The Cold War and Its Origins, 1917–1960*, vol. 1 (Doubleday, Garden City NY, 1961), pp. 48–97.

4. For a concise history of American anti-communism, see http://killinghope. org/bblum6/Intro2004.htm.
5. See Blum, *Killing Hope*, ch. 3.
6. *New York Times*, June 27, 1963, p. 12.
7. *USA Today*, October 11, 1999, p. 1.
8. *Washington Post*, May 12, 2009; see a similar story November 5, 2009.
9. Carolyn Eisenberg, *Drawing the Line: The American Decision to Divide Germany, 1944–1949* (Cambridge University Press, Cambridge, 1996); or see a concise review of this book by Kai Bird in *The Nation*, December 16, 1996.
10. See Blum, *Killing Hope*, p. 400 n8.
11. *Guardian*, March 7, 1985.
12. National Security Archive: www.gwu.edu/~nsarchiv. Search <Ford Timor>; William Blum, *Rogue State: A Guide to the World's Only Superpower* (Common Courage Press, Monroe ME, 2005), pp. 188–9.
13. *New York Times*, September 17, 1974, p. 22.
14. Michael Beschloss, *Taking Charge: The Johnson White House Tapes 1963–1964* (Simon & Schuster, New York, 1997), p. 306. All other sources for this section on Gordon can be found in *Washington Post*, December 22, 2009, obituary; *Guardian*, August 31, 2007; Blum, *Killing Hope*, ch. 27.
15. Frances Stonor Saunders, *The Cultural Cold War: The CIA and the World of Arts and Letters* (New Press, New York, 2000).
16. *Washington Post*, October 7, 2010.
17. Andreas Papandreou, *Democracy at Gunpoint: The Greek Front* (Doubleday, New York, 1970), p. 294.
18. *New York Times*, November 21, 1999.
19. *New York Times*, November 23, 1999.
20. *Washington Post*, October 21, 1973, p. C5.
21. *Washington Post Book World*, June 24, 2008, review of *One Minute to Midnight*.
22. *Khrushchev Remembers* (Andre Deutsch, London, 1971) pp. 494, 496.
23. Fred Kaplan, *The Wizards of Armageddon* (Simon & Schuster, New York, 1983), p. 246.
24. *Los Angeles Times*, September 23, 1994.
25. *Washington Post*, July 18, 2001.
26. BBC, August 14, 2004.
27. *Washington Post*, August 30, 2005, p. 10.
28. *Der Spiegel*, November 20, 2006, p. 24.
29. *Washington Post*, January 10, 2007, p. 7.
30. *Washington Post*, March 23, 2006, p. 21; see also *Washington Post*, May 26, 2004, p. A25 for a further example of same.
31. *Washington Post*, April 9, 2006, p. 2.
32. Associated Press, March 29, 2006.

CHAPTER 17

1. http://killinghope.org/superogue/system.htm.
2. *Washington Post*, February 26, 2010.
3. Associated Press, August 21, 2008; *Washington Post*, August 22, 2008.
4. Associated Press, March 2, 2008.
5. *Sunday Telegraph* (Sydney), August 10, 2003.
6. santafenewmexican.com/news/66424.html.
7. *Washington Post*, February 13, 2007, p. 14.
8. *Washington Post*, February 23, 2006.
9. Speaking at the 'Take Back America' conference, organized by the Campaign for America's Future, June 20, 2007, Washington, DC; this excerpt can be heard at democracynow.org.
10. Roger Morris (former member of the National Security Council), *Partners in Power: The Clintons and Their America* (Henry Holt, 1996), p. 415.
11. Ibid.
12. *National Review Online*, May 1, 2007.
13. *Fortune* magazine, July 9, 2007.

CHAPTER 18

1. *Washington Post*, March 22, 2007.
2. tomdispatch.com/post/174810.
3. *Los Angeles Times*, June 18, 1990.
4. Google <US military bases toxic>.

CHAPTER 19

1. US Senate, Permanent Subcommittee on Investigations, Committee on Homeland Security and Governmental Affairs, *The Role of Market Speculation in Rising Oil and Gas Prices*, June 27, 2006.
2. *Washington Post*, 'Wall Street Lobbies to Protect Speculative Oil Trades,' June 19, 2008, p. D1.
3. *Washington Post*, May 10, 2008, p. D3.
4. 'What To Do About the Price of Oil,' *Multinational Monitor*, May 28, 2008, www.multinationalmonitor.org/editorsblog.
5. *Washington Post*, September 25, 2008.
6. Column by Steven Pearlstein, *Washington Post*, August 3, 2005, pp. D1–2.
7. Wallace Peterson, *Silent Depression: The Fate of the American Dream* (W.W. Norton, New York, 1994).
8. *Washington Post*, May 26, 2004, p. A25; see also *Washington Post*, March 23, 2006, p. 21 for a further example of same.
9. Associated Press, August 11, 2011.
10. Agence France Presse, May 21, 2010, referring to a remark made in 2009.
11. *Los Angeles Times*, January 2, 1995.
12. *Washington Post*, September 24, 2003.
13. *New York Times*, November 3, 2010.
14. Jonathan Rowe, *Dollars & Sense* magazine, July–August 1999.
15. *Los Angeles Times*, April 15, 2006.

16. *Washington Post*, March 29, 2009.
17. 'Russia Now' (Moscow), insert in *Washington Post*, March 25, 2009.
18. *Los Angeles Times*, September 2, 1994.
19. Frank Bernack, Jr, Hearst Corporation president, address to the American Bar Association, early 1987, reported in *In These Times* magazine (Chicago), June 24-July 7, 1987.

CHAPTER 20

1. *The Nation*, June 4, 1990, pp. 763-4.
2. *Washington Post*, October 26, 2011.
3. Index on Censorship online, the UK's leading organization promoting freedom of expression, October 18, 2001.
4. *Independent*, April 24, 1999, p. 1.
5. *Bristol Evening Post*, April 24, 1999.
6. *Guardian*, April 24, 1999.
7. *The Pentagon Papers* (*New York Times* edition), pp. xii-xiii.
8. House of Representatives, *Congressional Record*, May 12, 1966, pp. 9977-8, reprint of an article by Morley Safer of CBS News.

CHAPTER 21

1. William Blum, 'Cuban Political Prisoners... in the United States,' http://killinghope.org/bblum6/polpris.htm.
2. *Washington Post*, February 25, 2008, p. A4.
3. Agence France Presse, December 1, 2008.
4. Haaretz.com, May 16, 2007.
5. Bill Van Auken, Global Research, July 18, 2008, www.globalresearch.ca.
6. *Chicago Tribune*, July 27, 2004.
7. *Chicago Tribune*, September 25, 2004.
8. House of Representatives, *Congressional Record*, June 21, 2005, p. S6897.
9. For the full Brzezinski interview, see killinghope.org/bblum6/brz.htm.
10. Associated Press, March 28, 2008.
11. See, for example, Peter Wehner, 'Why Republicans Like Obama,' *Washington Post*, February 3, 2008, p. B7.
12. www.whitehouse.gov/the_press_office/2010/09/23/remarks_president_united_nations_general_assembly.
13. http://harpers.org/subjects/JRMPublishersNote (June 17, 2009).
14. *New York Times*, October 30, 2007.
15. *New York Times*, December 27, 1977, p. 40.
16. *Lobster* magazine (Hull) no. 14, November 1987.
17. William Blum, *Rogue State: A Guide to the World's Only Superpower* (Common Courage Press, Monroe ME, 2005), pp. 199-200.
18. Carl Oglesby, *Ravens in the Storm: A Personal History of the 1960s Antiwar Movement* (Scribner, New York, 2008), *passim*.
19. Wikipedia entry for Anne Dunham.
20. George Cotter, 'Spies, Strings and Missionaries,' *The Christian Century* (Chicago), 25 March 1981, p. 321.
21. *Washington Post*, January 15, 2012.

22. Sam Smith was a longtime publisher and journalist in Washington, DC, now living in Maine. Subscribe to his marvelous newsletter, the *Progressive Review*, at www.prorev.com.
23. *Washington Post*, May 27, 2010.
24. Democratic Party function, Miami, FL, March 4, 2011, *Congressional Quarterly*, transcriptions.
25. *Los Angeles Times*, March 11, 2011.
26. The full speech can be read at comicism.tripod.com/350521.html.
27. *Killing Hope: US Military and CIA Interventions since World War II* (Zed Books, London, 2003), ch. 32.
28. Blum, *Rogue State*, ch. 23.

CHAPTER 22

1. *Sunday Telegraph*, July 18, 1999.
2. *Independent*, November 22, 1995.
3. *Far Eastern Economic Review* (Hong Kong), October 30, 1997, article by Nate Thayer, pp. 15 and 20.
4. *Washington Post*, May 11, 2007.
5. *Passionate Declarations* (HarperCollins, New York, 2003), p. 40; *Z Magazine*, May 2006, interview by David Barsamian.
6. *Democracy in America* (1840), ch. 16.
7. *New York Times*, December 25, 1992.
8. George Orwell, 'Notes on Nationalism,' p. 83, 84, in *Such, Such Were the Joys* (Harcourt Brace, New York, 1945).
9. Alan Colmes, *Red, White and Liberal* (Regan, New York, 2003), p. 30.
10. *The Outline of History* (London, 1920), vol. II, chapter 37, p. 782.
11. 'Letters on Patriotism,' 1869.
12. *International Herald Tribune*, February 25, 2003.

CHAPTER 23

1. *Christian Science Monitor*, November 29, 2004.
2. White House press briefing, March 20, 2008.
3. *Washington Post*, July 19, 2009.
4. *New York Times*, January 8, 1946, p. 3.
5. *New York Times*, January 11, 1946, p. 1.
6. Ibid., p. 4.
7. For more information about the soldiers' protests, see Mary-Alice Waters, *G.I.s and the Fight against War* (New York, 1967), a pamphlet published by *Young Socialist* magazine.

CHAPTER 24

1. Christopher Hitchens, *God Is Not Great: How Religion Poisons Everything* (Twelve Books, New York, 2007), p. 25.
2. www.soc.umn.edu/amp/AMPPublications.htm.
3. *Washington Post*, January 5, 2011.
4. *Washington Post*, September 5, 2010.

INDEX

abortion 232–4
Afghanistan
    and Soviet Union 83
    oil and gas pipelines as reason for
        war 80–81
Ahmadinejad, Mahmoud 88–94
Albania, backwardness of 109–10
Albright, Madeleine 19, 157, 312
An Inconvenient Truth (Al Gore) 243–4
Arab public opinion 100
Assange, Julian 131–6
atheism 324–6

Bennett, Tony 315–16
Berlin Wall 205–8
bin Laden, Osama, and William Blum
    281–4
Blair, Tony 276
Bolton, John 102, 310–11
bombing, US 33–4, 84–6; *see also* Serbia
Bosch, Orlando 51–2
Boxer, Barbara 112
Brazil 210–11
Brennan, John 31
British Guiana 21
Bulgaria 110
Bush, George H.W. 18–19, 108–9
Bush, George W. 18–19, 30, 55, 102,
    106–10, 117, 311

Cambodia/Khmer Rouge 116–18
capitalism 247–62

Cheney, Dick 45, 47, 75, 106–7
Chile 170–73, 178–9, 209, 214, 304
Chomsky, Noam 8, 64, 228, 338
Clinton, Bill 213
Clinton, Hillary, closet conservative
    240–42
Cold War, end of 103
conservatives, American 239–40
conspiracy theorists 134–5
Cuba 51–2, 142–3, 186–98

Davis, Angela 244–5
Debs, Eugene 11
Dershowitz, Alan 115
drones, US use of 126–7

Ecuador and WikiLeaks 139–40
Egypt and WikiLeaks 143
El Salvador 199–201
environment, US military greatest
    spoiler of 244–6

Ford, Gerald. 208–9
Fox News 68
France 35

Gaddafi, Muammar 19–20
Gates, Robert 36–7, 102
Gerassi, John 224–5
Germany
    in Afghanistan 81–2
    US teaching Germany how to kill

218–19
WikiLeaks 144
Google 27
Gorbachev, Mikhail 83
Gordon, Lincoln 209–11
Greece 212–14
Grenada 21
Guatemala 21

Haiti and WikiLeaks 143–4
Hicks, David 40–41
homosexuality 238
Honduras and WikiLeaks 139
Hughes, Karen 29, 76

ideology of Americans 230–32
India 111, 144–5
Indonesia 37–8, 208
International Atomic Energy Agency
     and WikiLeaks 137–8
Iran
     nuclear threat 95–8, 101, 103–5
     US myths about 88–92
     US sanctions 99–100
Iraq
     alleged reduction in violence 65–7,
          144
     informing US they had no WMD
          61–2
     loss of a secular state 324
     pre-war peace offer 20
     reception to US military occupiers
          69–70
     Saddam Hussein 'killing own people'
          75–6
     the phoney threat 74–5
Israel 88–99, 101–5, 119–20, 134–5, 141,
     144, 147, 176–7, 186–7, 275, 281, 284,
     286–8, 291, 296–7, 310, 315, 316

Japan 217–8
Johnson, Lyndon Baines, 210
Jones, James 118

Kosovo, 34, 42, 154–5, 158–60
Kubisch, Jack 214–15
Kucinich, Dennis 11–12

Latin America, emigration to US caused

by US policies 184–6
Ledeen, Michael 6–7
Legacy of Ashes: The History of the CIA
     (Tim Weiner) 277–80
Leno, Jay 90, 195, 274–5
Libya 19–20, 35, 92–3, 150–3, 161–9,
     274–5, 315–16

MacArthur, Douglas, General 45, 48,
     217, 227
Mailer, Norman 313
Manning, Bradley 132, 135–7
marijuana 239
Marshall Plan 22–5
Mexico 20–1
Middle East, US hostile acts in
     315–16
Moore, Michael 56, 197
Moussaoui, Zacarias 50–51
Mullen, Michael, Admiral 32
Murray, Craig 116
Muslims in America 326

National Public Radio (NPR) 195,
     269–72
NATO 156–9, 164, 223–4, 276
Nicaragua 181–4
Nobel Peace Prize 95
nuclear missile crisis, 1962 215–16

Obama, Barack
     and the empire, early warnings
          285–90
     Cairo speech compared to Hitler
          speech 298–302
     CIA background of him and his
          mother 292–4
     Indonesia and human rights 141
     not punishing US war criminals
          117
     poll of Arab people, very low
          standing in 101
     torture 121–22
     war lover 59–60, 167–8
     who is this man? 290–2, 297
Occupy movement 334–6
Ochs, Phil 227, 294
Oglesby, Carl 226
Orwell, George 44, 45, 276, 307

PanAm 103, bombing of 150–52
Panama 18
Panetta, Leon 96, 98, 116, 121–2
Paul, Ron 314
Pentagon, March on (1967) 227–9
Pletka, Danielle 99
police state, US as 132–3
population control 236–8
Posada, Luis 52
Powell, Colin 64–5, 312
Prince, Erik 18

Ratner, Michael 117–18
Reagan, Ronald 92
reconstruction not done by US 71–72
Rice, Condoleezza 6, 19, 111–13, 311
right to food, US opposition to 129–30
Rosenberg, Julius and Ethel 224–5
Rumsfeld, Donald 104, 107, 117, 275–6
Russia 35

Saudi Arabia and WikiLeaks 140–41
Scalia, Antonin 70
Scheuer, Michael 44
Schlesinger, Arthur, Jr 273–4
September 11, 2001 attack 148–50
Serbia
    US bombing Chinese embassy 34–5
    US bombing television station 276
Smith, Sam 295, 298, 316, 338

socialism 219–21, 264–8
Soviet Union 202–5, 215–16
Spain and WikiLeaks 138
Stone, I.F. 338
Sweden, myths about being progressive
        133–4, 140
Syria and WikiLeaks 145

Talbot, Phillips 212
terrorists
    motivation against US 316
    US fighting on same side as 165
Thomas, Helen 31
torture 114–22

United Kingdom and WikiLeaks 142,
    144
US soldiers, maltreatment of by US
    government 122–25

Venezuela 20, 112, 141–2, 170–81, 220
Vietnam 21, 317–18
Voight, Jon 68

Wiesel, Elie 94–5
WikiLeaks 99–100, 131–2, 136–45
Woolsey, James 2
World War II 21–2, 202

Zinn, Howard 272–4, 306, 338